Digital Evidence and Procedural Law in the UAE

Hany A. B. Ganah
Umm Al Quwain University, UAE

Ahmed Moustafa Aldabousi
https://orcid.org/0000-0002-9073-7254
Umm Al Quwain University, UAE

Amer Fakhoury
https://orcid.org/0009-0005-0826-6932
American University in the Emirates, UAE

Abdulghani Qasim Muthana Taher Al-Shuaibi
https://orcid.org/0000-0002-6679-0151
Umm Al-Quwain University, UAE

Abdelrehim Awad
https://orcid.org/0009-0005-3649-430X
University of Bisha, Saudi Arabia

IGI Global
Scientific Publishing
Publishing Tomorrow's Research Today

Vice President of Editorial	Melissa Wagner
Director of Acquisitions	Mikaela Felty
Director of Book Development	Jocelynn Hessler
Production Manager	Mike Brehm
Cover Design	Jose Rosado

Published in the United States of America by
IGI Global Scientific Publishing
701 East Chocolate Avenue
Hershey, PA, 17033, USA
Tel: 717-533-8845 | Fax: 717-533-7115
Website: https://www.igi-global.com E-mail: cust@igi-global.com

Library of Congress Cataloging-in-Publication Data

Names: Ganah, Hany A. B., 1973- editor
Title: Digital evidence and procedural law in the UAE / edited by Hany A. B. Ganah, Ahmed Moustafa Aldabousi, Amer Fakhoury, Abdulghani Qasim Muthana Taher Al-Shuaibi, Abdelrehim Awad.
Description: Hershey : IGI Global Scientific Publishing, 2026. | Includes bibliographical references and index. | Summary: "This book provides a practice-first treatment of digital evidence and procedural law"-- Provided by publisher.
Identifiers: LCCN 2026009770 (print) | LCCN 2026009771 (ebook) | ISBN 9798337379616 hardcover | ISBN 9798337379623 paperback | ISBN 9798337379630 ebook
Subjects: LCSH: Electronic evidence--United Arab Emirates | Admissible evidence--United Arab Emirates | Procedure (Law)--United Arab Emirates | Criminal law--United Arab Emirates | Criminal procedure--United Arab Emirates | Smart contracts--United Arab Emirates | Blockchains (Databases)--Law and legislation--United Arab Emirates | Artificial intelligence--Law and legislation--United Arab Emirates | Cryptocurrencies--Law and legislation--United Arab Emirates
Classification: LCC KMV1676.7 .D54 2026 (print) | LCC KMV1676.7 (ebook)
LC record available at https://lccn.loc.gov/2026009770
LC ebook record available at https://lccn.loc.gov/2026009771

British Cataloguing in Publication Data
A Cataloguing in Publication record for this book is available from the British Library.

Table of Contents

Detailed Table of Contents

The rapid expansion of virtual reality and metaverse environments has transformed commercial, social, and legal interactions, giving rise to a new category of disputes that challenge traditional legal frameworks. Arbitration, as a flexible and transnational dispute resolution mechanism, has emerged as a preferred method for resolving disputes arising within these immersive digital environments. However, conventional arbitration rules were primarily designed for physical and territorial contexts, raising concerns about their suitability for virtual reality–based disputes. This study examines the adequacy of existing arbitration frameworks in addressing disputes arising in virtual environments and explores the need for specialized arbitration rules tailored to the unique characteristics of virtual reality.

Digital transformation has shifted the evidentiary center of gravity in modern disputes from paper documents to electronically generated traces such as instant-messaging communications, mobile device artifacts, platform records, and cloud audit logs. In the United Arab Emirates (UAE), this shift is reinforced by reforms that recognize electronic evidence and modern communication tools within civil, commercial, and criminal proceedings, while preserving core principles of relevance, legality, authenticity, and judicial evaluation of probative value. Yet the abundance of digital evidence does not automatically translate into legal reliability. Messaging records can be selectively captured, edited, or presented without context; cloud logs can be misinterpreted, exported without provenance, or lost because of short retention windows; and cross-border infrastructures complicate acquisition and verification.

Virtual currencies are: One of the recent technological inventions resulting from the digital technological revolution in the fields of communications, information systems, and banking industry. There are more than 4,000 virtual currencies, the most famous of which is Bitcoin, which appeared in 2009 by an anonymous programmer (Satoshi Nakamoto) who adopted the idea of virtual currency to change the prevailing traditional currencies and replace them with a new currency that preserves the privacy of the seller and buyer and is not subject to supervision by banks or governmentsThe transactions are conducted via a peer-to-peer protocol (P2P) without a central server, Amid the challenges posed by the growing virtual currency market, it has become essential to explore legal frameworks to regulate this sector, not only to capitalize on its profits but also to establish a tax system for the revenues it generates. This humble study aimed to address this issue and examine the foundations of the tax treatment for virtual currency activitie

This research provides a descriptive and analytical study of the use of technology in compulsory enforcement procedures by outlining the legal framework and the most prominent digital applications, and platforms implemented within the legal system of the United Arab Emirates, in a comparative context with the French legal system. The study is divided into two main parts: the first examines the conceptual and regulatory framework governing the use of technology in compulsory enforcement, while the second addresses the principal forms of its practical application. The research concludes that the use of technological tools in compulsory enforcement has become an established judicial practice in both legal systems, albeit with variations in the level of regulation and the breadth of application. It further recommends extending the experience applied in the Emirate of Dubai to the other Emirates and strengthening institutional digital integration between the relevant judicial and enforcement authorities.

This study examines the impact of the COVID-19 pandemic on contractual obligations within the labor market. It posits that the pandemic qualifies as a force majeure event, potentially suspending or limiting contractual obligations due to its unforeseen nature. The study also identifies obligations that remain unaffected by the pandemic, thereby precluding parties from using it as a pretext to evade their commitments. It recommends seeking amicable solutions and establishing specialized committees, particularly for minor cases that cannot sustain litigation. Additionally, it suggests legislative reform in the Civil Transactions Law to clarify the definition and scope of force majeure, thereby preventing judicial confusion and ensuring that it is not limited to natural calamities, as some rulings by the Dubai Court of Cassation have relied on their interpretation of the explanatory memorandum of the Federal Civil Transactions Law.

The study aims to provide a clear understanding and a general overview of corporal punishment in Islam compared to corporal punishment in other legal systems. It sheds light on the key regulations governing the implementation of corporal punishment in Islam in contrast to modern criminal policies. The two researchers seek to refute the criticisms raised about this form of punishment that are based on personal biases rather than solid evidence and reasoning. Their objective is to clarify for contemporary scholars that corporal punishments in Islam are not merely a continuation of ancient punitive practices. Instead, Islamic punishments are unique because they are governed by strict regulations that ensure they are fair and just, while also respecting human dignity and showing mercy, even during the execution of such punishments. This principle was exemplified by the Prophet of Mercy (peace be upon him) in both word and deed, as reflected in the Quranic verse: "And We have not sent you except as a mercy to the worlds." (Surah Al-Anbiya, 107).

Undoubtedly, the legal profession, like other fields, is influenced by the rapid developments occurring in society, which require keeping up with these advancements and dealing with them in a positive and realistic manner. This has enhanced the ability of law to adapt to rapid technological changes, especially considering the information revolution and the digital transformation that the world is experiencing today. Technology has become an essential tool in enhancing knowledge and improving the efficiency of legal practice, while maintaining the human and ethical aspects that distinguish this profession. This research reviews the legal and technological challenges facing the legal profession in light of developments in artificial intelligence, with a focus on its impact on legal practice and finding solutions to these challenges.

Blockchain technology and smart contracts are revolutionizing legal and commercial transactions worldwide. These innovations enhance efficiency, automation, and security in contract execution while reducing reliance on intermediaries. However, their adoption presents legal challenges related to enforceability, regulatory oversight, and dispute resolution. This research examines the UAE's legal framework governing blockchain and smart contracts, analysing their recognition under contract and commercial law, as well as the roles of key regulatory UAE authorities, including the Securities and Commodities Authority ("SCA") and the Virtual Assets Regulatory Authority ("VARA").

Foreword

Digital transformation is reshaping every dimension of legal practice in the United Arab Emirates, and nowhere is that shift more consequential than in the handling of digital evidence. From mobile devices and cloud platforms to social media trails, encrypted communications, and emerging forms of data generated by connected systems, disputes and investigations increasingly turn on digital traces. The central question facing courts, practitioners, and scholars is no longer whether digital evidence will appear, but how it should be collected, preserved, authenticated, evaluated, and challenged—consistently, fairly, and in accordance with procedural safeguards.

This book, *Digital Evidence and Procedural Law in the UAE*, arrives at an important moment for the region's legal landscape. By bringing together scholarly and practitioner-oriented contributions, the volume aims to clarify the procedural implications of digital evidence across the litigation lifecycle: discovery and disclosure, chain of custody, admissibility and probative value, expert testimony, cross-border data access, and the delicate balance between effective justice and the protection of rights. The resulting dialogue is timely, practical, and directly relevant to the evolving needs of the UAE's courts and legal community.

One of the strengths of this edited collection is its ability to connect doctrinal discussion with the realities of practice. Digital evidence often presents complexity not found in traditional documentary material: metadata, device forensics, platform policies, algorithmic transformations, and the risk of alteration or misinterpretation. Procedural law must therefore provide clear routes for verification, contestation, and judicial reasoning. The chapters in this volume contribute to that goal by examining how legal standards and procedural principles can be applied to contemporary technologies while maintaining the integrity of due process.

The book's focus on the UAE context is especially valuable. The UAE is a leading hub for commerce, innovation, and international dispute resolution, and its legal system continues to develop in response to rapid technological change and cross-border transactions. As business activities expand through digital channels, and as individuals' interactions are increasingly mediated through platforms, the demand for reliable frameworks governing electronic evidence will only intensify. This volume supports that development by offering structured analysis, comparative insights where appropriate, and actionable perspectives for policy, adjudication, and advocacy.

I also appreciate the book's broad relevance to its intended audience. Academics and graduate students will find a foundation for further research into the doctrinal and methodological challenges of digital evidence. Practitioners and in-house counsel will benefit from applied discussions that illuminate litigation strategy and procedural compliance. Judges, arbitrators, investigators, and experts will find useful reflections on evidentiary assessment and on the interface between technical findings and legal reasoning. In this sense, the book contributes both to scholarship and to professional capacity-building.

It is a pleasure to acknowledge the editorial leadership behind this publication. The editors—Hany Bakr (Umm Al Quwain University), Ahmed Aldabousi (Umm Al Quwain University), Amer Fakhoury (American University in the Emirates), Abdulghani Al-Shuaibi (Umm Al Quwain University), and Abdelrehim Awad (University of Bisha)—have advanced an agenda that responds to pressing contemporary questions. Their collaboration underscores the value of joint academic efforts across institutions and jurisdictions, and it provides a platform for rigorous discussion of procedural law in the digital age.

As a legal professional, I have seen how the quality of justice can hinge on the quality of evidence and the procedures that govern it. Digital evidence can strengthen fact-finding, protect rights, and enhance accountability—yet it can also create new vulnerabilities when rules and practices lag behind technology. I trust that this volume will serve as a meaningful reference for those seeking to navigate these challenges with competence, integrity, and a commitment to the rule of law.

I commend the editors and contributors for their work and I encourage readers to engage with the insights presented throughout the chapters. The discussions offered here will support more confident adjudication, more effective advocacy, and more informed scholarly debate—ultimately strengthening the UAE's legal ecosystem as it continues to evolve alongside technological innovation.

Mohamed Nagib Saleh
Al Nagib Legal Consultancy, Dubai, UAE

Preface

This book was developed in response to a structural transformation that now affects legal practice, dispute resolution, enforcement, regulation, and professional responsibility across virtually every jurisdiction: the migration of legally relevant facts from paper-based records and physically localised transactions to digitally generated, electronically stored, and algorithmically mediated forms of evidence. In the United Arab Emirates, this transformation is especially significant. The UAE has positioned itself as a regional hub for commerce, finance, logistics, innovation, and digital governance, and this institutional setting has made questions of electronic proof, technological compliance, jurisdiction, and procedural modernisation impossible to treat as secondary issues. Courts, regulators, arbitrators, enforcement officers, and legal professionals increasingly confront disputes in which the decisive evidence is found in messages, logs, cloud records, platform data, blockchain entries, electronic contracts, or AI-assisted workflows. This volume, therefore, examines how legal systems - and specifically the UAE legal framework - can respond to these changes in a principled, practical, and procedurally defensible manner.

The central purpose of this book is to connect doctrinal legal analysis with contemporary evidentiary realities. Rather than approaching technology as an external or purely technical subject, the chapters in this volume treat technology as part of the procedural architecture of modern law. They ask how evidence is collected, preserved, authenticated, challenged, and evaluated when legal disputes involve digital devices, online communications, virtual assets, cross-border infrastructures, environmental monitoring tools, automated execution mechanisms, or artificial intelligence applications. Across the volume, a shared theme emerges: legal validity in the digital era depends not only on substantive rights and duties, but also on the reliability of the evidentiary process, the integrity of documentation, the legality of acquisition, and the procedural safeguards that make adjudication credible.

The topic fits squarely within the world today because legal and commercial life are now inseparable from digital systems. Contracts are negotiated and executed through electronic platforms; communication is increasingly platform- and mobile-based; assets can exist in decentralised or tokenised form; algorithms may assist professional decisions; and even conventional forms of public regulation, such as enforcement proceedings or environmental complaints, increasingly depend on electronic records. At the same time, new legal risks have become more visible: fabricated screenshots, incomplete message exports, weak chains of custody, cross-border data barriers, uncertain jurisdiction in cyber-enabled wrongdoing, opaque algorithmic outputs, and tensions between procedural efficiency and due process. As states seek to strengthen digital governance while preserving fairness and legal certainty, scholarship must offer frameworks that are both analytically rigorous and operationally useful. This book is intended to contribute to that need by focusing not merely on abstract legal adaptation, but on how procedural systems can remain trustworthy when evidence, transactions, and professional practice are increasingly digital.

The primary audience for this book includes legal scholars, judges, arbitrators, practising lawyers, public prosecutors, enforcement officials, compliance officers, policymakers, postgraduate students, and advanced researchers working at the intersection of law and technology. It is also relevant to professionals in digital forensics, cybersecurity governance, data compliance, and institutional risk management who need to understand how technical records are translated into legally persuasive proof. Because the book combines doctrinal analysis, comparative reasoning, and practice-oriented procedural guidance, it is especially suitable for readers who require more than a descriptive overview. The chapters are designed to support teaching, scholarly debate, legislative reflection, and professional application in courts, arbitration, regulatory settings, and legal advisory work.

CHAPTER OVERVIEW

The opening chapter of the volume, which deals with WhatsApp messages and cloud logs under the UAE legal framework, establishes the book's evidentiary foundation. It explains why digital proof should be treated as a process rather than a single file. It develops a practical framework based on lawful acquisition, authentication and attribution, and integrity preservation through documented chain-of-custody procedures. By focusing on two of the most common modern evidence types - instant-messaging records and cloud-generated logs - the chapter addresses a recurrent problem in contemporary litigation: how apparently persuasive digital materials can lose evidentiary weight if provenance, completeness, or reliability cannot be demonstrated. Its importance lies in providing a workable bridge between legal doctrine and digital forensics practice.

The second chapter turns to compulsory enforcement procedures and examines how technology is being integrated into the final stage of judicial protection. This chapter is important because enforcement is where legal rights are translated into real-world outcomes. By analysing electronic notifications, electronic case management, digital attachments, and electronic auction mechanisms, and by comparing the UAE framework with French law, the chapter shows how procedural modernisation can improve efficiency while also raising questions about due process, data protection, and the legal limits of technological intervention. It offers a valuable perspective on how digitalisation affects not only adjudication but also post-judgment implementation.

The third chapter addresses corporal punishments through the lens of procedural legitimacy, evidentiary reliability, and institutional restraint. Its importance lies in repositioning a sensitive and often normatively charged subject within a framework of proof, documentation, admissibility, proportionality, and error avoidance. By connecting Islamic jurisprudential categories such as hudud, qisas, and ta'zir with modern due process expectations and severity-sensitive evidentiary safeguards, the chapter demonstrates that debates about punishment cannot be separated from the quality of the evidentiary process. It is particularly significant for showing how traditional legal foundations can be examined while remaining attentive to contemporary concerns about procedural justice and reliability.

The fourth chapter studies pandemic-related contract disputes under UAE law and highlights the procedural role of digital evidence in proving disruption, impossibility, hardship, notice, mitigation, and performance history. This contribution is especially important because the pandemic made clear that emergency conditions often generate not only substantive legal questions - such as force majeure and exceptional circumstances - but also highly practical evidentiary disputes. The chapter shows how emails, platform notices, transaction data, shipment records, and digital correspondence can become central to judicial determinations concerning risk allocation, contractual adaptation, and liability. In doing so, it extends the book's core argument into the commercial sphere and illustrates how crisis-driven disputes still depend on disciplined evidence governance.

The fifth chapter examines noise pollution in the UAE from the standpoint of procedural enforcement and digital proof. Although environmental complaints are sometimes treated as minor or purely administrative matters, this chapter demonstrates that they raise serious issues of public order, regulatory compliance, evidentiary documentation, and legal challenge. By focusing on how noise-related violations are recorded, authenticated, measured, contested, and enforced - including the role of digital monitoring, electronic complaints, and administrative records - the chapter expands the book's scope and shows that digital evidence is not confined to courts and commercial disputes alone. Its importance lies in applying the logic of evidentiary integrity to a concrete regulatory field with direct social impact.

The sixth chapter addresses criminal jurisdiction in the age of modern technology and examines how cyber-enabled conduct complicates traditional territorial models of criminal law. This is one of the most practically important contributions in the book because transnational wrongdoing often involves conduct, servers, victims, and evidentiary traces distributed across multiple states. By analysing the UAE framework alongside comparative examples, the chapter clarifies how jurisdiction can be asserted, limited, and coordinated in a manner consistent with legality, sovereignty, and procedural fairness. It also underscores the evidentiary dimension of jurisdiction: modern jurisdictional effectiveness depends not merely on doctrinal authority, but on the ability to preserve, obtain, and present reliable digital evidence across borders.

The seventh chapter focuses on the role of artificial intelligence in arbitration for disputes arising in virtual reality and metaverse environments. This chapter is important because it pushes the discussion beyond present-day litigation into emerging transactional and dispute-resolution spaces in which identity, evidence, ownership, and harmful conduct may all be mediated through immersive digital platforms. By examining how AI tools may support case management, evidence organisation, pattern detection, and procedural efficiency in arbitration, while also raising concerns about fairness, transparency, bias, and enforceability, the chapter offers a forward-looking contribution. It demonstrates that future procedural debates will not be limited to digitising old systems; they will increasingly involve designing dispute-resolution models for entirely new forms of digital interaction.

The eighth chapter examines virtual currencies in relation to legal classification, taxation, enforcement, and digital evidence in the UAE. Its importance lies in clarifying one of the most contested areas of contemporary legal regulation: the distinction between cryptocurrencies, electronic money, and state-recognised legal tender, and the procedural consequences that follow from that distinction. By exploring the tax implications, anti-money-laundering concerns, consumer-protection issues, and evidentiary challenges arising from pseudonymity and decentralised transfer systems, the chapter provides a coherent framework for understanding how virtual assets intersect with public regulation and adjudication. It also reinforces the book's larger concern with the need for legally intelligible documentation in environments shaped by technical complexity.

The ninth chapter analyses the legal framework of blockchain and smart contracts in the UAE. This contribution is important because blockchain-based execution mechanisms challenge conventional legal assumptions about consent, interpretation, performance, breach, and remedies. The chapter explains how automation can enhance efficiency and transactional certainty while also raising questions about enforceability, coding errors, regulatory oversight, and dispute resolution when contractual logic is embedded in technical systems. By situating these questions within the UAE legal context, the chapter helps readers evaluate when smart-contract structures can be integrated into existing legal doctrine and when additional regulatory clarification may be necessary. It is an essential chapter for understanding how technological architecture can shape procedural outcomes itself.

The tenth chapter examines the legal profession in the age of artificial intelligence and considers how AI is changing research, drafting, document review, client interaction, and professional judgment. This chapter is especially important because it shifts the focus from legal systems and disputes to the legal profession itself. If lawyers, judges, and legal institutions increasingly rely on digital tools, then questions of accountability, confidentiality, data protection, professional ethics, and quality control become central to the legitimacy of legal practice. By addressing both the opportunities and risks created by AI-assisted legal work, the chapter ensures that the volume concludes with a broader institutional reflection: procedural law in the digital era is shaped not only by new evidence and new disputes but also by new modes of professional decision-making.

Taken together, the chapters in this volume are linked by a common methodological and substantive contribution. Methodologically, they combine doctrinal analysis with a practical concern for implementation, documentation, and procedural credibility. Substantively, they demonstrate that digital transformation is no longer a peripheral topic in legal studies. It now affects evidence, jurisdiction, contract performance, regulatory enforcement, arbitration, asset classification, professional ethics, and institutional design. The book, therefore, contributes to the field by assembling diverse but interconnected case studies that show how the UAE legal environment can serve as a meaningful site for analysing broader global questions about law, technology, and procedural justice. It also contributes by insisting that legal modernisation must remain anchored in legality, transparency, reliability, and human oversight.

This book does not claim that technology alone resolves legal problems, nor does it assume that procedural adaptation should come at the expense of due process or fairness. Instead, it advances a more disciplined proposition: the future of legal systems depends on their ability to integrate technological change without sacrificing evidentiary rigour, institutional accountability, and the normative values that make legal decision-making legitimate. For that reason, the volume is intended not simply as a collection of topical discussions, but as a coherent contribution to ongoing debates in digital evidence, procedural reform, and law-and-technology scholarship. We hope that the analyses gathered here will support more reliable adjudication, better-informed policy development, and deeper scholarly engagement with the evolving relationship between legal procedure and digital transformation in the UAE and beyond.

Acknowledgement

Umm Al Quwain University extends its sincere appreciation and profound gratitude to the University's Board of Trustees for their continued support of scientific research.

The Board's unwavering commitment to promoting academic excellence and advancing scholarly initiatives has been instrumental in the successful completion of this publication. This support reflects a clear strategic vision aimed at strengthening the research ecosystem, enhancing the University's academic and research standing, and contributing effectively to the service of society.

The College of Law at Umm Al Quwain University extends its sincere appreciation to Counselor Mohamed Nagib Saleh, Owner and Director of Al Nagib Legal Consultancy – Dubai, for his generous financial support of this scholarly work.

His contribution played a significant role in bringing this book to publication and reflects a strong commitment to supporting academic initiatives and advancing legal research.

This sponsorship stands as a distinguished example of constructive collaboration between legal professional practice and academic institutions, contributing to the development of legal scholarship and the advancement of specialized research.

Chapter 1

The Function of Artificial Intelligence in Arbitration for Resolving Virtual Reality Disputes

Ahmed Moustafa Aldabousi
http://orcid.org/0000-0002-9073-7254
Umm Al Quwain University, UAE

Abdulghani Al-Shuaibi
http://orcid.org/0000-0002-6679-0151
Umm Al Quwain University, UAE

Layla Saeed Alateibi
Umm Al Quwain University, UAE

Mohamed Nagib Saleh
Al Nagib Legal Consultancy, UAE

Abdelrehim Awad
http://orcid.org/0009-0005-3649-430X
University of Bisha, Saudi Arabia

ABSTRACT

The rapid expansion of virtual reality and metaverse environments has transformed commercial, social, and legal interactions, giving rise to a new category of disputes that challenge traditional legal frameworks. Arbitration, as a flexible and transnational dispute resolution mechanism, has emerged as a preferred method for resolving disputes arising within these immersive digital environments. However,

DOI: 10.4018/979-8-3373-7961-6.ch001

conventional arbitration rules were primarily designed for physical and territorial contexts, raising concerns about their suitability for virtual reality–based disputes. This study examines the adequacy of existing arbitration frameworks in addressing disputes arising in virtual environments and explores the need for specialized arbitration rules tailored to the unique characteristics of virtual reality.

INTRODUCTION

Rapid technological innovation has led to the emergence of immersive virtual environments, including virtual reality and the metaverse. Within these digital domains, users engage directly with content, unlike traditional passive learning models. This heightened user engagement has streamlined processes, reduced operational costs across multiple industries, and facilitated new forms of communication. As a result, business opportunities have expanded, attracting increased investment and prompting companies to prioritize enhancing user experiences in virtual environments.

Despite these advancements, significant legal challenges have emerged, as disputes arising within virtual environments necessitate a reassessment of existing legal frameworks to determine their adequacy for digital contexts. Arbitration has become a central mechanism for resolving such disputes and developing effective legal responses. This situation prompts a critical inquiry: Are current arbitration regulations adequate for virtual environments, or is the development of specialized rules required to address the unique characteristics of these disputes?

Addressing these evolving challenges requires examining the role of arbitration. Arbitration serves as a primary alternative to judicial proceedings and has developed to closely mirror court processes. Historically, arbitration functioned as an early means of achieving justice in ancient societies. In response to global developments, arbitration has become a preferred dispute resolution mechanism, valued for its efficiency and confidentiality. It allows parties to appoint one or more arbitrators to resolve disputes outside the court system, resulting in enforceable awards issued through a streamlined, private process.

1.1 Research Problem:

1. Assess the effectiveness of conventional arbitration rules in resolving disputes specific to virtual reality environments.
2. Identify the absence of specialized legal regulations addressing the resolution of virtual reality-related disputes.
3. Address the need to develop tailored arbitration rules to address the unique challenges of virtual reality disputes.

4. Examine legal and regulatory barriers to effective collaboration in virtual arbitration and propose steps to overcome them.

1.2 Research Questions

Based on the identified research problems, this study seeks to answer the following questions:

1. What constitutes the virtual world from a legal and technological perspective?
2. In what ways do disputes arising in virtual reality differ from disputes in the physical world?
3. What are the conventional rules governing arbitration, and to what extent are they effective in resolving virtual reality disputes?
4. Is there a need to develop specialized arbitration rules specifically designed for virtual reality environments?
5. How can legislators and legal systems effectively address the emerging challenges of virtual arbitration?

1.3 Research Objectives

The objectives of this research are as follows:

1. To evaluate the extent to which conventional arbitration rules correspond to disputes occurring in virtual reality contexts.
2. To propose legal and procedural adjustments to arbitration frameworks to better accommodate virtual reality disputes.
3. To suggest the development of intelligent and technology-driven arbitration systems that ensure fairness, transparency, and procedural efficiency in virtual dispute resolution.
4. To clarify the legal and practical challenges faced by parties and arbitrators operating within virtual arbitration environments.

1.4 Significance of the Study

1.4.1 Theoretical Significance

From a theoretical perspective, this study contributes to bridging the gap between traditional arbitration frameworks and the evolving legal needs of virtual reality environments. It offers a forward-looking legal analysis that integrates dispute resolution theory with emerging digital technologies, thereby enriching contemporary arbitration scholarship (Feng & Shen, 2025).

1.4.2 Practical Significance

Practically, this research provides policymakers, legislators, and arbitrators with concrete guidance for designing arbitration frameworks capable of addressing the distinctive challenges posed by virtual reality disputes. The findings aim to support the development of effective, enforceable, and technologically responsive arbitration mechanisms suitable for digital and metaverse-based interactions (Aldabousi, 2023).

2. SMART ARBITRATION AND ITS EVOLUTION

Smart arbitration stems from technological innovation across multiple sectors and has become a crucial method for dispute resolution. This section defines smart arbitration, delineates technological integration, and specifies the newly established procedural rules.

2.1 The Idea of Smart Arbitration and How Technology Fits In

Smart arbitration is based on a mutual agreement between parties, conducted entirely via electronic means until the arbitral award is issued. This method involves sending electronic communications between parties and the arbitral tribunal and completing digital forms through arbitration centers operating on dedicated digital platforms (Al-Adba, 2025).

The arbitration process advances through digital procedures, including hearings on online platforms (utilizing or omitting audio-visual tools), electronic exchange of briefs, evidentiary documents, and communications, and examination of witnesses in a digital format. The process concludes with the electronic delivery of the arbitral award. This aligns with Article (33), paragraph 3 of Federal Law No. (6) of 2018 on Arbitration: "Sessions may be conducted by modern communication means without necessitating physical presence."

2.2 Smart Arbitration

Smart arbitration is embedded in electronic contracts via blockchain technology, serving as an arbitration clause or agreement to resolve disputes arising from automated contracts during negotiation, formation, or execution. This enhances fairness and reliability for users, promoting broader adoption and supporting blockchain-based business transactions.

Smart arbitration is an agreement between parties to use electronic or smart tools for an efficient arbitration process. Arbitrators may be individuals or bodies, with procedures culminating in an arbitral award applying either traditional or electronically determined law, or the rules of equity for traditional or non-traditional contracts (Surana, Dembla, & Bihani, 2022).

The most up-to-date rules for smart arbitration can be found in Federal Law No. (6) of 2018 on Arbitration in the United Arab Emirates, especially in Articles 7, 24, 28, 33, 35, and 41.

Article (7/2) of the UAE Arbitration Law states that: "(a) [The arbitration agreement shall be valid] if it is included in a document signed by the parties, or contained in correspondence or other written means of communication exchanged between them, or concluded by electronic communication in accordance with the applicable legislation in the State concerning electronic transactions, As stated in Article (24/1):

1 This paragraph's rules will apply unless the parties agree otherwise, as follows:

(a) Any written communication shall be considered received if delivered personally to the addressee, or at their place of business, habitual residence, known postal address, or the address specified in the arbitration agreement or the document governing the relationship subject to arbitration.

If none of these addresses can be found after the necessary searches, the written communication will be considered received if it is sent by registered mail, courier service, or any other method that gives written proof of an attempt to deliver it to the addressee's last known place of business, home, or postal address.

The term "postal address" includes any fax number or email address that the parties used to talk to each other before, or that one party told the other about in writing.

(b) A message will be considered received on the day it is delivered in accordance with this Law. If there is no proof that the transmission was wrong, a fax or email will be considered received on the date it was sent, as shown in the transmission data.

If the communication is sent or received before 6:00 p.m. in the country where it is received, it will be considered received. If it is sent or received after that time, it will be considered received the next day (Aboelazm, 2025).

2 When figuring out time limits under this Law, the period will start on the day after the day the communication or any other correspondence was received.

If the last day of the period is a holiday or a day when the addressee's business is closed, the period will be extended until the first working day after that, Days off and official holidays that happen during this time will be counted (Tsuda, Ichino, & Shimizu, 2023)

3 This Article's rules don't apply to communications made through court procedures.

1 The parties may agree on how the arbitration will be carried out and choose a location for it, either in person or online using modern technology or in digital environments. If there is no such agreement, the arbitral tribunal will decide this based on the facts of the case and whether the venue is well suited to the parties.

2 The arbitral tribunal must give or send the parties the minutes of the hearings.

3 The arbitration center will give the necessary tools to hold the arbitration hearings using modern technology or in digital environments, if they follow the rules and standards that apply in the State.

Also, Article (33), paragraph 3, of Federal Law No. (6) of 2018 on Arbitration says that: Hearings may be conducted via up-to-date communication methods that do not necessitate the physical presence of the parties, Article (35) of the same law says that: The arbitral tribunal may hear witnesses, including expert witnesses, through up-to-date communication means that do not require their physical attendance at the hearing and Article (41/6) also says that, An arbitral award shall be deemed issued at the seat of arbitration as provided in Article (28) of this Law, even if it is signed by the members of the arbitral tribunal outside the seat of arbitration, and regardless of the manner of signing whether signed by the arbitrators in person, or the award was sent for each member to sign individually, or signed electronically—unless the parties agree otherwise."

From these rules, the lawmaker wants the arbitration agreement to be in writing. If it is not, it is not valid, even if it was made through social media, email, or other electronic means. The lawmaker has also allowed electronic notification, electronic arbitration, and the use of contemporary communication technologies to hear witnesses. The lawmaker also didn't require a specific method for signing the arbitral award or a specific place for issuing it, meaning the award could be signed electronically (Arjmand & Kondori, 2025).

Traditional arbitration is frequently criticized for its time-consuming and costly nature. In contrast, smart arbitration provides a flexible and efficient method for resolving disputes within digital environments. Ensuring fairness and accessibility requires the development of regulatory systems that are compatible with these emerging technologies (Aboelazm, 2025).

3. VIRTUAL REALITY DISPUTES: LEGAL CHARACTERISTICS

There are two parts to the term "virtual reality." The first word is "reality," which means all the physical and non-physical events and experiences a person goes through and learns from. The second word is "virtual," which means something imagined or close to reality. The term refers to a type of imitation or simulation of reality or truth in three-dimensional virtual environments designed to work with devices that support that technology.

Virtual reality technology is not limited by the rules and ideas of the real world. This means that virtual environments can show ideas or situations that don't exist in the real world. For example, someone could virtually fly between buildings and landmarks in a city.

We break down the different kinds of virtual reality into three main groups:

1 Full Simulation: This means fully experiencing the virtual world through head-mounted displays, headphones, gloves, omnidirectional treadmills, or suspension devices. People often use this kind of thing for games and fun.
2 Semi-Full Simulation: This creates a virtual environment that is only partially immersive, but users can still interact with some parts of it. Most of the time, it is used for learning and training.
3 Non-Full Simulation: This is the most common type. For example, mid-level video games are a type of non-fully immersive virtual reality experience.

3.1 Legal Problems with Virtual Disputes

There is no question that virtual disputes entail significant legal risks and challenges. The most important problem is that there aren't enough laws to govern, regulate, and resolve these kinds of disputes. This is especially true because these disputes occur in an external digital space that lacks fixed features or defined characteristics to which traditional laws can be meaningfully applied (Al-Sherman & Aldabousi, 2024).

Some of the legal problems that come up in virtual disputes are:

a. There aren't many laws that deal with problems that come up in the virtual world.
b. Figuring out which court should hear these kinds of cases.
c. A disagreement between laws
d. It's hard to make sure that the people involved are who they say they are and that the digital contracts are real.
e. Protecting and keeping data private
f. The lack of technical knowledge in arbitration and the courts

These challenges significantly hinder the resolution of disputes, resulting in complications regarding the validity of judgments and extending the time required to achieve justice and final settlement.

3.2 How to Use Arbitration in Virtual Reality

Smart arbitration is a new and improved version of traditional arbitration, which is one of the other ways to settle disputes. Smart arbitration is the same as regular arbitration, except that the rules for arbitration are different in the virtual world. To explain what smart arbitration is, we first need to look at the general definition of arbitration. It is an agreement to resolve a dispute with a specific person or group, rather than going to court.

Smart arbitration has gone by many names, like online arbitration or web-based arbitration, but they all mean the same thing. It is a process in which arbitration takes place over an international communication network using audio and video methods, without the need for the parties or arbitrators to be in the same place (Aldabousi, Awad, Hassan, Abdullah, & Ghonim (2025).

This definition makes it clear that smart arbitration is different because it uses up-to-date communication technologies, especially the Internet, which are based on information and communication systems. Because this network is widely used in legal transactions, especially business transactions, a new type of electronic transaction, e-commerce, has emerged. As a result, smart arbitration emerged as an improved version of traditional arbitration that addresses the unique nature of electronic transactions and the problems they pose. This is because it uses the same medium as electronic transactions: electronic means.

Since electronic means are what make smart arbitration unique, a question arises: Does the entire arbitration process have to be conducted electronically for it to be smart arbitration, or is it enough to use up-to-date communication technologies at any point to make it electronic and smart?

Because e-commerce disputes differ from other types of disputes, there are significant questions about how best to resolve them. This prompted a review of conventional dispute resolution methods and their evolution to more effectively suit the nature of electronic disputes. This made smart arbitration well-known, and many legal systems around the world, including the US, quickly set up systems that let people use these tools.

In this part, we will examine the steps a smart arbitration system follows in its procedural system. These steps include going to the arbitral institution, forming the arbitral tribunal, and finally deciding what law applies to smart arbitration agreements.

When there is a disagreement, the person making the claim sends an electronic request for arbitration to the other party or to the mutually agreed-upon arbitral institution. After that, the arbitrator or arbitral tribunal is selected electronically, and the parties exchange claims, defenses, and documents electronically. After arbitration, a specific date is set for the issuance of the award. The award is then signed electronically and sent to parties by email or other electronic means.

Smart arbitration follows many of the same steps as regular arbitration, but the main difference is that everything is done electronically. As a result, the main differences between the two systems are how they notify the parties, where arbitration is held, and how they enforce the arbitral award.

3.2.1 Filing the dispute (request for arbitration)

Anyone who wants to use smart arbitration must visit the chosen arbitral center's website and complete the required online form. This form is usually already filled out on the center's website. It usually includes the names of the parties, what they do, their email addresses, the nature and circumstances of the dispute, the purpose of the request, the type of settlement sought, and a list of evidence.

Each side must also provide the names of its representatives, specify how they want to be contacted by email or fax and choose the number of arbitrators, the best way to handle the dispute, and the length of the arbitration. The parties must also submit all documents and evidence backing their claims, as well as a copy of the arbitration agreement.

The Virtual Arbitration Court and the WIPO Arbitration and Mediation Center are two examples of arbitration centers that use English as their official working language.

3.2.2 Submitting the dispute to arbitration

The arbitral center will decide whether to accept jurisdiction over the dispute after receiving the arbitration request. If the center agrees to take the case, it sends an email to the second party (the respondent) notifying them and providing a response form (a statement of defense). If the respondent agrees to arbitration, they must include all relevant information and evidence, and both parties must pay the registration fees.

The arbitration center then creates a dedicated dispute page on a specific electronic platform and provides both sides with login information so they can view the page and read about the case. The center then explains its role and gives the arbitrator the option to accept or decline the case.

3.2.3 Setting up the Arbitral Tribunal in Smart Arbitration

Arbitration, whether traditional or electronic, is essentially the same; the difference resides solely in the methods employed, as smart arbitration uses the internet to facilitate audiovisual procedures without requiring the physical presence of the parties.

Because arbitration is based on agreement, the parties usually decide how to establish the arbitral tribunal, whether it will be in person or online. Most of the time, smart arbitration is done through arbitral institutions that use internet platforms. The parties usually use lists of arbitrators prepared by these bodies. The center usually maintains a list of qualified arbitrators, and the parties can choose whether the arbitrator will serve as the sole arbitrator or as part of a panel.

Some people think this system limits the parties' freedom to choose arbitrators, depending on the rules of each arbitral institution. For instance, under the rules of the International Chamber of Commerce (ICC), the institution has significant power to appoint arbitrators, even if the parties have already agreed on the number and names of the arbitrators. This is because the ICC Court only sees this as a suggestion that needs to be confirmed.

No matter how the arbitrator is chosen, they must be a real person with full civil rights. If the arbitrator is a legal entity, one or more of its members must be selected as the arbitrator. The arbitrator must also be well-versed in electronic commerce, since arbitration, like the courts (Alhiniti & Zaid, 2026), calls for careful consideration of technical issues. Also, the arbitrator must be fair, independent, and have a good reputation. If any of these conditions are not met, the arbitrator can be challenged. The appointed arbitrator must agree to perform the task assigned to them for the arbitral tribunal to be properly constituted.

However, in smart arbitration, it is harder to maintain the arbitrator's neutrality and independence because the process relies entirely on electronic communications and does not require the parties to be in the same place.

3.2.4 Start of the arbitration

The arbitration process begins online before the arbitral tribunal on the date set. This date is sent to both parties after the smart arbitration center provides the respondent's information and gives them enough time to submit extra information or update any already submitted information. The parties can also choose their own representatives, no matter where they are from. Smart arbitration and traditional arbitration use the same basic steps, but the main difference is the technology used. Smart arbitration doesn't require the parties or witnesses to be present in person, as all information and documents are sent electronically.

The arbitral tribunal issues a decision on the dispute and sends it in writing once all submissions have been received. The decision can be made with a simple majority vote, and the chair and members of the tribunal must sign it. When the award is not unanimous, the opinion of any member who disagrees is noted. The arbitral award must include the decision itself, the date and place it was made, and the costs and fees of the arbitrators, experts, and any other costs. The parties can agree to leave out these details of the award (Aldabousi, 2023).

3.3 A Comparison of Smart Arbitration and Regular Arbitration

3.3.1 How quickly and easily can the deal be made

One problem with traditional arbitration agreements is that they take a long time because the parties usually must be there in person. Smart arbitration agreements, on the other hand, can be completed quickly, regardless of how far apart the parties are (Aldabousi, 2022). This is because they are simple and cheap, and they don't require anyone to move.

Different from traditional arbitration agreements, which are often signed on paper, smart arbitration agreements made online do not require any paper-based documentation.

A comparison of traditional and smart arbitration demonstrates that smart arbitration necessitates advanced technical infrastructure and the creation of new legal frameworks. Emphasizing the training of legal professionals and the integration of emerging technologies is essential to ensure that virtual disputes are resolved efficiently and equitably.

3.3.2 Legal Problems and Holes in Smart Arbitration

Legal scholars hold divergent views on this issue, leading to two primary perspectives.

The first group thinks that arbitration is "smart," even if only one stage of the process uses modern communication, while the others use more traditional methods.

The second group, on the other hand, says that arbitration can't be called smart arbitration unless the entire process is conducted electronically, from drafting the arbitration agreement in digital form to completing all steps, with neither party nor the arbitrators present in person, and finally issuing an electronic arbitral award.

It seems the second opinion is more correct because smart arbitration is an arbitration system in which technology replaces the physical meeting of arbitrators and the parties involved in the dispute. The whole dispute is handled electronically, using methods such as fax, email, or specialized online platforms. The arbitral award is also sent electronically to all parties involved (Ramadan, Abdelsalam, Qasim, & Aldabousi, 2025).

It is not accurate to classify arbitration as "electronic arbitration" merely because electronic methods are used at certain stages, as contemporary arbitration invariably incorporates up-to-date communication tools at various points.

3.4 Smart Arbitration Risks

As technology becomes increasingly important across many aspects of life, smart arbitration has become a good way to resolve international business disputes. But this kind of arbitration raises many legal issues that lawmakers need to fully address.

Smart arbitration offers some benefits because it is conducted electronically, but it also poses risks and challenges. The most important risks of smart arbitration can be summed up as follows:

a. No Guarantee of Confidentiality in Arbitration

One downside of smart arbitration is that hackers could breach confidentiality, putting the privacy of the entire arbitration process at risk. One of the main reasons why parties prefer arbitration to litigation is that it keeps the details of the dispute and its resolution private. This is important for merchants and businesses that want to keep their trade secrets and sensitive information safe from competitors.

In traditional arbitration, confidentiality is usually guaranteed because only the parties to the case can hear it. In court, hearings are usually public, unless there are special circumstances. However, this guarantee isn't always possible in smart arbitration. This is because arbitration is done online, and each side receives a unique access code (password) that grants them access to the case platform, where they can meet with the arbitrator or the other side and view documents and evidence related to the case.

However, to obtain these access codes, technical staff who are not involved in the dispute must be involved to ensure the login is secure. This means the codes are no longer private to the parties arguing, potentially compromising the confidentiality of the arbitration process.

You can reduce this risk by encrypting all arbitration-related data and giving the electronic platforms that hold its systems to keep it safe from hacking and spying.

b. One of these risks is fear, especially on the part of the weaker part of arbitration, in general, and smart arbitration in particular. This fear stems from the possibility that the arbitrator might not follow the rules meant to protect the weaker party under national law, especially if that party is a consumer. Such a failure could render the arbitral award invalid and unenforceable.

3.5 Legal Gaps in the Rules for Virtual Arbitration

The legal gaps in the rules governing virtual arbitration differ and have different reasons. In short, these gaps are:

1.There is no law that applies, and there are gaps in how legal and international procedures are defined. There are often legal gaps because it is hard to figure out which national or international legal framework governs the procedures of smart arbitration. This makes the law unclear, which makes it hard to figure out which steps to take.

2 There is no single legal framework: There are big differences between how different countries' laws deal with smart arbitration. This makes it hard to know if arbitration procedures and awards are valid and enforceable in this context.

3 Hard to Find the Seat of Arbitration: Because arbitration proceedings happen online, it's hard to figure out where the legal seat of arbitration is. This raises many questions about the law and the court's authority.

4 Proof of Procedures: Smart arbitration makes it hard to prove that the legal steps were taken, like sending and receiving messages, signing contracts, and making sure that electronically issued awards are accepted.

5 Protecting Personal Data: Smart arbitration involves dealing with a lot of personal data, which raises legal issues about how to protect it and follow privacy rules.

6 Electronic Signatures: Electronic signatures are an important part of smart arbitration. There is, however, a difference between countries in how legally valid and enforceable they are, which makes it hard to use smart arbitration consistently everywhere.

7 Judicial Jurisdiction: A key question that smart arbitration raises is which court has the power to look at challenges to smart arbitration awards. This problem becomes even more complicated because smart arbitration spans borders, meaning the parties and the arbitration institutions may be in different legal jurisdictions. This means there needs to be clear rules for determining jurisdiction so that awards can be enforced effectively.

8 The law that applies to the smart arbitration agreement: Figuring out what law applies to the smart arbitration agreement is very important because it affects how the arbitration process works and whether the awards are legal. There are two main schools of thought in legal scholarship:

A. The Law of the Seat of Arbitration: This view says that the law that applies to the arbitration agreement is the law of the seat of arbitration. This is based on the idea that the local law of the state where the arbitration takes place governs the arbitration process.

B. The Law Set by the Arbitral Institution:

The arbitral institution in charge of the dispute determines which law applies. This method gives you more freedom, but it can be hard to handle when laws from different countries conflict.

The main challenge in smart arbitration arises when the relevant law is not explicitly established. It is very hard to determine the law in the jurisdiction where arbitration takes place, as it occurs in an online environment. This raises an important question: should the law of the place where the service is provided apply, or should the law of the arbitrator's home apply?

Granting the arbitral tribunal the authority to determine the applicable law is considered the most effective solution, as it enables the selection of the most appropriate legal framework for each case.

When it comes to the law the parties have chosen to apply, if they agree to arbitration, the law governing the arbitration agreement is the law they have chosen. Most national laws, especially those governing international business contracts, support this approach.

4. INSTITUTIONAL AND TECHNICAL REQUIREMENTS FOR VIRTUAL ARBITRATION

Smart arbitration has become a useful way to settle disputes as technology advances rapidly. It addresses the problems with traditional arbitration related to time, cost, and location. Traditional arbitration centers are now facing challenges that require them to change how they operate to keep pace with digital transformation. This means using technology for case management, hearings, and the enforcement of awards.

This study examines the adaptation of traditional arbitration centers to digital means, the establishment of advanced technical infrastructure, and the enforcement of digital awards. It also offers solutions to improve their efficiency and strengthen their role in resolving disputes in the information age.

First, how traditional arbitration centers have changed to work with smart arbitration

4.1 The Idea of Smart Arbitration

Smart arbitration is a new way to settle disputes that use technology to get around old problems like time, money, and distance. It uses tools such as video conferencing, electronic signatures, and digital case management platforms, making it a quick and effective alternative to traditional arbitration.

4.2 Why Smart Arbitration Is Important

Speed of Proceedings, Smart arbitration gets things done faster than standard methods, which can take a lot longer. Cost Efficiency It cuts down on costs for travel, lodging, and printing because everything is done online, Worldwide Access, People from different countries can take part without being there in person, which makes it perfect for international disputes.

4.3 Smart Arbitration Tools

a) Video-conferencing services like Zoom and Microsoft Teams are used for virtual hearings.

b) Case-Management Systems: These help with filing papers, keeping track of deadlines, and sending in electronic evidence.

c) Electronic Signatures: Making sure that contracts and other legal documents are valid and can be enforced.

d) d. Real-Life Examples of Smart Arbitration

e) E-commerce companies like Amazon and eBay use smart arbitration to settle disputes between buyers and sellers.

f) Financial Institutions: Banks and other financial service providers use electronic platforms to settle disagreements that come up over contracts and services.

4.3 Problems with Traditional Arbitration Centers

A. Traditional Work Culture, Resistance to Change: Traditional arbitrators often stick with what they know, Not Enough Digital Skills: Some employees don't know enough about technology.

B. Weak Infrastructure, not having modern technology or digital case management systems, some areas have internet networks that aren't very stable.

C. Rules and Laws, in many countries, inure is no definite legal framework for smart arbitration, The law is slow to catch up with the fast changes in technology.

D. Problems with trust and security, worries with respect to privacy when data is stolen, the dangers of digital forgery and changing electronic evidence.

E. The First Cost of Going Digital, building a digital environment takes a lot of money, like training staff, upgrading equipment, and buying software.

4.4 Steps Toward Adapting to Smart Arbitration

A. Developing Digital Infrastructure: Creating specialized platforms for smart arbitration in collaboration with software developers, upgrading equipment and securing networks to ensure strong data protection.

B. Training Human Resources:Training arbitrators and administrative staff on the use of digital arbitration platforms., Offering continuous technical training to keep pace with technological developments.

C. Amending Legal Regulations:Issuing legislation that recognizes electronic evidence and electronic arbitral awards, Regulating the use of digital tools to guarantee transparency and procedural fairness.

D. Strengthening Trust in Smart Arbitration: Awareness efforts to educate parties about the benefits of smart arbitration.

4.5 The technical and technological bases of smart arbitration

Smart arbitration is built on virtual platforms that create an electronic space for quickly and easily handling disputes. These platforms apply technology to ensure clarity and speed, while also making workflows easier and case management more efficient. This makes arbitration processes easier and faster in arbitration centers.

4.5.1 Key Factors Contributing to the Effectiveness of Virtual Arbitration Platforms

Virtual arbitration platforms function effectively when they are designed in a manner that balances technological sophistication with user accessibility. Several interrelated factors contribute to the operational success of these platforms.

First, ease of use is a fundamental requirement. Both disputing parties and arbitrators must be able to navigate platform interfaces intuitively without requiring advanced technical expertise. User-friendly design enhances participation, reduces procedural delays, and minimizes the risk of technical disputes undermining the arbitration process.

Second, flexibility and accessibility are essential characteristics. Virtual platforms should enable access from different geographical locations and across multiple devices, including computers, tablets, and smartphones. This flexibility reinforces arbitration's traditional advantages of efficiency and convenience, particularly in cross-border disputes.

Third, security and data protection play a decisive role in the credibility of virtual arbitration. Robust encryption mechanisms are required to protect sensitive data, communications, and arbitral records from unauthorized access or cyber threats.

Without adequate security guarantees, parties may be reluctant to engage fully in digital dispute resolution.

Finally, system integration significantly enhances platform efficiency. Effective virtual arbitration platforms should support electronic payment systems, video conferencing tools for virtual hearings, and secure document management systems. Seamless integration ensures procedural continuity and reduces reliance on external or fragmented technologies.

4.5.2 Establishing Virtual Arbitration Platforms

The establishment of effective virtual arbitration platforms requires a structured and collaborative approach. The initial step involves assessing the specific needs of the parties and arbitration institutions, including the nature of disputes, procedural requirements, and expected case volume. This assessment ensures that the platform's design aligns with practical arbitration demands.

Subsequently, collaboration with technical experts is necessary to develop customized platforms tailored to institutional or client-specific requirements. Generic solutions may not adequately address the complexities of arbitration proceedings, particularly in high-value or technically complex disputes.

Once developed, platforms must undergo rigorous testing to ensure operational efficiency, cybersecurity resilience, and procedural reliability. Continuous testing helps identify vulnerabilities and ensures compliance with legal and technical standards. Moreover, regular system updates are essential to accommodate technological advancements and evolving cybersecurity risks.

4.5.3 Required Technical Infrastructure

A. Systems and Hardware

Effective virtual arbitration depends on robust technical infrastructure, including high-capacity servers capable of securely managing case files, communications, and procedural data. In addition, reliable video conferencing technologies are essential to facilitate virtual hearings, witness examinations, and deliberations.

B. Cybersecurity Technologies

Cybersecurity constitutes a core pillar of virtual arbitration infrastructure. Advanced data encryption tools are required to safeguard confidential information, while intrusion detection and prevention systems are necessary to protect platforms against cyberattacks and unauthorized access.

C. Connectivity Requirements

High-speed and stable internet connectivity is indispensable to ensure uninterrupted arbitration sessions. Technical contingency plans, including backup servers and alternative communication channels, must be in place to mitigate service disruptions and maintain procedural continuity.

D. Technical Personnel

The operation of virtual arbitration platforms requires specialized technical staff, including IT professionals and information security officers. These experts are responsible for system maintenance, security monitoring, and rapid response to technical incidents.

4.5.4 Technical Challenges in Establishing Virtual Arbitration Platforms

A. High Financial Costs

One of the primary challenges lies in the high costs associated with developing and maintaining digital arbitration platforms. Significant financial investment is required not only for initial development but also for periodic system upgrades to keep pace with technological advancements.

B. Legal Compatibility

Legal challenges arise from inconsistencies between national and international legal frameworks governing digital dispute resolution and smart arbitration. Divergent rules concerning electronic evidence, digital signatures, and procedural validity may hinder the uniform application of virtual arbitration.

C. Trust and User Acceptance

Trust remains a critical concern in virtual arbitration. Some users may be reluctant to adopt new technologies, while others may question the authenticity and integrity of digital documents. The absence of universally accepted mechanisms for verifying electronic evidence further exacerbates these concerns.

Proposed Solutions to Address These Challenges

A. Financial Support Mechanisms

Providing financial support in the form of grants or low-interest loans to arbitration centers can facilitate investment in technical infrastructure and digital transformation initiatives.

B. Training and Capacity Building

Comprehensive training programs should be established to enhance the technical competencies of arbitrators, administrative staff, and legal practitioners. Such programs foster confidence in digital systems and improve the overall effectiveness of virtual arbitration.

C. Enhancing Trust and Reliability

Trust can be strengthened using certified cybersecurity standards and internationally recognized security certificates for arbitration platforms. Additionally, providing immediate technical support ensures that technical issues are resolved promptly, minimizing disruptions to proceedings.

The Impact of Digital Infrastructure on the Future of Arbitration

Robust digital infrastructure has the potential to transform access to justice by making arbitration services more accessible, efficient, and cost-effective. Virtual arbitration platforms enable individuals and small businesses to resolve disputes swiftly without the financial and logistical burdens associated with traditional proceedings. As digital infrastructure continues to evolve, it is likely to play a central role in shaping the future of arbitration and advancing the broader concept of digital justice.

4.6 Enforcement of Awards Given Through Smart Arbitration

Enforcing awards in smart arbitration means making electronically issued arbitral awards into decisions that can be carried out in the real world. To ensure that everyone follows these awards, the judicial system, the parties involved, and the relevant institutions must work together.

Getting an “original” copy of an electronic arbitral award is hard because there is no standard idea of what an authentic document or a certified copy is. When an electronic award is copied, several identical copies are created. But if the goal of asking for an original or certified copy is to make sure the award is real and that no changes or forgeries have been made, this can be done with data protection and cryptographic technologies, or by using a trusted third party to verify the arbitrators' electronic signatures and confirm that they really belong to the arbitrators.

Still, an award made through smart arbitration won't be enforceable in a certain state unless that state has passed laws on electronic commerce that treat electronic writing and signatures as legally valid as written documents and handwritten signatures.

4.7 Problems with Making Electronic Arbitral Awards Happen

A. Domestic legal systems cannot keep up with how quickly electronic commerce contracts are changing, Recognition of electronic awards:

Some states do not legally recognize arbitral awards made through smart arbitration platforms, Conflicts between domestic and international laws make it hard to enforce arbitral awards in disputes that cross borders.

B. Questions About Whether Smart Arbitration Procedures Are Valid:

In states where courts are not legally required to enforce arbitral awards, enforcing recognition of an arbitral award may be difficult. Article II (1) of the New York Convention on the Recognition and Enforcement of Foreign Arbitral Awards requires signatory countries to recognize arbitration agreements and enforce foreign arbitral awards. However, this duty is not absolute. These include the requirement that the arbitration agreement be signed, and that the arbitral award be properly authenticated (Wu (2025).

These conditions call for verifying their fulfillment through electronic dispute resolution methods, which, in turn, require a review and expansion of the customary notions of writing and signature to adapt to technological developments that have influenced both.

C. The Arbitrator's Failure to Follow Required Rules:

Parties, especially the weaker party to the contract, are often afraid to go to arbitration, in general and smart arbitration in particular, because they fear the arbitrator won't follow the mandatory rules of the applicable national law.

D. Checking to see if the arbitration agreement is valid

The New York Convention provides that an arbitration agreement is valid if it complies with several laws, including the law of the state where the arbitral award was rendered. This ensures that you can figure out which country the award was given in, which means that the award was given in a specific national jurisdiction. But this assumption doesn't work when the award is made and written on an electronic platform over communication networks (Al-Adba, 2025).

Also, the New York Convention has rules that require arbitration proceedings to take place in a specific place or in the territory of a specific state. So, if someone breaks the procedural rules of that state, the arbitral award may not be recognized or enforced.

E. Finding the Place of Arbitration

The smart arbitration system lacks a physical seat of arbitration, which is why these legal questions arise. The seat is set only figuratively or virtually, since neither the parties nor the arbitrators meet in person. Instead, the proceedings take place online via electronic communication networks (Weerasinghe, Macdonald, Fiani, et al., 2025).

So, the problems and issues that smart arbitration brings up, which make people question its usefulness and effectiveness, can be listed as follows:

I. Technical and technological problems, especially in specialized adjudication processes.

II. Different levels of security and privacy in electronic communications and differences in how well systems work together.

III. The risk of private information being leaked in arbitration cases that are held online.

IV. Problems with putting digital files in order and holding online hearings.

V. Problems that come up when trying to make sure that data is real and that it is correctly documented.

4.8 Problems with the process structure, such as issues of commitment, reliability, and figuring out where the arbitration will take place.

• Problems with arbitral awards, such as formal requirements, binding force, and public policy that governs enforcement, Improving the ways that Smart Arbitration makes sure that people follow the rules

A. Changing laws in both the US and the world

I. Adding smart arbitration to domestic laws by giving electronic arbitral awards full legal status.

II. Working together on a global scale by signing international agreements that make sure that arbitral awards are enforced across borders.

III. Regular updates to the law to keep up with changes in technology and real needs.

B. Giving digital tools that help

I. Systems for tracking enforcement to keep an eye on how well parties are following arbitral awards.

II. Electronic authentication systems to make sure that evidence and awards are real and safe.

C. Helping the Parties

I. Legal support offices to help people understand and follow the rules for electronic arbitration.

II. Technical support services to help with any technical problems that come up during the compliance process.

D. Making things clearer

I. Recording all steps of the process electronically to make sure they are clear and honest.

II. Periodic reports that give the parties updated information on how the award enforcement is going.

4.8.1 How Smart Arbitration Awards Are Enforced

I. The New York Convention: It is very important for enforcing international arbitration awards, such as smart arbitration awards.

II. The European Union: Some EU countries have put in place integrated systems that make it easy and quick to enforce electronic arbitral awards made through smart arbitration.

4.8.2 Local Success Stories

Some Gulf countries have set up electronic systems to make it easier to enforce business judgments using online platforms. This saves time and effort, How enforcing awards will affect the future of smart arbitration (Tsuda, Ichino, & Shimizu, 2023).

A. Getting people to trust the digital system

When arbitral awards are enforced successfully, it makes people more confident that smart arbitration is a good alternative to traditional arbitration.

B. Getting people to use the digital system.

People and businesses are more likely to use electronic platforms to settle disputes because it is easy to enforce arbitral awards.

C. Encouraging New Ideas

Smart arbitration technologies will get more investment if arbitral awards are enforced quickly and effectively.

D. Helping with international disputes

Smart arbitration awards between parties from different countries improve international trade and cooperation. Traditional arbitration centers must transition to smart arbitration by enhancing their technological capabilities and adopting advanced digital frameworks. Furthermore, continuous training for arbitrators and regular legal updates are essential to ensure the effectiveness and sustainability of arbitration in the digital era.

Recent scholarship highlights that the legitimacy of AI-assisted dispute resolution depends on transparency, fairness, and explainability in automated decision-support (Angerschmid et al., 2022). In addition, emerging guidance and comparative analyses emphasize disclosure, due process safeguards, and institutional governance when AI tools are used in arbitration (Perera & Tan, 2025; Azab & Ismail, 2024), while doctrinal discussions propose national-level frameworks to support AI-enabled arbitration systems (Labanieh et al., 2025).

5. CONCLUSION

Smart arbitration faces significant legal and legislative challenges that require comprehensive, systematic solutions to establish a stable legal environment, foster trust among parties, and enhance the credibility of this dispute-resolution method. Accordingly, it is imperative to develop national and international laws that keep pace with technological advancements and align with international standards, thereby increasing efficiency and reliability.

6. RECOMMENDATIONS

1 It is recommended that arbitration centers organize legal seminars and workshops to educate stakeholders concerning the role and significance of smart arbitration and virtual environments.

2 To enhance the security, transparency, and integrity of documentation, it is advisable for responsible authorities to incorporate blockchain technology and NFT tokens into electronic records and electronic signatures utilized in smart arbitration.

3 Regular updates to the legal frameworks governing smart arbitration are recommended to fill gaps that hinder the efficiency and timeliness of dispute resolution in digital contexts.

4 Greater collaboration between competent authorities and arbitration centers is encouraged to establish unified standards for smart arbitration and ensure consistency in related legal notions and procedures.

5 Courts are encouraged to develop innovative mechanisms to facilitate the enforcement of smart arbitration awards, thereby enhancing the credibility and standing of smart arbitration institutions within the contemporary justice system.

6 It is recommended to strengthen security measures for online transactions.

7 Amendments to the Evidence Law under Federal Decree-Law No. (35) of 2022 are recommended, notably regarding provisions for electronic evidence in civil and commercial transactions.

REFERENCES

Aboelazm, K. (2025). The effects of Supreme Constitutional Court decision of unconstitutionality legislative omission: A comparative study. *Lex Scientia Law Review*, *9*(2), 1446–1483. Advance online publication. DOI: 10.15294/lslr.v9i2.8801

Aboelazm, K. S. (2025). A new era of public procurement: Critical issues of procuring artificial intelligence systems to produce public services. *International Journal of Law and Management*. https://doi.org/DOI: 10.1108/IJLMA-06-2024-0208

Al-Adba, N. M. M. A. (2025). AI and the future of decision-making in international arbitration: Redefining the boundaries of human judgment. *International Arbitration Law Review*, *28*(3), 172–192.

Al-Sherman, N., & Aldabousi, A. M. (2024). The complementary penalties enforced to combat corporate crimes in UAE law. *Pakistan Journal of Criminology*, *16*(3), 635–648. DOI: 10.62271/pjc.16.3.635.648

Aldabousi, A. M. (2022). Legal problems of conclusion of intelligent software agent for smart commercial contracts in the era of blockchain: U.A.E as a model. *Universidad y Sociedad*, *14*(S3), 713–728. https://rus.ucf.edu.cu/index.php/rus/article/view/3005

Aldabousi, A. M. (2023). The legal problems facing the conclusion of cloud computing contracts. *Universidad y Sociedad*, *15*(3), 602–611. https://rus.ucf.edu.cu/index.php/rus/article/view/3815

Aldabousi, A. M., Awad, A., Hassan, H. E. M., Abdullah, S. S., & Ghonim, A. (2025). Arbitration in Islamic banking: Exploring legal and practical implications for dispute resolution. *Banks and Bank Systems*, *20*(2), 15–28. DOI: 10.21511/bbs.20(2).2025.02

Alhiniti, Y., & Zaid, M. Y. A. (2026). Future prospects of electronic commercial arbitration in light of modern technologies and artificial intelligence. In *Studies in Systems, Decision and Control*. https://www.scopus.com/pages/publications/105027061756

Angerschmid, A., Zhou, J., Theuermann, K., Chen, F., & Holzinger, A. (2022). Fairness and explanation in AI-informed decision making. *Machine Learning and Knowledge Extraction*, *4*(2), 556–579. DOI: 10.3390/make4020026

Arjmand, S., & Kondori, N. F. (2025). Identifying functions and benefits of artificial intelligence in judgement using the metasynthesis method. Iranian Journal of Information Processing and Management. https://jipm.irandoc.ac.ir/article_728675_en.html

Azab, R. S., & Ismail, H. H. (2024). AI as a tool to enhance digital arbitration effectiveness: Analytical study under Silicon Valley Arbitration Center guidelines. *Edelweiss Applied Science and Technology*, *8*(6), 1723–1734. DOI: 10.55214/25768484.v8i6.2333

Feng, S., & Shen, W. (2025). Selecting arbitrators by AI: Theoretical analysis and institutional responses. *International Journal of Legal Discourse*, *10*(2), 333–360. DOI: 10.1515/ijld-2025-2018

Labanieh, M. F., Alshamsi, A. A. S. S., Ayub, Z. A., & Wahab, H. A. (2025). The potential benefits of establishing an AI-arbitration legal framework in Malaysia. Multidisciplinary Science Journal. https://malque.pub/ojs/index.php/msj/article/view/10180

Perera, D., & Tan, A. (2025). AI guidelines in international arbitration: Revolutionary or cautionary? A comparative analysis. *Journal of International Arbitration*. https://www.scopus.com/pages/publications/105018928452

Ramadan, S. A., Abdelsalam, T., Qasim, A., & Aldabousi, A. M. (2025). The role and impact of legal legislation in achieving sustainable development goals: An applied study on UAE legislation. In *Studies in Systems, Decision and Control*. Springer., DOI: 10.1007/978-3-031-96641-5_4

Surana, S., Dembla, S., & Bihani, P. (2022). Identifying contradictions in the legal proceedings using natural language models. *SN Computer Science*, *3*(3), 187. DOI: 10.1007/s42979-022-01075-3

Tsuda, K., Ichino, J., & Shimizu, K. (2023). Gender effects on physical contact in social VR. In *Lecture Notes in Computer Science (including subseries Lecture Notes in Artificial Intelligence and Lecture Notes in Bioinformatics)*. https://www.scopus.com/pages/publications/85171473708

Weerasinghe, M., Macdonald, S., Fiani, C., et al., & Khamis, M. (2025). Beyond mute and block: Adoption and effectiveness of safety tools in social VR, from ubiquitous harassment to social sculpting. *IEEE Transactions on Visualization and Computer Graphics*. https://www.scopus.com/pages/publications/105004050119

Wu, Y. (2025). Arbitrators in the virtual world: The evolution of independence and impartiality and the safeguarding of procedural justice in metaverse dispute resolution. Arbitration: The International Journal of Arbitration. *Mediation and Dispute Management, 91*(4), 360–386. DOI: 10.54648/AMDM2025027

KEY TERMS AND DEFINITIONS

Arbitration Agreement: A written agreement by which parties submit disputes to arbitration rather than courts, including electronic formation where legally recognised.

Attribution: Linking a digital act or record (avatar action, account event, transaction) to a specific person or controlled device/account.

Authentication: The process of demonstrating that a digital exhibit is genuine and what it purports to be (source, creation, and integrity).

Chain of Custody: Documented handling history of evidence from collection to presentation to ensure integrity and prevent tampering claims.

Cybersecurity in Arbitration: Technical and organisational safeguards protecting confidentiality, integrity, and availability of arbitration communications and evidence.

Electronic Evidence: Digitally stored or transmitted information used to prove facts (logs, recordings, platform records, metadata, smart-contract traces).

Metaverse: A network of persistent virtual environments where users, avatars, and digital assets interact for work, commerce, and social activity.

Online Dispute Resolution (ODR): Technology-enabled dispute resolution processes (negotiation, mediation, arbitration) conducted partly or fully through digital platforms.

Seat of Arbitration: The legal place of arbitration that determines the procedural law (lex arbitri) and court supervision, even if hearings occur online.

Virtual Hearing: An arbitration hearing conducted remotely via video/online platforms, requiring identity verification, integrity controls, and equal participation.

Virtual Reality (VR): A computer-generated immersive environment in which users interact with simulated spaces via headsets, sensors, and digital interfaces.

Virtual Reality Dispute: A conflict arising from conduct, transactions, or harms occurring in VR/metaverse environments (e.g., digital asset theft, contract breach, harassment).

Chapter 2
From WhatsApp Messages to Cloud Logs: Admissibility, Authentication, and Chain-of-Custody of Digital Evidence Under the UAE Legal Framework

Tarek Abdelsalam
Umm Al Quwain University, UAE

George Nabil Micheal
http://orcid.org/0000-0002-0712-4247
Institute of Public Administration, Saudi Arabia

Esraa Taha Khudhair Shujairi
University of Baghdad, Iraq

Saad Ali Ramadan
http://orcid.org/0000-0003-0043-6982
Umm Al Quwain University, UAE

ABSTRACT

Digital transformation has shifted the evidentiary center of gravity in modern disputes from paper documents to electronically generated traces such as instant-messaging communications, mobile device artifacts, platform records, and cloud audit logs. In the United Arab Emirates (UAE), this shift is reinforced by reforms that recognize electronic evidence and modern communication tools within civil, commercial, and criminal proceedings, while preserving core principles of relevance, legality,

DOI: 10.4018/979-8-3373-7961-6.ch002

authenticity, and judicial evaluation of probative value. Yet the abundance of digital evidence does not automatically translate into legal reliability. Messaging records can be selectively captured, edited, or presented without context; cloud logs can be misinterpreted, exported without provenance, or lost because of short retention windows; and cross-border infrastructures complicate acquisition and verification.

1- INTRODUCTION

Digital evidence now routinely determines outcomes in civil, commercial, and criminal disputes. Many facts that used to be evidenced by signed paper documents are instead captured in electronic traces: a supplier confirms delivery through an instant message; a manager authorizes payment by email; a cloud tenant administrator changes access permissions through a console; a security platform logs a sequence of authentication attempts before a suspected intrusion. These traces exist in multiple forms and layers: message databases on devices, exported transcripts in files, metadata created by applications, and server-side records generated by platforms. They can be copied instantly, presented selectively, and interpreted in ways that either clarify or distort the factual narrative.

The technical characteristics of digital evidence challenge traditional evidence concepts in several ways. First, the notion of an "original" becomes ambiguous because identical copies can exist across devices and systems. Second, the same evidentiary content can be represented through different artefacts with very different reliability profiles: a screenshot, an exported transcript, a database extraction, or a forensic image. Third, digital evidence is often volatile and context-dependent. Normal device use can modify databases; logs can be rotated; cloud services can compress or normalize records; and timestamps can be stored in different time bases. Fourth, digital evidence frequently implicates privacy and cross-border jurisdiction issues because it may contain personal data and may be stored in geographically distributed infrastructures.

The UAE is a particularly relevant jurisdiction for examining these dynamics. As a regional hub for commerce, finance, logistics, and technology, the UAE faces disputes that involve multinational platforms, cross-border cloud infrastructures, and rapidly evolving communication practices. Its legislative reforms have modernized evidentiary and procedural frameworks to accommodate electronic records and modern means of communication as proof. At the same time, the UAE procedural environment retains core legal expectations: evidence must be relevant, should be obtained lawfully, and must be sufficiently reliable for judicial reliance. The result is that digital evidence is not excluded as a category, but it is frequently contested on questions of authenticity, attribution, completeness, and integrity.

Two evidence types illustrate the stakes. The first is WhatsApp-style messaging evidence. Litigants often submit screenshots or partial exports that appear compelling but are vulnerable to manipulation and missing context. Opponents challenge them by alleging fabrication, selective capture, identity uncertainty (who controlled the account), or post-hoc editing. The second is cloud logs and platform records. These machine-generated records are powerful because they can document actions such as access, downloads, permission changes, and administrative operations. Yet cloud logs raise their own vulnerabilities: a party may not preserve them in time; exports may be incomplete; fields may be misunderstood; and cross-platform correlations may be necessary to draw reliable conclusions. Because cloud evidence is mediated through provider interfaces, courts also need assurance about provenance and continuity.

This chapter therefore treats digital evidence reliability as a process rather than a file. It proposes an integrated framework anchored in a triad that aligns legal doctrine with technical practice: lawful acquisition (including proportionality and authority), authentication and attribution (for persons and systems), and integrity preservation through a documented chain-of-custody (CoC). The triad reflects the core concerns of digital forensics scholarship. Antwi-Boasiako and Venter propose a structured admissibility assessment model that unifies technical and legal requirements into an evaluative process rather than a purely formal legal question (Antwi-Boasiako & Venter, 2017). Narasimhan and Kala emphasize that CoC is a central mechanism for ensuring integrity and admissibility, highlighting best practices that translate directly into courtroom credibility (Narasimhan & Kala, 2024). For cloud evidence, Nasreldin and colleagues identify acquisition and CoC challenges unique to distributed infrastructures and suggest cryptographic mechanisms as part of integrity and confidentiality controls (Nasreldin et al., 2015). Lucien's systematic review likewise highlights trustworthiness and CoC as recurring barriers in cloud evidence that directly influence admissibility (Lucien, 2024).

The chapter aims to support practical implementation under UAE procedural reforms. It does not provide legal advice; rather, it articulates a defensible approach to collecting, documenting, and presenting digital evidence so that courts can evaluate it efficiently and consistently. To keep the narrative coherent and accessible, the chapter uses limited headings and emphasizes integrated workflows, courtroom communication, and documentation tools. The appendices provide a chain-of-custody template and practical checklists that can be adopted in investigations and litigation preparation.

2- LEGAL AND INSTITUTIONAL LANDSCAPE FOR DIGITAL EVIDENCE IN THE UAE

The UAE legal environment for digital evidence is best understood as an interlocking architecture rather than a single statute. For civil and commercial disputes, the central instrument is the Evidence Law in Civil and Commercial Transactions (Federal Decree-Law No. 35 of 2022). This law recognizes that proof may be established by electronic means and accommodates electronic documents, correspondence, and modern communication tools as evidentiary categories. The practical significance is that electronic records are not treated as exceptional materials; they are incorporated into ordinary evidentiary evaluation. Courts therefore focus less on whether a WhatsApp transcript or a cloud audit export is admissible in principle, and more on whether it is sufficiently reliable and lawfully acquired to carry probative weight in the case at hand.

The Evidence Law operates alongside the Electronic Transactions and Trust Services regime (Federal Decree-Law No. 46 of 2021). While this regime is often associated with electronic commerce and digital signatures, its concepts are foundational for evidence disputes because it articulates the legal recognition of electronic records and trust services that support identity, integrity, and non-repudiation. In many digital disputes, authentication is strengthened when evidence is linked to recognized trust mechanisms: an electronic signature certificate, a trusted timestamp, an electronic seal, or a documented trust service relationship. Even when such mechanisms are not used, the trust services framework clarifies what kinds of technical controls can function as legally meaningful authenticity indicators.

Procedural law shapes the lifecycle of evidence in litigation and investigation. The Civil Procedure Code (Federal Decree-Law No. 42 of 2022) governs how parties submit documents, challenge evidence, request disclosure or production, and rely on expert analysis. As litigation processes become increasingly digitized, procedural rules interact with electronic filing, electronic notifications, and document management systems. For criminal matters, the Criminal Procedure Law (Federal Decree-Law No. 38 of 2022) is especially relevant because it governs investigation powers, seizure, search, and the procedural legality of obtaining and preserving evidence. In criminal proceedings, the legality of acquisition can be central: digital artefacts may be excluded or discounted if collected without competent authorization or in a manner inconsistent with procedural safeguards.

The UAE cybercrime framework (Federal Decree-Law No. 34 of 2021 on Countering Rumors and Cybercrimes) influences digital evidence practice by emphasizing the illegality of unauthorized access and misuse of information systems. This matters in two ways. First, it shapes the substantive legal context of cyber and digital offences. Second, it reinforces the evidentiary principle that evidence should be lawfully obtained. A party that obtains evidence through unauthorized access risks both legal liability and evidentiary vulnerability because the court may view the evidence as tainted or unreliable. In parallel, the UAE Personal Data Protection Law (Federal Decree-Law No. 45 of 2021) and related compliance practices affect internal investigations and corporate evidence collection. While civil litigation often involves parties who are free to preserve evidence within their lawful control, organizations must still consider proportionality and data minimization when collecting employee communications or customer records. Overbroad evidence collection can create privacy risk and can weaken credibility if the court perceives the process as intrusive rather than targeted.

Institutionally, digital evidence is operationalized by investigators, forensic analysts, expert witnesses, and litigators. Courts evaluate not only the content of an artefact but also the narrative of how it was obtained, preserved, and interpreted. This is why digital evidence disputes frequently hinge on process documentation rather than on substantive content alone. Garrie and Morrissy emphasize that judges require clarity about the content and quality of digital forensic evidence. Quality includes the ability to demonstrate the integrity of the evidence and to communicate the meaning of technical traces without exaggeration (Garrie & Morrissy, 2014). The UAE's evidentiary modernization therefore creates an implicit demand for professionalization: parties are expected to substantiate authenticity and continuity claims through demonstrable handling procedures.

Cross-border technology platforms and cloud infrastructures amplify these demands. Messaging platforms may store limited server-side metadata because of encryption and privacy architectures; cloud services may store logs in regional data centers; and provider cooperation can be shaped by contractual terms and legal processes. In some cases, the best evidence is not available through the provider and must be obtained from devices or organizational tenants. In other cases, the provider's audit records are the most objective evidence. A realistic UAE-ready approach must therefore combine legal awareness with technical pragmatism: the evidence handler must preserve what is available, document limitations transparently, and corroborate across sources to support reliability. This chapter's framework builds precisely on that alignment.

3- A UAE-ORIENTED TECHNO-LEGAL FRAMEWORK FOR ADMISSIBILITY AND WEIGHT

The admissibility of digital evidence is often described as a gatekeeping problem: the court admits evidence if it is relevant and not excluded by legal rules. In digital disputes, however, admissibility and probative weight depend on a hybrid of legal standards and technical practice. An electronic artefact is not self-authenticating merely because it exists as a file. The court must be satisfied that the artefact is what it claims to be, that it is attributable to a person or system in a legally meaningful way, and that it has not been altered in the journey from acquisition to presentation. Because these questions are simultaneously legal and technical, a coherent framework is necessary to avoid ad hoc and inconsistent reasoning.

This chapter proposes a triadic framework: lawful acquisition, authentication and attribution, and integrity preservation through chain-of-custody. Lawful acquisition asks whether the evidence was obtained through an authority basis consistent with UAE procedural and substantive law, and whether the scope of acquisition was proportionate to the evidentiary need. In civil and commercial disputes, lawful acquisition often rests on participant access (a party's own messages), contractual control (organizational systems), or court-directed production. In criminal investigations, it rests on competent authorization and compliance with procedural safeguards. Proportionality matters across contexts because digital evidence collection can easily become overbroad, capturing vast quantities of personal data. A targeted, documented scope signals reliability and fairness.

Authentication and attribution ask whether the evidence is genuine and whether it can be linked to a person or system. For messaging evidence, authentication includes demonstrating that the record reflects actual messages exchanged and that it is complete for the relevant period. Attribution includes linking the account identifier (phone number or username) to a person and addressing plausible alternative explanations, such as shared devices or account compromise. For cloud logs, authentication includes demonstrating that the records originated from the relevant cloud service and tenant and were exported using reliable, documented methods. Attribution includes linking events to accounts, roles, and devices and explaining what the log fields mean. Comparative scholarship reinforces that attribution and credibility are recurring issues even in jurisdictions that formally recognize electronic evidence. Matis's analysis of messaging evidence in Slovak criminal proceedings emphasizes that relevance and authenticity disputes persist, and that credibility often depends on how convincingly identity linkage and continuity are demonstrated (Matis, 2025; Albatal et al., 2025).

Integrity preservation through chain-of-custody is the mechanism that makes authenticity claims demonstrable. CoC is the sequential documentation and accountability for custody, management, control, transfer, analysis, and disposition of evidence from collection to court (Narasimhan & Kala, 2024). For digital evidence, CoC must address two risks: content alteration and interpretive distortion. Content alteration is mitigated through cryptographic hashing, secure storage, controlled access, and audited transfers. Interpretive distortion is mitigated through transparent methodology and reproducibility: the expert should explain how the evidence was processed and what assumptions were used. Nasreldin et al. highlight that cloud evidence acquisition and integrity are complicated by distributed architectures, and that cryptographic mechanisms such as encryption and digital signatures can support confidentiality and chain-of-custody when evidence is acquired from cloud environments (Nasreldin et al., 2015). Lucien's systematic review likewise identifies that trustworthiness and CoC controls are central challenges affecting admissibility in cloud settings (Lucien, 2024).

The triadic framework clarifies the relationship between admissibility and probative weight. Evidence may be admitted but assigned little weight if authentication and integrity are weak. This is common with screenshots and informal exports. Screenshots can be persuasive visually, but they are vulnerable because they usually lack provenance, metadata, and continuity evidence. Courts may admit them as indicative materials while preferring stronger corroboration. Conversely, evidence may be admitted and carry strong weight when the party can demonstrate lawful acquisition, transparent authentication, and robust CoC controls. The framework therefore encourages parties to design their evidence handling strategy at the point of collection, not after a dispute has escalated.

Operationally, the framework can be implemented through an "evidence narrative" for each key artefact. The narrative should answer five questions in plain language: (1) What is the evidence and what fact does it support? (2) Where did it come from and who controlled the source? (3) How was it collected and what tools were used? (4) What integrity controls were applied and how is chain-of-custody documented? (5) How were the relevant excerpts selected and interpreted? When these questions are answered consistently, courts can evaluate reliability efficiently, and opposing parties have fewer grounds to raise procedural objections. The following sections elaborate the CoC pillar and then apply the framework to messaging evidence and cloud logs, with an emphasis on UAE-ready workflows and courtroom communication.

4- CHAIN-OF-CUSTODY AND INTEGRITY PRESERVATION IN DIGITAL FORENSICS

Chain-of-custody (CoC) is often summarized as a form, but in contested digital evidence it is better understood as an integrity system. CoC is the process and documentation that enable an independent reviewer to reconstruct the evidentiary journey from discovery through courtroom presentation: who collected the evidence, what happened to it, who accessed it, how it was stored, and how integrity was verified. The core idea is continuity and accountability. Antwi-Boasiako and Venter argue that digital evidence admissibility depends on a harmonized assessment that integrates technical and legal controls; CoC functions as the evidence of that harmonization because it makes integrity and provenance auditable (Antwi-Boasiako & Venter, 2017).

Digital CoC has two intertwined dimensions: custody of physical devices and custody of extracted datasets. Device custody matters for evidence that resides on phones, laptops, and storage media. Normal use can change databases, update metadata, or overwrite logs. If a device is central to a dispute, preservation should minimize changes and document the state of the device at the time evidence is identified. Data custody matters because analysis and presentation are performed on copies and derivatives. A master evidence package should be preserved, hashed, and stored securely. Working copies for analysis should be created deliberately and documented. Each derivative should be traceable to the master package.

Narasimhan and Kala emphasize that CoC is crucial for ensuring reliability and admissibility and outline best practices that translate directly into procedural defensibility (Narasimhan & Kala, 2024). These best practices include unique evidence identifiers; time-stamped entries for each transfer and action; clear identification of handlers and their roles; secure storage with restricted access; and integrity verification through hashing. Hashing is particularly useful because it creates a cryptographic fingerprint of a file or package. When calculated at acquisition and re-verified at later stages, hash matching provides strong evidence that the artefact has not changed. The key is that hashing must be applied systematically: the method and tool should be documented, and hashing should be performed on the preserved master files rather than on edited derivatives.

Cloud evidence introduces additional CoC complexities. In cloud environments, the evidence source is not a seized device but a service environment controlled partly by a provider. Evidence may be fragmented across virtualized layers and may be accessible only through provider interfaces and APIs. Nasreldin et al. emphasize that cloud evidence acquisition faces challenges in ensuring authenticity and integrity because of distribution and virtualization, and they suggest cryptographic mechanisms to support confidentiality and chain-of-custody (Nasreldin et al., 2015). In cloud contexts, CoC therefore includes administrative access governance. The handler should document who had administrative rights, which role was used to export logs, what filters and settings were applied, and whether the export action itself is captured in audit logs. The goal is to show that the export process was transparent and repeatable, not selective and opaque.

CoC is also a courtroom communication challenge. Garrie and Morrissy explain that judges must evaluate the quality of digital forensic evidence, and that quality includes integrity and methodological clarity (Garrie & Morrissy, 2014). A CoC record that exists but is not explained can still fail to persuade. Therefore, CoC should be summarized in the evidence narrative: when it was collected, where it was stored, who accessed it, and what integrity checks were performed. In contested cases, the proponent should anticipate common challenges: "The screenshot was edited"; "The export could be incomplete"; "The logs were selected"; "The device could have been used by someone else"; "The expert processed the data without controls". The strongest response is a combination of disciplined CoC documentation and transparent methodology.

Because CoC disputes are common, standardization is valuable. Template-based documentation reduces omissions and improves consistency across cases. The appendices provide a CoC log template and checklists designed for both device-based and cloud-based evidence. The templates are intentionally simple so they can be used not only by forensic laboratories but also by organizations conducting internal investigations. Internal investigations frequently become litigation, and weaknesses in early evidence handling can later be exploited. A disciplined CoC is therefore a practical risk management tool as well as an evidentiary requirement.

5- WHATSAPP-STYLE MESSAGING EVIDENCE: ADMISSIBILITY, AUTHENTICATION, AND HANDLING

Messaging applications have become a dominant channel for personal and business communication, and their evidentiary role has expanded accordingly. In the UAE context, modern means of communication are recognized as evidence categories in civil and commercial disputes, but the practical question is reliability. Messaging evidence is frequently submitted in weak forms, especially screenshots, that invite disputes about authenticity, completeness, and attribution.

The starting point is lawful access and proportionality. When a party is a participant in a conversation, access through their own device is generally lawful. Problems arise when parties attempt to obtain evidence from another person's device without authority, or when employers collect employee communications without clear policy notice and lawful basis. Because messaging datasets can include sensitive personal and third-party content, proportional collection is important. A defensible approach is to define the relevant timeframe and conversational context and to collect only what is necessary to prove or disprove the disputed facts.

Acquisition method is decisive. Messaging evidence can be presented as (a) screenshots, (b) platform chat exports, (c) backups (device or cloud), or (d) forensic extractions of application databases. Each has different reliability. Screenshots are visually compelling but easily manipulated and typically lack metadata. Exports generated through platform functions are stronger because they provide structured records, but they still may omit metadata present in databases and can be generated selectively. Backups can preserve broader context but may introduce complexity in verifying completeness. Forensic extraction is typically the most robust because it can capture databases, metadata, and supporting artefacts under controlled conditions, but it requires specialized tools and skills.

Authentication for messaging evidence has two layers: identity linkage and content authenticity. Identity linkage connects the account identifier (phone number, account name) to a person. This may be supported by subscription ownership, device ownership, contact lists, profile information, and corroborating communications (emails referencing the same facts, transaction records, or witness testimony). Content authenticity concerns whether the messages were actually exchanged and whether the record is complete and unedited. A key vulnerability is selective presentation. Parties sometimes present only fragments that support their case. The strongest approach is to preserve the full conversation for the relevant timeframe and then present relevant excerpts transparently. If excerpts are presented, the selection method should be explained, and the complete preserved record should be available for court review if required.

Chain-of-custody is essential because the source device often contains the best evidence. Preservation steps should minimize changes to the device and document its state at acquisition. If a forensic extraction is performed, the extraction method and tool versions should be documented, and the extracted image should be hashed. If an export is performed, the export file and any associated media should be hashed and stored as a master package. Working copies for highlighting or translation should be derived from the master package and documented as derivatives. In contested cases, an expert may be needed to explain what artefacts were collected, what metadata exists, and whether manipulation indicators are present.

Messaging evidence also raises interpretive challenges. Voice notes, images, and emojis can change meaning; timestamps may be affected by device settings; and language translation can distort nuance. Therefore, interpretation should be conservative and corroborated. Comparative scholarship reinforces that courts worldwide face similar challenges with messaging evidence. Matis notes that even when electronic evidence is accepted formally, disputes about authenticity and credibility persist, and courts often rely on corroboration and procedural rigor to resolve them (Matis, 2025). This insight is directly applicable to UAE practice: formal recognition does not remove the need for robust authentication and integrity practices.

When presented effectively, messaging evidence can be powerful. The court should receive a concise reliability statement, relevant excerpts, and a CoC and hash manifest. The narrative should avoid technical overreach. Instead of claiming that messages are "impossible to fake," the proponent should explain why, given the acquisition method, documentation, integrity controls, and corroboration, the evidence is sufficiently reliable to support the factual conclusion. The next section examines cloud logs, where the evidence is often machine-generated and requires different acquisition and interpretation disciplines.

6- CLOUD LOGS AND PLATFORM RECORDS: ACQUISITION, TRUSTWORTHINESS, AND INTERPRETATION

Cloud logs and platform records are increasingly decisive in disputes because organizations rely on cloud services for storage, identity management, collaboration, and infrastructure operations. Many contested facts involve access and actions rather than written agreements: who accessed a file, when permissions changed, whether an account performed an administrative action, or whether suspicious login attempts occurred. Cloud audit logs provide time-stamped records of such events and can be more objective than human recollection. Yet they are not automatically self-explanatory or automatically trustworthy; reliability depends on prompt preservation, provenance documentation, and correct interpretation.

Cloud forensics literature identifies recurring obstacles. Alenezi highlights constraints on cloud data acquisition, multi-tenancy, virtualization, encryption, privacy barriers, and tool limitations (Alenezi, 2023). These obstacles mean that investigators often cannot create traditional forensic images of server hardware. Instead, they export logs and snapshots through provider tools. Nasreldin et al. describe cloud evidence acquisition and emphasize challenges in ensuring authenticity and integrity; they note that encryption and digital signatures can support confidentiality and chain-of-custody, but acquisition workflows must account for cloud architecture realities (Nasreldin et al., 2015). Lucien's systematic review similarly concludes that trustworthiness and chain-of-custody challenges in cloud environments affect admissibility and that procedural discipline and standardization remain gaps (Lucien, 2024). These findings imply that cloud log evidence is only as persuasive as the process that produces it.

The first practical challenge is retention and volatility. Many cloud platforms have default log retention periods that may be short. If a party does not preserve logs promptly, they may be overwritten or become inaccessible. Therefore, cloud evidence handling should begin with rapid identification and preservation. Organizations should implement legal hold procedures, and investigators should export relevant logs as soon as practicable. Preservation should also include documenting logging configurations: what logs were enabled, at what level, and for what period. If logging was disabled or insufficient, that limitation should be recorded transparently because it affects the scope of defensible inference.

The second challenge is provenance and authentication. Cloud logs must be authenticated by showing that they originate from the relevant cloud service and tenant and that the export method is reliable. Best practice is to export logs using provider-native tools (administrative consoles or official APIs) and to document tenant identifiers, account roles used for export, filters applied, export timestamps, and file formats. If the export action itself generates an audit event, that event should be preserved as meta-evidence of provenance. The proponent should also preserve provider documentation describing log semantics and fields, because courts may require contextual explanation.

The third challenge is time normalization and correlation. Cloud logs often use UTC timestamps and may record events across multiple services with different event identifiers. Misinterpreting time bases can distort narratives, especially when an action is close in time to a security alert. Therefore, the evidence handler should document time zone conversions and verify clock assumptions. Correlation is equally important. A single log stream may be ambiguous; correlating across identity logs, multi-factor authentication events, endpoint telemetry, email alerts, and ticketing systems can support stronger conclusions.

Chain-of-custody for cloud logs has distinctive features. The evidence source is a service environment and the collector often has administrative access rather than physical control. CoC therefore includes documentation of access governance: who had admin rights, what roles and permissions were used, and how exports were stored and protected. After export, logs should be packaged as a master bundle, hashed, and stored in secure vaulting. Any parsing, filtering, or visualization should be performed on working copies, and derived datasets should be documented as derivatives. This disciplined approach helps counter allegations that logs were selected or modified.

Cross-border issues may limit what is available. Cloud data can be stored in multiple jurisdictions, and provider cooperation may depend on legal processes. In some civil disputes, parties may not have access to provider-side records beyond what the tenant controls permit. A defensible approach is transparency: document what was available, what was not, what requests were made, and why. Courts can weigh evidence in light of reasonable availability, especially when the proponent demonstrates that it preserved what it could and sought corroboration elsewhere.

Finally, presentation is critical. Raw logs can overwhelm courts and invite misunderstanding. A persuasive approach is to build a timeline narrative that presents key events and references the underlying log extracts as exhibits. The timeline should explain selection criteria and provide enough context for verification. Expert testimony may be needed to explain log semantics, limitations, and the defensible scope of inferences. Courts are generally receptive to cloud logs when they are presented as a transparent, auditable process rather than as opaque technical assertions.

7- EXPERT REPORTS, COURTROOM COMMUNICATION, AND EVIDENCE QUALITY

Digital evidence frequently requires expert interpretation because electronic traces are embedded in technical systems that generate structured records with specialized semantics. Judges and litigators can evaluate relevance and legal issues, but provenance, integrity controls, and log meaning often require expert explanation. This reliance on experts means that the quality of expert reporting becomes a central determinant of evidentiary weight. Garrie and Morrissy emphasize that courts should not treat digital forensic evidence as inherently reliable or inherently suspect; instead, they should evaluate its content and quality, including method transparency and integrity assurances (Garrie & Morrissy, 2014).

A high-quality expert report should align with the triadic framework. First, it should explain the authority basis and scope of acquisition. Second, it should explain the acquisition method and support authentication and attribution. Third, it should document integrity preservation and chain-of-custody. This structure keeps the report closely connected to the legal questions the court must answer. It also reduces the risk that the report becomes an overly technical narrative that does not translate into evidentiary relevance. Transparency is essential: the report should identify tools used (including versions), describe key steps, and explain why those steps are appropriate. Reproducibility should be the guiding principle: another competent expert should be able to follow the method and obtain the same outputs from the same evidence package.

CoC should be embedded into expert reporting. Narasimhan and Kala highlight that CoC is crucial for reliability and admissibility and provide best practices that can be integrated into expert methodology (Narasimhan & Kala, 2024). The expert should reference the CoC log as an exhibit and should summarize key CoC events: receipt, storage, access controls, creation of working copies, and hash verification events. When hash values are used, the report should explain the hashing algorithm, the tools used to compute hashes, and the verification steps. This enables the court to understand integrity verification without needing deep cryptographic expertise.

Experts should also distinguish between artifact integrity and interpretation integrity. Artifact integrity concerns whether the evidence bundle has been altered; interpretation integrity concerns whether the conclusions drawn are justified. For example, a cloud log entry may indicate that an account accessed a file. Interpreting that entry as "the accused stole the file" may be unjustified without additional context, such as download confirmation, data exfiltration indicators, or endpoint telemetry. Expert neutrality requires careful language: describe what the data shows, identify plausible alternative explanations, and cxplain why a particular infcrence is more consistent with the available evidence.

Courtroom communication complements expert reporting. Even a strong expert report can fail to persuade if the evidence is not presented coherently. A practical approach is to prepare a concise reliability statement for each major artefact: what it is, how it was obtained, how integrity was preserved, and what it proves. The statement should avoid exaggerated claims and should anticipate common challenges. For messaging evidence, the statement should address completeness and identity linkage. For cloud logs, it should address provenance, retention, and time normalization. When limitations exist, they should be acknowledged with mitigation strategies such as corroboration across sources.

Evidence quality can also be improved through organizational readiness. Organizations that anticipate disputes should implement evidence readiness programs: enable appropriate logging, establish retention policies, implement legal hold procedures, train staff in evidence preservation, and maintain secure evidence vaulting. Lucien's systematic review of cloud evidence trustworthiness underscores that CoC and standardization challenges remain persistent barriers (Lucien, 2024). Evidence readiness is therefore not only a compliance activity but also a litigation resilience strategy.

In summary, expert reporting and courtroom communication are not peripheral tasks. They are the mechanisms by which technical reliability becomes legally persuasive. The next section examines emerging enhancements, particularly blockchain-based chain-of-custody systems, and evaluates how they may strengthen auditability while acknowledging their limits.

8- BLOCKCHAIN AND EMERGING ENHANCEMENTS FOR CHAIN-OF-CUSTODY

Blockchain has attracted attention in digital forensics because it can create tamper-evident records of events without relying on a single administrator. In chain-of-custody contexts, the proposed advantage is that each custody event - collection, transfer, access, analysis, verification - can be recorded on a distributed ledger. Because entries are cryptographically linked and append-only, unauthorized modification becomes difficult to conceal. A blockchain record can therefore function as an auditable custody trail that supports integrity claims, particularly when evidence passes through multiple organizations or handling teams.

Al-Khateeb, Epiphaniou, and Daly conceptualize the chain-of-custody as a distributed ledger application for modern digital forensics, emphasizing that blockchain can record custody events and integrity proofs and thereby strengthen admissibility arguments (Al-Khateeb et al., 2019). Miller and Singh propose a blockchain-based approach that combines immutability with smart contract logic for access control, suggesting that blockchain can enhance integrity verification and transparency in evidence handling (Miller & Singh, 2024). Related work in blockchain-based CoC for digital forensics proposes similar benefits: improved auditability, reduced single-point-of-failure risks, and greater transparency for custody events (Chopade et al., 2019; Igonor et al., 2025). These proposals respond to a real vulnerability: traditional

CoC logs are sometimes maintained in ordinary documents or case management systems that can be altered, lost, or incompletely recorded.

Yet blockchain is not a substitute for lawful acquisition or for correct forensic collection. A blockchain record can show that a hash existed at a particular time and that custody events were recorded, but it cannot guarantee that the evidence content is authentic or that the initial acquisition was lawful. Authentication and lawful acquisition remain separate pillars. If an artefact is fabricated before it is hashed, blockchain will preserve the hash of a fabricated file. If evidence is obtained through unauthorized access, blockchain auditability does not cure illegality. Courts may still exclude the evidence or discount it on fairness grounds.

Blockchain also introduces practical considerations. Evidence often contains sensitive personal data and confidential information. Recording evidence content on a blockchain is generally inappropriate; most proposals therefore record only hashes and metadata. Even metadata can be sensitive because it can reveal investigative targets or case details. Governance rules must therefore define who can write to the ledger, who can read from it, and how access is audited. In many contexts, a permissioned blockchain is more realistic than a public chain. Implementing such systems requires institutional capacity, technical expertise, and clear policies.

For UAE practice, blockchain-based CoC is most plausible in institutional settings where evidence handling is standardized and disputes about continuity are high-stakes: law enforcement evidence management, large enterprise incident response programs, and regulated sectors with strong governance requirements. In such settings, blockchain can function as an additional layer of auditability. Smart contracts can enforce access permissions and ensure that every access event is recorded. Blockchain may be particularly useful when evidence passes between organizations, such as between internal security teams, external forensic consultants, and legal counsel. However, in ordinary civil disputes involving individuals or small businesses, blockchain CoC infrastructure may be impractical. In those contexts, conventional CoC documentation combined with hashing and secure storage can satisfy reliability requirements when applied consistently.

It is also important to recognize that cloud platforms increasingly provide native features that support tamper-evident evidence preservation. Immutable storage options, key management services, access auditing, and export manifests can create auditability without introducing external blockchain systems. The principle is the same: create a verifiable trail of custody events and integrity checks. A pragmatic UAE-ready approach is therefore incremental: implement robust baseline controls first, then add blockchain-based enhancements where governance and infrastructure support them and where they meaningfully reduce dispute risk.

In summary, blockchain can strengthen the auditability of chain-of-custody, but it is not an evidentiary miracle. Its value lies in governance support for continuity, not in replacing lawful acquisition, authentication, or careful interpretation. The final section consolidates the chapter into an actionable workflow for UAE digital evidence practice and provides templates and checklists for implementation.

9- A CONSOLIDATED UAE-READY WORKFLOW AND RECOMMENDATIONS

The analysis in this chapter can be consolidated into a workflow that practitioners can implement without excessive technical overhead. The workflow is designed to satisfy the admissibility triad: lawful acquisition, authentication and attribution, and integrity preservation through chain-of-custody. It applies to messaging evidence and cloud logs, and it is adaptable to other digital evidence types. The workflow is presented as phases that can be incorporated into organizational policies, internal investigations, and litigation preparation. The guiding idea is to treat evidence handling as evidence design: actions taken at collection determine later admissibility and weight.

Phase 1: Authority and scope. Before collecting any data, define the authority basis and scope. In civil and commercial disputes, identify whether the evidence is collected from a participant device, an organizational system under contractual control, or a production mechanism. In criminal contexts, confirm competent authorization. In organizational investigations, align collection with workplace policies, consent notices, and privacy compliance requirements. Scope should be defined by timeframe, custodians, systems, and relevance. A clear scope supports proportionality and reduces allegations of fishing expeditions.

Phase 2: Preservation. Digital evidence is volatile. Messaging applications can delete or overwrite records; devices can change databases with normal use; cloud platforms can rotate logs. Preservation should be prompt and documented. For messaging evidence, preservation may involve securing the source device, minimizing changes, and performing a documented export or forensic extraction as soon as practical. For cloud logs, preservation may involve enabling audit logging, extending retention where possible, applying legal hold procedures, and exporting relevant logs. Preservation should also include documenting system configurations that affect evidence generation, such as logging settings and retention policies.

Phase 3: Acquisition and documentation. Acquire evidence using methods that are forensically reasonable and explainable. For messaging evidence, prefer structured chat exports or forensic extraction over screenshots. If screenshots are used, treat them as illustrative and corroborate with stronger artefacts. For cloud logs, export using provider-native tools and document tenant identifiers, roles used, filters applied, export timestamps, and file formats. Record tool versions and settings.

When conversion or parsing is needed, document conversion steps and preserve original exports.

Phase 4: Integrity verification and chain-of-custody. Immediately after acquisition, compute hashes for evidence packages and record them. Open a CoC log and update it for every transfer, access, conversion, and analysis action. Store the master package in secure, access-controlled storage. Create working copies for analysis and record their hashes. In cloud contexts, preserve original exports as authoritative sources and treat parsed datasets as derivatives. Where possible, use storage systems that provide access auditing and immutability controls. The aim is to ensure that any party can verify continuity and integrity.

Phase 5: Analysis and correlation. Digital evidence becomes more persuasive when correlated across sources. Messaging records can be correlated with emails, transaction documents, delivery records, and witness testimony. Cloud logs can be correlated with identity provider logs, multi-factor authentication records, endpoint telemetry, and security alerts. Analysis should be documented: selection criteria, filters applied, and assumptions used. Where assumptions are unavoidable (for example, time conversions), they should be stated and justified.

Phase 6: Presentation and explanation. Present evidence with clarity and transparency. Provide a concise reliability statement for each key artefact: what it is, where it came from, how it was acquired, and how integrity was preserved. Provide relevant excerpts with clear referencing and pagination, and explain how excerpts were selected. Attach the CoC summary and hash manifest. Where technical interpretation is necessary, provide an expert report structured around lawful acquisition, authentication, and integrity preservation. Avoid overclaiming. Courts are persuaded by transparency and reproducibility, not by absolute assertions.

Several recommendations follow for UAE stakeholders. For courts, standardized expectations for digital evidence submission packages can reduce disputes. Minimum requirements could include a provenance statement, CoC summary, and hash manifest for contested electronic exhibits. Courts can encourage standardized expert report structures aligned with the triadic framework. For investigators and forensic practitioners, the recommendation is disciplined documentation and avoidance of informal evidence handling, such as using personal devices for evidence copies or sharing evidence bundles without controlled access. For organizations, the recommendation is evidence readiness: configure logging, retention, and access auditing; train staff; and establish incident response preservation steps.

These recommendations align with the literature. Nasreldin et al. emphasize cloud evidence acquisition and chain-of-custody challenges and the role of cryptographic mechanisms (Nasreldin et al., 2015). Lucien identifies trustworthiness and CoC as recurring barriers in cloud environments affecting admissibility (Lucien, 2024). Narasimhan and Kala emphasize CoC best practices as essential to integrity and admissibility (Narasimhan & Kala, 2024). Antwi-Boasiako and Venter advocate structured techno-legal admissibility assessment rather than ad hoc evaluation (Antwi-Boasiako & Venter, 2017). Blockchain-based approaches (Al-Khateeb et al., 2019; Miller & Singh, 2024; Chopade et al., 2019) illustrate how custody auditability can be strengthened, but the chapter emphasizes that baseline discipline is the primary driver of reliability.

Ultimately, UAE procedural reforms provide the legal infrastructure to accept digital proof, but they also raise expectations for evidence handling. When digital evidence is collected and presented as a defensible process, courts can focus on substantive resolution rather than procedural conflict. The appendices provide practical tools to support implementation: a chain-of-custody log template and checklists for messaging and cloud evidence. These tools can be integrated into litigation preparation, internal investigations, and evidence management policies to improve the reliability and persuasiveness of digital proof under UAE procedural reforms.

10- EXTENDED PRACTICAL APPLICATION: BUILDING COURT-READY EVIDENCE PACKAGES FOR WHATSAPP AND CLOUD LOGS

This section extends the chapter with a pragmatic, court-oriented discussion of how digital evidence packages are built and defended in real disputes. The aim is to translate the triadic framework (lawful acquisition, authentication/attribution, and integrity through chain-of-custody) into concrete artefacts that can be filed in a UAE proceeding and withstand challenge. The discussion uses hypothetical scenarios for illustration, because the evidentiary steps are generally stable across sectors: the facts change, but the reliability questions raised by opposing parties are highly repetitive. The value of standardizing the package is that it narrows the dispute. Instead of litigating broad accusations such as "these messages are fake" or "these logs were manipulated," the parties and the court can focus on specific, verifiable questions: What was the source? Who controlled it? What method produced the export? What integrity checks were applied? What parts are excerpts and what parts are the preserved master record?

A court-ready package typically contains four layers. Layer 1 is the narrative layer: a concise statement (often one to three pages) that identifies the factual proposition to be proved and explains, in plain language, how the digital artefact supports that proposition. Layer 2 is the provenance layer: documents that link the artefact to its source and to the relevant person or system. For messaging evidence, provenance materials can include SIM ownership or subscription records, device custody documentation, and contemporaneous business records that show the same phone number or account identifier was used in the relationship. For cloud logs, provenance materials can include tenant identifiers, administrative role descriptions, screenshots of logging configuration at the relevant time, and an export "receipt" showing how the logs were generated. Layer 3 is the integrity layer: hash manifests, packaging records, and chain-of-custody logs showing continuity from acquisition to presentation. Layer 4 is the analytic layer: curated excerpts, timelines, correlation tables, and (where needed) expert explanations, all explicitly linked back to the preserved master exports so the court can verify that the analytic layer is not cherry-picked or altered.

Hypothetical scenario A (commercial dispute): two companies negotiate delivery terms and penalty clauses through WhatsApp because the operational teams are communicating rapidly across sites. Later, one party alleges that the other agreed to a reduced price and waived penalties; the opponent denies that such agreement occurred and claims the chat screenshot presented in court is fabricated. In this scenario, the most common weaknesses are (1) reliance on screenshots rather than a defensible export, (2) lack of identity linkage beyond a saved contact name, and (3) lack of completeness (only the favorable messages are shown). A strengthened approach begins with collecting the relevant chat record as a structured export from the device of the party who participated in the conversation. The export should include media and should cover the relevant timeframe. Immediately after export, the proponent should compute a SHA-256 hash of the export file(s) and record it in a hash manifest. The export should be stored as the "master package" in secure storage, and the chain-of-custody log should start at this point. All later work—translation, highlighting, excerpting, timeline building—should be done on working copies derived from the master package, with their own hashes and derivation notes. This practice does not guarantee that the opponent will accept authenticity, but it prevents the court from being forced to decide based on a fragile screenshot alone.

Identity linkage in scenario A must be treated as an evidentiary problem rather than as a mere assumption. A WhatsApp contact label ("Manager Ahmed") proves nothing about identity because labels are user-defined. Instead, the proponent should establish linkage through converging indicators. Examples include: contracts or invoices that list the same phone number; emails or letters where the alleged counterparty signs off with the same number; call records showing repeated communication with the number during the relationship; delivery notes that reference the number; or witness statements from employees who routinely communicated with that number as part of business performance. If the dispute is acute, the proponent may request that the court order inspection of the counterparty's device or request a forensic examination, but even without that, multi-source corroboration increases weight. The key is to show that attribution is the most reasonable explanation, not the only possible explanation. Courts often evaluate proof on a balance of plausibility, and attribution becomes stronger when alternative hypotheses (such as impersonation or number reuse) are addressed explicitly in the narrative.

Completeness is another recurring vulnerability. Messaging evidence is easy to excerpt, which creates a "selective capture" challenge. A proponent should preserve the full conversation for the relevant period in the master package, even if only a small subset will be filed as an exhibit. The exhibit should clearly state that it is an excerpt and should define the selection criteria. For example: "Pages 4–12 reproduce the messages from 12–18 March 2025 relevant to delivery pricing and penalty waiver; the full exported conversation from 1 January to 31 May 2025 is preserved in the master package and can be produced if requested." This approach balances relevance and proportionality. It reduces the risk that the court views the evidence as cherry-picked, while avoiding unnecessary disclosure of unrelated personal content. Where privacy is sensitive, a court can order limited disclosure or supervised inspection, but the proponent must demonstrate that a full record exists and is preserved with integrity (Awad & Aldabousi, 2024).

Hypothetical scenario B (employment dispute): an employer alleges that a staff member disclosed confidential information to a competitor and relies on WhatsApp messages that include attachments, voice notes, and screenshots. The employee denies authorship and argues that the phone was accessible to other people and that the employer accessed the device unlawfully. This scenario highlights the interaction of lawful acquisition and privacy with evidentiary weight. The employer's first task is to demonstrate a lawful basis for collecting evidence. In corporate investigations, lawful basis is strengthened by clear workplace policies that inform employees of acceptable use, monitoring rights, and investigation procedures. The employer should document consent notices, policy acknowledgements, and the limited scope of the collection. Even when lawful access exists, proportionality remains important: collecting entire device content or unrelated conversations can trigger privacy concerns under data protection principles. Therefore, the employer should document scope limitation (timeframe, relevant contacts, relevant keywords) and the steps taken to minimize exposure of irrelevant personal data (Ghonim & Awad, 2024).

Attribution challenges in scenario B are best addressed by combining messaging artefacts with device and system artefacts. Messaging databases often store metadata that screenshots omit, such as message identifiers, internal timestamps, attachment references, and, in some systems, encryption-related flags. If a forensic extraction is performed, an expert can describe how the artefacts were obtained and how they relate to the application's internal storage. However, even without deep forensic extraction, attribution can be supported by contextual correlation: did the same employee use the same number for payroll contact, HR updates, or project coordination? Were the attachments also found in corporate email or shared drives? Did the employee's corporate account access logs show contemporaneous uploading of the same files to external services? When multiple evidence streams converge on the same narrative, attribution becomes more persuasive and courts are less likely to accept a generic denial of authorship.

This scenario also illustrates why "content authenticity" and "lawful acquisition" should not be conflated. Even if a message is authentic, unlawful access can undermine admissibility or weight and can create separate legal exposure. Conversely, lawful access does not automatically prove authenticity if the evidence was handled informally. The proponent should therefore explain both dimensions separately: (1) the lawful basis and proportional scope, and (2) the technical integrity controls and chain-of-custody steps that preserve the artefact. Separating the issues helps the court focus on the correct question at each stage, rather than collapsing reliability into a single contested claim. It also aligns with best-practice recommendations that treat chain-of-custody as a core reliability foundation (Narasimhan & Kala, 2024).

Hypothetical scenario C (cyber incident dispute): a company alleges that an external actor compromised its cloud environment and exfiltrated data. The defense claims that the company's own employees performed the actions or that the logs are incomplete. Here, cloud logs and platform records are central, but their probative value depends on correct preservation and interpretation. The first risk is retention. If the company fails to preserve audit logs promptly, the most relevant period may be overwritten. Therefore, incident response playbooks should include immediate log export and secure retention. The second risk is provenance. A proponent should document the exact cloud tenant, the services involved, and the roles used to export logs. If logs were exported via an API, the request parameters, time range, and query filters should be documented. If the platform provides an export manifest or checksum, that should be preserved in the master package and referenced in the chain-of-custody record.

A common failure mode in cloud log evidence is "semantic overreach": treating a log entry as proof of an actor's intent or identity beyond what the record can support. For example, an audit log may show that a particular access key was used to retrieve an object, but it may not identify the human user who operated the key. Attribution may require correlation with identity provider logs, multi-factor authentication events, device telemetry, and administrative change logs. Time normalization is also critical. Logs may be in UTC, while human activity narratives are in local time. A disciplined package therefore includes a time conversion table and explicitly states the time basis used in each exhibit. Where correlation is performed, the methodology should be described: how records were joined, what identifiers were matched (user IDs, session IDs, IP addresses), and what uncertainties remain. Courts are more likely to accept a careful, bounded inference than a sweeping conclusion that ignores technical ambiguity.

In scenario C, chain-of-custody includes governance of administrative access. Because cloud evidence is collected through privileged roles, opponents may argue that administrators could have altered or filtered logs. The practical mitigation is to use provider-native immutability controls where available, to export logs promptly, and to preserve original exports as authoritative sources. The evidence package should show who had administrative rights at the relevant time, what roles were used, and how access was controlled. Where feasible, storing exports in immutable storage (write-once-read-many controls) and enabling access auditing strengthens integrity arguments. Again, the point is not to claim impossibility of manipulation; it is to demonstrate that the process made manipulation detectable and unlikely, and that the evidence handler took reasonable steps to preserve integrity in a manner consistent with cloud forensics scholarship (Nasreldin et al., 2015; Lucien, 2024).

Across these scenarios, a small set of "failure modes" explains most adverse outcomes in digital evidence disputes. Failure mode 1 is informal capture: screenshots, forwarded messages, or copied-and-pasted text without provenance. Failure mode 2 is missing continuity: files passed between people without documentation, stored on personal devices, or edited for presentation without preserving originals. Failure mode 3 is weak attribution: assuming that a phone number equals a person, or that a cloud key equals a user, without corroboration. Failure mode 4 is selective extraction: presenting only favorable parts without demonstrating that a complete record exists. Failure mode 5 is interpretive overreach: drawing conclusions that exceed what the technical record can support. The triadic framework is essentially a response to these failure modes. It provides a checklist of what must be addressed so that the court is not forced to choose between two competing stories without a reliability foundation.

An additional issue that deserves explicit attention in UAE proceedings is language and translation. Messaging evidence frequently involves Arabic and English mixed with regional dialects, emojis, and shorthand. If the court relies on translated extracts, translation must be treated as a transformation step in the evidence chain, not as a neutral rendering. Best practice is to preserve the original-language record in the master package, to produce a working copy for translation, and to document who performed the translation, what method was used, and how disagreements were handled. When the translation is critical to meaning, the proponent should consider presenting both the original excerpt and the translation side by side, or providing a certified translation where required. The integrity of the evidence does not guarantee the integrity of interpretation; translation is one of the most common pathways by which interpretation integrity can be challenged without attacking the artefact itself.

Finally, evidence packages should be designed for the court's cognitive needs. Courts are persuaded not merely by the volume of data but by clarity, structure, and verifiability. A strong package allows the judge to follow the reasoning path: from a preserved master export, to a hash manifest that proves integrity, to a chain-of-custody record that proves continuity, to excerpts that are clearly identified as selections, and to a narrative that explains why those excerpts matter. This is consistent with the emphasis on evidence content and quality in digital forensic courtroom analysis (Garrie & Morrissy, 2014). When the package is built this way, disputes become narrower and more technical: a challenger must identify a specific break in custody, a specific missing segment, or a specific attribution gap. That is precisely what a reliability-oriented legal system should encourage, because it enables fair adjudication based on evidence quality rather than on rhetorical suspicion.

11- CONCLUSION

Digital evidence will continue to dominate UAE disputes because communication, transactions, and operational events are increasingly digital. The UAE's legislative reforms and institutional modernization recognize this reality and provide legal foundations for electronic documents, modern communication means, and machine-generated records to function as proof. Yet digital evidence does not become reliable simply by being digital. Messaging records can be selectively captured and edited; cloud logs can be lost, misunderstood, or exported without provenance; and cross-border infrastructures can complicate acquisition and verification.

This chapter proposed a triadic framework - lawful acquisition, authentication and attribution, and integrity preservation through chain-of-custody - to align legal doctrine with practical digital forensics discipline. The framework is consistent with structured admissibility assessment thinking in digital forensics scholarship (Antwi-Boasiako & Venter, 2017) and with cloud forensic research emphasizing trustworthiness and integrity controls (Nasreldin et al., 2015; Lucien, 2024; Alenezi, 2023). Applied to WhatsApp-style messaging evidence, the framework highlights that screenshots without provenance and continuity are weak, while structured exports and forensic extractions supported by identity linkage, hashing, and chain-of-custody are stronger. Applied to cloud logs, it highlights that machine-generated records require prompt preservation, provider-native exports, provenance documentation, time normalization, and cautious interpretation supported by correlation and expert explanation.

The chapter also evaluated blockchain-based chain-of-custody approaches. Distributed ledger systems can strengthen auditability of custody events and reduce manipulation risk in custody logs, but they do not substitute for lawful collection, correct acquisition, or accurate interpretation. Their value is therefore best understood as governance enhancement in institutional contexts, not as a universal replacement for disciplined evidence handling.

The practical message for UAE stakeholders is that digital evidence reliability is primarily an outcome of disciplined process. When evidence is collected promptly, preserved with integrity controls, documented in an auditable chain-of-custody, and communicated clearly through structured narratives and expert reports, courts can evaluate it efficiently and consistently. Conversely, informal handling practices create procedural vulnerability and can lead to exclusion or devaluation even when the underlying facts are genuine. By adopting the workflows and documentation tools proposed in this chapter, litigants, investigators, and organizations can reduce admissibility disputes and strengthen the evidential value of WhatsApp messages, cloud logs, and other digital artefacts under UAE procedural reforms.

AI USE DECLARATION

The authors used an artificial intelligence–assisted writing tool (QuillBot) solely for language editing, including rephrasing sentences for clarity and improving grammar and readability. No AI tools were used for study design, data collection, statistical analysis, interpretation of results, or generation of scientific content. The authors reviewed and verified all revisions and take full responsibility for the accuracy and integrity of the manuscript.

REFERENCES

Al-Khateeb, H. M., Epiphaniou, G., & Daly, H. (2019). Blockchain for modern digital forensics: The chain-of-custody as a distributed ledger. In Jahankhani, H., Kendzierskyj, S., Jamal, A., Epiphaniou, G., & Al-Khateeb, H. (Eds.), *Blockchain and clinical trial: Securing patient data* (pp. 149–168). Springer., DOI: 10.1007/978-3-030-11289-9_7

Albatal, S., Awad, A., & Aldabousi, A. M. (2025). The influence of social media marketing on customer knowledge management: The role of confidentiality in UAE public banks. *Banks and Bank Systems*, *20*(1), 1–10. DOI: 10.21511/bbs.20(1).2025.01

Alenezi, A. M. (2023). Digital and cloud forensic challenges. arXiv. https://arxiv.org/abs/2305.03059

Antwi-Boasiako, A., & Venter, H. (2017). A model for digital evidence admissibility assessment. In Peterson, G., & Shenoi, S. (Eds.), *Advances in digital forensics XIII* (pp. 23–38). Springer., DOI: 10.1007/978-3-319-67208-3_2

Awad, A., & Aldabousi, A. M. (2024). Analyzing the impact of viral marketing on brand equity dimensions in Egypt's home appliances sector: A customer and legal perspective. *Innovative Marketing*, *20*(4), 100–111. DOI: 10.21511/im.20(4).2024.09

Chopade, M., Khan, S., Shaikh, U., & Pawar, R. (2019). Digital forensics: Maintaining chain of custody using blockchain. In 2019 Third International Conference on I-SMAC (IoT in Social, Mobile, Analytics and Cloud) (pp. 744-747). IEEE. https://doi.org/DOI: 10.1109/I-SMAC47947.2019.9032693

Garrie, D. B., & Morrissy, J. D. (2014). Digital forensic evidence in the courtroom: Understanding content and quality. *Northwestern Journal of Technology and Intellectual Property*, *12*(2), 121–128. https://scholarlycommons.law.northwestern.edu/njtip/vol12/iss2/1/

Ghonim, A., & Awad, A. (2024). Leveraging e-marketing for enhancing customer knowledge management: A systematic review of tourism strategies in the Saudi Arabian context. *Journal of Ecohumanism*, *3*(8), 2729–2745. DOI: 10.2478/jeh-2024-0056

Igonor, O. S., Amin, M. B., & Garg, S. (2025). The application of blockchain technology in the field of digital forensics: A literature review. *Blockchains*, *3*(1), 5. DOI: 10.3390/blockchains3010005

Lucien, L. R. (2024). Challenges of trustworthy of digital evidence and its chain of custody on cloud computing environment: A systematic review. In Proceedings of the 26th International Conference on Enterprise Information Systems (ICEIS 2024) (Vol. 2, pp. 240-246). SCITEPRESS. https://doi.org/DOI: 10.5220/0012702800003690

Matis, J. (2025). Digital evidence and its use for criminal proceedings. *Analytical and Comparative Jurisprudence*, *5*(3), 121–126. DOI: 10.24144/2788-6018.2025.03.3.19

Miller, A., & Singh, A. (2024). Chain of custody and evidence integrity verification using blockchain technology. In Proceedings of the International Conference on Cyber Warfare and Security (Vol. 19, Issue 1, pp. 168-176). Academic Conferences International. https://doi.org/DOI: 10.34190/iccws.19.1.2025

Moussa, A. F. (2021). Electronic evidence and its authenticity in forensic evidence. *Egyptian Journal of Forensic Sciences*, *11*(1), 34. DOI: 10.1186/s41935-021-00234-6

Narasimhan, P., & Kala, N. (2024). Ensuring the integrity of digital evidence: The role of the chain of custody in digital forensics. International Journal of Scientific Research in Computer Science. *Engineering and Information Technology*, *10*(6), 2438–2450. DOI: 10.32628/CSEIT2410612443

Nasreldin, M. M., El-Hennawy, M., Aslan, H. K., & El-Hennawy, A. E. (2015). Digital forensics evidence acquisition and chain of custody in cloud computing. *International Journal of Computer Science Issues*, *12*(1), 153–160. https://www.ijcsi.org/papers/IJCSI-12-1-1-153-160.pdf

United Arab Emirates. (2021). Federal Decree-Law No. (34) of 2021 on countering rumors and cybercrimes. UAE Legislation. https://uaelegislation.gov.ae/en/legislations/1526/download

United Arab Emirates. (2021). Federal Decree-Law No. (45) of 2021 on the protection of personal data. UAE Legislation. https://uaelegislation.gov.ae/en/legislations/1972/download

United Arab Emirates. (2021). Federal Decree-Law No. (46) of 2021 on electronic transactions and trust services. Telecommunications and Digital Government Regulatory Authority. https://tdra.gov.ae/-/media/About/Trust-Services/Laws-and-regulations/Federal-Decree-Law-No-46-OF-2021-On-Electronic-Transactions-and-Trust-Services-EN.ashx

United Arab Emirates. (2022). Federal Decree-Law No. (35) of 2022 promulgating the law of evidence in civil and commercial transactions. UAE Legislation. https://uaelegislation.gov.ae/en/legislations/1612/download

United Arab Emirates. (2022). Federal Decree-Law No. (38) of 2022 promulgating the criminal procedures law. UAE Legislation. https://uaelegislation.gov.ae/en/legislations/1609/download

United Arab Emirates. (2022). Federal Decree-Law No. (42) of 2022 promulgating the civil procedure code. UAE Legislation. https://uaelegislation.gov.ae/en/legislations/1602/download

ADDITIONAL READING

8. Council of Europe – Budapest Convention on Cybercrime. (evidence cooperation). https://www.coe.int/en/web/cybercrime/the-budapest-convention

1. Evidence Law, U. A. E. (Federal Decree-Law No. 35 of 2022) – official portal. https://uaelegislation.gov.ae/en/legislations

7. INTERPOL Cybercrime – Digital evidence guidance (gateway). https://www.interpol.int/en/Crimes/Cybercrime

6. ISO/IEC 27037: Guidelines for identification, collection, acquisition and preservation of digital evidence (catalog). https://www.iso.org/standard/44381.html

5. NIST Guide to Integrating Forensic Techniques into Incident Response. (SP 800-86). https://csrc.nist.gov/publications/detail/sp/800-86/final

4. SWGDE Best Practices for Digital Evidence (documents). https://www.swgde.org/documents

2. UAE Electronic Transactions & Trust Services Law (Federal Decree-Law No. 46 of 2021) – official portal. https://uaelegislation.gov.ae/en/legislations

3. UAE Personal Data Protection Law. (Federal Decree-Law No. 45 of 2021) – official portal. https://uaelegislation.gov.ae/en/legislations

KEY TERMS AND DEFINITIONS

Admissibility: The legal threshold for a court/tribunal to receive evidence; distinct from the weight given after evaluation.

Attribution: Linking evidence to a person/system (e.g., account control, device ownership, admin role).

Authentication: Demonstrating that an artefact is genuine and derived from a reliable source without material alteration.

Chain of Custody (CoC): A documented record of evidence handling, transfer, storage, and integrity checks from acquisition to court.

Cloud Audit Log: Machine-generated record of actions/events in cloud services (logins, changes, downloads) used to reconstruct activity.

Digital Evidence: Information of probative value stored or transmitted in digital form, including device artefacts, communications, and platform logs.

Electronic Document: A document created, stored, or communicated electronically, potentially admissible if authenticity and integrity are demonstrated.

Forensic Image: A bit-for-bit copy of a storage medium/device created under controlled conditions for analysis and verification.

Hash Value: A cryptographic fingerprint used to verify that a file or evidence package has not changed.

Metadata: Data about data (timestamps, device identifiers, file properties) supporting provenance and event sequencing.

Preservation Order/Request: A request to keep logs/data from deletion while legal process is pursued, critical given short retention windows.

Probative Weight: The persuasive value assigned to evidence after considering reliability, completeness, and corroboration.

APPENDIX I

Chain-of-Custody Log Template (Digital Evidence)

This template can be adapted for device-based evidence (e.g., mobile phone acquisition) and cloud-based evidence (e.g., audit log exports). It is designed to document continuity, access, and integrity verification in a form that is easy to audit and explain in court.

Table 1.

Case/Reference Number	
Evidence Item ID	
Evidence Description	
Source (Device/System/Tenant)	
Legal Basis/Authorization (order/policy/consent)	
Collector (Name, Role, Organization)	
Collection Method/Tool/Version	
Collection Date/Time (include time zone)	
Initial Evidence Package Location (vault/path)	
Initial Hash (SHA-256) and Hash Tool	

Table 2. Transfer and access history (add rows as needed)

Date/Time	From (custodian)	To (custodian)	Purpose	Action Taken	Storage Location/ Medium	Hash Verified (Y/N)

APPENDIX II

Practical Checklists

Messaging (WhatsApp-style) evidence checklist:

- Confirm lawful access and define scope (participants, timeframe, relevance).
- Prefer structured chat exports or forensic extraction; avoid relying solely on screenshots.
- Preserve context by keeping the complete conversation for the relevant period in the master evidence package.
- Document acquisition method (device/account, steps taken, tool or export function, date/time).
- Link account identity to person (subscription ownership, device custody, corroboration across records).
- Hash exported files and media immediately; preserve a master package and create controlled working copies.
- Maintain chain-of-custody log for every transfer, access, conversion, and analysis action.
- Prepare a concise reliability statement and use an expert report where authenticity is contested.

Cloud log and platform record evidence checklist:

- Confirm lawful authority and proportional scope; document the basis for administrative access and collection.
- Identify relevant log sources and confirm retention settings (audit logs, authentication logs, admin events, API logs).
- Preserve promptly due to retention limits; apply legal hold and export relevant logs as soon as practical.
- Export using provider-native tools; document tenant ID, roles used, filters applied, export settings, and timestamps.
- Normalize time references; document UTC/time zone conversions and clock synchronization assumptions.
- Hash export packages; store master copies securely with restricted access and auditable storage.
- Treat parsed or filtered datasets as derivatives; preserve original exports as authoritative sources.
- Correlate logs with other evidence streams (MFA events, endpoint telemetry, email alerts, ticketing systems).

- Use expert explanation to clarify log semantics, limitations, and the scope of defensible inferences.

Chapter 3
Virtual Currency Tax Avoidance in the United Arab Emirates:
Central Digital Currency

Haytham Mohmed Sherif
http://orcid.org/0009-0008-4340-7616
Federal Tax Authority, Egypt

Tarek Abdelsalam
Umm Al Quwain University, UAE

Ahmed Ibrahim Hassan
http://orcid.org/0009-0002-0601-0755
Abu Dhabi University, UAE

Mohamed Elawwa
Federal Tax Authority, UAE

Mostafa Metawea
Mansoura University, UAE

ABSTRACT

Virtual currencies are: One of the recent technological inventions resulting from the digital technological revolution in the fields of communications, information systems, and banking industry. There are more than 4,000 virtual currencies, the most famous of which is Bitcoin, which appeared in 2009 by an anonymous programmer (Satoshi Nakamoto) who adopted the idea of virtual currency to change the prevailing traditional currencies and replace them with a new currency that

DOI: 10.4018/979-8-3373-7961-6.ch003

preserves the privacy of the seller and buyer and is not subject to supervision by banks or governmentsThe transactions are conducted via a peer-to-peer protocol (P2P) without a central server, Amid the challenges posed by the growing virtual currency market, it has become essential to explore legal frameworks to regulate this sector, not only to capitalize on its profits but also to establish a tax system for the revenues it generates. This humble study aimed to address this issue and examine the foundations of the tax treatment for virtual currency activitie

INTRODUCTION

This chapter examines the evolution of virtual currencies and their relationship to traditional money, differentiating cryptocurrencies from electronic money and legal tender. It analyzes regulatory and enforcement challenges arising from decentralization, pseudonymity, and cross-border transferability, with emphasis on tax implications, money laundering risks, and consumer protection. The chapter also highlights the UAE's emerging approach to regulating virtual assets and outlines procedural considerations for collecting, preserving, and presenting digital evidence in virtual-currency cases.

Virtual currencies are among the most recent technological innovations resulting from the digital revolution in communications, information systems, and the banking industry. Bitcoin, the most prominent cryptocurrency, was proposed as a peer-to-peer electronic cash system and later launched in 2009 (Nakamoto, 2008).

The transactions are conducted via a peer-to-peer protocol (P2P) without a central server, relying on modern encryption techniques to enhance security. It is a currency that exists only on the internet through electronic wallets, without a central authority issuing it like paper money. (Sherif, 2020)

Since the main purpose of virtual currencies is to eliminate financial intermediaries and replace existing money, explaining the nature of barter operations and then the emergence of money is essential to understand the essence of virtual currencies and their relation to money. (European Central Bank, 2015)

First: Barter operations:

Before humans invented money, they needed to use goods and services as tools for exchange to be traded for other goods and services held by others. The ability to acquire what the other side possessed depended on what goods and services they accepted. Trade exchanges between individuals and populations were carried out through trade contracts known as barter, which is the process of exchanging goods for other goods, or services for other services, or any combination of goods and services, without a standardized medium of exchange like money.

Second: Emergence of money:

Money is one of the fundamental elements on which modern economic systems are based. It can be defined as "any medium of exchange accepted universally for fulfilling obligations," and it significantly contributes to organizing economic transactions between individuals and nations. Since its emergence, money has gone through many stages of development, starting from the use of metal coins, then paper currency, up to digital and virtual money in the present era. It is a key element in understanding the development of the global economy and the trade relations among countries and peoples.

Third: Traditional money from an Islamic law perspective:

Muslims historically used metallic money such as the Dinar, which is mentioned in the Holy Qur'an:

"And among the People of the Scripture is he who, if you trust him with a Dinar, will return it to you unless you persistently stand over him" (Surah Al-Imran, 75).

The Dinar and the Dirham are the currencies known during the Prophet Muhammad's time, and before and after him. The Arabian Peninsula used the Dinar in dealings with the Romans and the Persians with the Dirham. Although the Dirham, in terms of its quality, was considered inferior to the Dinar (since the Dinar was made of gold and the Dirham of silver), both had their importance, standing, and specific rulings in Islamic jurisprudence.

And:

- The effective means of preventing the existence of money from the nonexistent — i.e., imaginary money that could generate more imaginary wealth — is through certainty of possession*. This is because such speculative money could lead to the creation of fictitious wealth, which is unlawful in Islamic law. The Prophet (peace be upon him) said:
- _"Gold for gold, silver for silver, wheat for wheat, dates for dates, salt for salt — equal in weight and in kind, hand-to-hand; if these types differ, then sell as you wish, provided that it is hand-to-hand."_ (Sahih Al-Bukhari (3/74)

Study Problem:

- The study aims to answer the following questions:
- How do virtual currencies affect tax revenues?
- What is the stance of different countries on virtual currencies?

Importance of Study:

- To clarify the position of the financial system on virtual currencies issued without central bank oversight and to highlight the potential risks of using these currencies on the national economy.
- To explain the legal recourse mechanisms for fraud cases involving virtual currencies, as they have become a reality.

Study Methodology:

The researcher followed the inductive method and the analytical deductive method, tracing relevant religious texts and the opinions of classical and contemporary Islamic jurists to understand the legal framework for dealing with virtual currencies.

Study Plan:

Based on the above, the study will be divided as follows:

CHAPTER ONE: THE NATURE OF VIRTUAL CURRENCY

The topic of money and finance is gaining increasing importance from the perspective of modern economics due to the significant developments in money and finance in modern civilization, especially over the past three centuries. These changes include substantial transformations in all forms of money generated and circulated in vast quantities unprecedented in human history. Additionally, new forms of money have emerged, whether in the form of industrial goods, services, or new benefits. All these developments have led to the expansion and evolution of financial markets to accommodate the need to exchange these large quantities of money in various forms. This exchange meets the needs of modern society, which have diversified, increased, and advanced in line with the progression of contemporary life, achieving a high standard of living. Due to the importance and effectiveness of money in economic life and its immense impact on human conditions, systems, and societies, numerous questions have arisen about it throughout history, especially among economic researchers.

Virtual digital currencies can be defined as a type of currency available exclusively in digital form on the internet. They have no physical existence but possess characteristics like physical currencies. They are known as "Cryptocurrency". The word Crypto is short for "Cryptograph".

Virtual Currency vs. Electronic currency:

This new cryptocurrency is entirely different from the concept of electronic currency, which has recently emerged. The European Commission (1998) defined electronic currency as: "Monetary value stored electronically on an electronic device, such as a card or computer memory. It is accepted as a means of payment by a provider affiliated with the issuing institution and is made available to users as an alternative to physical cash, enabling electronic transfers of payments with a specified value"(Bank for International 1996) .

At the Basel Conference (1996), electronic currency was defined as:" Monetary value in the form of credit units stored electronically or on an electronic device held by the consumer")Al-Sherman, N., & Aldabousi, A. M. (2024). Moreover, this concept is fundamentally different from virtual currency, which is not regulated by governments or central banks. Instead, it is exchanged between individuals using a new technology known as "Blockchain ". These definitions raise questions about their compatibility with the traditional definition of money, which is:" Anything that is widely accepted in exchange for goods and services and for the repayment of debts" ..

Virtual Currency vs. Traditional Currency:

Virtual currency differs from traditional currency in the following ways: Firstly, Virtual currencies are not backed by any government or legal entity, nor are they issued by a central authority. Instead, they rely on a peer-to-peer network to maintain consistency, Secondly, unlike traditional currencies such as the US Dollar, Chinese Yuan, or Euro, which are controlled by regulations and laws, the value of virtual currencies is determined solely by supply and demand. The price is set by the highest rate at which people are willing to trade them. Thirdly, virtual currencies are exchanged electronically through peer-to-peer (P2P) networks without the involvement of banks or third-party regulatory bodies. This makes them less susceptible to economic and political issues that typically affect traditional currencies. An ongoing debate suggests that the growing acceptance of virtual currencies could be linked to negative perceptions of traditional banking systems, especially following the 2008 financial crisis.

Similarities between Virtual Currencies and Traditional Currencies:

Both virtual currencies and traditional currencies are used to purchase goods and services. Although most transactions involving virtual currencies occur online, an increasing number of businesses now accept them in exchange for goods and services, including grocery stores, food retailers, and car rental companies. Additionally, commercial transactions using virtual currencies are quite similar to online banking systems. Users can send virtual currencies to digital wallets or to other users using private keys, and public keys. This allows virtual currencies to be exchanged within communities. From another point, unlike traditional currencies, there is no tangible or digital file representing virtual currencies. Instead, only the transaction records are visible on a ledger called the Blockchain.

In addition to direct merchants, individuals can buy and sell virtual currencies through online exchanges, such as Bit stamp and Coinbase. However, unlike traditional currencies (like the US Dollar), virtual currency holders may lack access to physical cash or cash-convertible instruments. Since virtual currencies are decentralized and lack a third-party regulator, neither the sender nor the recipient needs a bank account. Transactions can be anonymous if users can hide their IP addresses, as cryptocurrencies exist purely as data. In traditional banking transactions, there is a potential issue of double-spending, such as bounced checks. In these cases, a third party or centralized system typically acts as a safeguard. However, this is not necessary for virtual currencies due to their design. Blockchain technology maintains records of transactions among all users, preventing double-spending. (Eyal, I., & Sirer, E. G. (2014))

In light of the above, this chapter is divided as follows:

1. First Subsection: Centralized and Decentralized Virtual Currencies.
2. Second Subsection: Countries' Stances on Virtual Currencies.
3. Third Subsection: Virtual Currencies and Tax Revenues.

First Subsection: Decentralized Virtual Currencies

Firstly: Decentralized Virtual Currencies

Virtual currencies are based on Blockchain technology and are expected to become an essential part of many transactions. Just like any new technology that blurs the line between reality and fiction like how most people use the internet today without understanding the underlying technologies and standards Blockchain could ultimately become deeply embedded and invisible in our daily lives. It is characterized by several features that distinguish it from legal tender and electronic currency. Its mechanism is based on a code generated through an algorithm that uniquely identifies each user without revealing their identity. It is stored in a secure digital wallet that sends and receives funds, making it impossible to identify the owner or trace or monitor the commercial transactions that occur .

Most importantly, it is a monopolistic currency concentrated in the hands of a few who own advanced computers and have expertise in information technology. This is due to the complexity of the mathematical calculations required for a user to become a miner and obtain the currency. This monopoly poses a threat to the future of the global economy, as those in control can manipulate it according to their own interests. Thus, it is an imaginary currency with no physical existence and no intrinsic value. It is an unregulated currency, meaning it is not backed by any official, institutional, or private entity. It is used exclusively over the internet and within institutions and companies that accept it. It can also be exchanged for fiat currencies like the US dollar or the euro through encrypted online transactions. Trade transactions occur directly between individuals without the need for a bank intermediary. There are no set limits for spending or purchases, unlike various credit cards.

The most popular types of decentralized digital currencies:

Bitcoin is not the only important currency in the field of virtual currencies, even though it has managed to convince many companies worldwide to invest in it and has been accepted in numerous countries and markets. Today, it sits at the top of the cryptocurrency world, with its prices reaching record levels in the exchanges that trade it (Aldabousi, 2022), However, at the same time, some economic experts consider it to be highly volatile. They believe that its prices depend on speculation, adventurous trading, and betting, which makes the risk of loss significantly high. Additionally, there is the possibility of hacking and cyberattacks.

Secondly: Central Digital currency

Centralized digital currencies are controlled by the issuing state. They are based on Blockchain technology, governed by precise regulations, and financially backed by the issuing authorities. These currencies can be referred to as Official Digital Money. In 2008, a person or group using the pseudonym Cypherpunk published an article under the name Nakamoto on the website White Paper. This article described Bitcoin as an innovative form of virtual currency composed of encrypted codes, explaining the protocol for creating and managing it as a means of exchange and an electronic payment system. What distinguishes Bitcoin from other electronic or digital currencies in the field of financial technology, which existed earlier, is its independence from any central authority and its immunity from the control of governments and central banks, both in issuance and circulation. As a result, on January 3, 2009, the first Bitcoin was created as the world's first encrypted virtual currency. This was followed by the emergence of many other types of virtual currencies, the most popular being Bitcoin Cash, Ethereum, Monero, Dash, Litecoin, EOS, Cardano, and NEO, among others. Today, the number of virtual currencies has exceeded 1,800. All of them adopted the same operating system as Bitcoin, which has become a general model for all virtual currencies.)Ahmed Qasim Farah:2019).

Many major institutions see a promising aspect in these currencies. A report by the World Bank revealed that "cryptocurrencies" could fundamentally transform payment methods and business practices. It also indicated that they could be introduced as a tool to combat corruption, provided that certain conditions are met

The use of encrypted currencies also enables instant transactions and borderless transfer of ownership, reducing the time and cost associated with transactions, as it eliminates the need for financial intermediaries. If digital currency transactions are regulated by central governments, or if an international body is established to oversee and regulate these currencies imposing fees, taxes, and other regulatory measures, digital currencies could become secure assets. This would contribute to creating a new business environment and facilitate faster and safer trade operations.

Characteristics of Central Digital Money:

Centralized digital currencies are issued and controlled by the issuing state, governed by precise regulations, and financially backed by the issuing authorities. They can be referred to as “Official Digital Money.”

Many major institutions see a promising aspect in these currencies. A report from the World Bank revealed that “encrypted currencies” could fundamentally transform payment methods and business practices, suggesting they could be used as a tool to combat corruption if certain conditions are met.

The bank believes that cryptocurrency ensures the security of transactions and can be adopted as a payment method in a project when each user's identity is verified. This contrasts with traditional payment methods. While most cryptocurrencies keep user identities anonymous and use encryption to identify users, they can also include personal information, such as a unique identification number, making the cryptocurrency non-anonymous. Additionally, the use of encrypted currencies allow for instant transactions and borderless transfer of ownership, which reduces transaction time and cost by eliminating the need for financial intermediaries.

According to the World Bank report, cryptocurrencies can be used more widely. Governments or development institutions can either utilize an existing non-anonymous cryptocurrency or create their own digital currency, giving it a name such as “Clean Currency.” The value of this cryptocurrency could be determined by market factors, and it is recommended to peg it to a fiat currency to minimize volatility. The report suggests that blockchain databases should include additional data stored regularly to provide sufficient information for fraud and corruption prevention. Additionally, transaction verification should ensure that the additional data meets the requirements of a smart contract, which includes logical clauses programmed in the code to trigger actions according to contract terms.

If digital currency transactions are regulated by central governments or by establishing an international body to oversee currency regulation, taxation, and other regulatory measures, digital currency could become a secure means of payment. This would contribute to creating a new business environment and facilitate faster and safer commercial transactions. Furthermore, the key characteristics required for traditional currency are also present in digital currencies, including:

- Methods of acquiring and securing digital currency.
- The ability to transfer it as part of financial transactions.
- Availability of physical means, such as smartphones, to support these transfers.
- Availability of sufficient financial services for deferred payments and direct payment systems to securely and flexibly support all services.

The Most Popular Types of Central Digital Currencies:

The Central Bank of the UAE granted preliminary approval to "AED Stablecoin" to issue its own digital currency under the "Payment Token Services Regulation" issued on June 7, 2024.

In January 2024, the United Arab Emirates conducted its first cross-border transaction using digital currency through the mBridge platform. This infrastructure was developed in collaboration with four central banks: the Hong Kong Monetary Authority, the Central Bank of the UAE (CBDC), the Digital Currency Institute of the People's Bank of China, and the Bank of Thailand. This technology aims to enhance the international payment system using central bank digital currencies, reinforcing the UAE's position as a leading hub for fintech and digital innovation.

Additionally, the Virtual Assets Regulatory Authority (VARA) operates independently from other federal regulatory bodies, giving it the authority to effectively regulate the cryptocurrency industry within Dubai. All Virtual Asset Service Providers (VASPs) in Dubai must obtain licenses from VARA, which imposes strict requirements on financial resources, risk management, and compliance with anti-money laundering and counter-terrorism financing laws.

Second subsection: The Position of Countries on Virtual Currencies

The following table illustrates the continuous increase in the number of countries dealing with virtual currencies in recent times. Like many central banks that are taking practical steps to issue digital currencies equivalent to the national fiat currencies, these digital currencies are used without any differences in value compared to official paper currencies.

Table 1. Top countries by cryptocurrency ownership rate in 2023

Country	Cryptocurrency Ownership Rate
United Arab Emirates	%30.4
Vietnam	%21.2
United state	%15.6
Iran	%13.5
Philippines	%13.4
Brazil	%12.0
Saudi Arabia	%11.4
Singapore	%11.1

continued on following page

Table 1. Continued

Country	Cryptocurrency Ownership Rate
Ukraine	%10.6
Venezuela	%10.3
United Arab Emirates	%30.4

Sources: Triple-A Company – in Jovial Capital State

Third subsection:Virtual currencies and their effects on inflation and tax revenues

It is relatively ineffective for countries to address the issue of combating criminal activities resulting from the use of virtual currencies on an individual basis. Given that virtual currencies can be accessed from anywhere in the world thanks to their decentralized, borderless virtual systems, there is a pressing need for a comprehensive legal framework capable of addressing any of their illicit uses whether related to money laundering, account hacking, terrorism financing, or tax evasion.

This should be established based on uniform and mutually agreed-upon principles among most countries, in a way that enhances international cooperation in regulating this matter. The unilateral regulation of virtual currencies by a single country would be of little use in isolation from the collective efforts of others.

The legal risks associated with virtual currency trading can be summarized as follows:

1. Difficulty in identifying the parties involved in transactions.
2. Traders resort to virtual currencies to avoid paying taxes imposed on their profits, leading to tax evasion that is difficult for governments to detect.
3. Challenges in tracking trading operations and identifying the parties involved due to the nature of virtual currency transactions, Examples of the risks that may affect users of virtual currencies include.(Obaid, 2018)

In November 2022, the American virtual currency trading platform FTX declared bankruptcy following a sharp decline in cryptocurrency prices, with at least one billion USD of client funds disappearing from the platform. This came after FTX failed to raise billions of dollars to avoid bankruptcy, as traders rushed to withdraw six billion USD within just 72 hours upon learning of the fraud. FTX issued an official statement on Twitter announcing that its crypto trading subsidiary "Alameda," along with around 130 affiliated companies, had initiated, Chapter 11 bankruptcy proceedings under U.S. bankruptcy law.

In the same month, block.Fi, another virtual currency platform, also declared bankruptcy and began creditor protection procedures under Chapter 11 of the U.S. Bankruptcy Code, along with eight affiliated companies. This made it the second platform to collapse in November 2022, following FTX, leading to severe instability in the virtual currency market. The cryptocurrency market lost approximately USD 3.7 billion in 2022 due to fraud and hacking incidents.

Experts are divided into two main groups on this matter:

The first group defends the cryptocurrency market, arguing that such issues occur in all other markets, and that the root cause lies in the absence of legal regulation of blockchain technology, The second group believes that the FTX collapse is clear evidence of the fragility and unreliability of these markets, predicting that they will eventually collapse entirely.

Mechanisms to Counter the Risks of Virtual Currency Transactions

In the United States, the Bank Secrecy Act (BSA) regulates the operations of financial institutions responsible for processing transactions related to money laundering. This law applies to all entities classified as small-scale banking institutions, requiring them to establish appropriate mechanisms for maintaining records and transaction data including foreign exchange operations, check cashing, issuing or selling traveler's checks, selling prepaid receipts, or conducting money transfers within the United States.

The Financial Crimes Enforcement Network (FinCEN) of the U.S. Department of the Treasury oversees compliance requirements for small and medium-sized financial firms. Under the 2017 Uniform Regulation of Virtual Business Act, companies engaging in virtual currency activities are required to comply with anti-money laundering (AML) standards. Each such company must adopt internal policies and procedures to prevent money laundering, fraud, and terrorism financing in accordance with established mechanisms. The purpose is to ensure that all virtual currency transactions comply with federal AML laws, while also requiring companies to identify and disclose the material risks associated with virtual currencies to their users.

The European Union, through Regulation (EU) 2024/1624, published in the Official Journal of the European Union on June 19, 2024, imposed obligations on virtual currency exchanges and related entities, including: mandatory registration of exchanges with the competent authorities in their jurisdictions; conducting customer due diligence procedures; preparing reports on suspicious activities when necessary; and maintaining records of individuals purchasing virtual currencies (Aldabousi, 2022)

The Impact of Virtual Currencies on Inflation Rates

Inflation occurs when supply exceeds demand, leading to a decline in the value of goods or currencies. For instance, when more U.S. dollars are printed than necessary, inflation occurs because there are more dollars in circulation while the quantity of goods remains the same, causing prices to rise.

The same principle applies to digital currencies. Suppose a project has a total market capitalization of $100,000and 10,000 tokens; each token would then be worth $10. However, if the number of tokens suddenly doubles to 20,000, the price per token would drop to $5. This illustrates how inflation affects digital currencies. Therefore, digital currency inflation is one of the most difficult challenges facing crypto projects.

Central banks issue traditional fiat currencies only under strict conditions typically backed by reserves of precious metals (e.g., gold) or a basket of stable currencies such as the USD, GBP, or JPY.

In contrast, virtual currencies rely on computing systems that engage in mining, which requires significant computational effort to produce new coins. As a result, it is not easy to create and distribute new coins in the market. Well-known projects such as Bitcoin, Litecoin, and Monero follow this model, and their prices are typically high because substantial effort and energy are required to produce them. The combination of intrinsic value, practical utility, and controlled inflation tends to sustain high market prices.

Bitcoin Inflation

Bitcoin serves as a prime example of how controlled inflation in a digital currency can be beneficial. Since its creation in 2008, Bitcoin's price has risen continuously from virtually no value at inception to around $27,000 per coin today, having peaked at $69,000 in 2021

The secret lies in the optimal balance between moderate inflation and strong demand ensuring that demand consistently exceeds supply. Each time new Bitcoins are mined and introduced to the market, the available supply increases (a form of inflation), but the demand rises even faster, driving the price upward. Maintaining this demand-over-supply ratio remains one of the greatest challenges facing virtual currencies, .

Inflation in Proof-of-Stake (PoS) Projects:

When supply exceeds demand, prices plummet. Examining most cryptocurrency charts reveals a common pattern: an initial rapid price surge followed by a sharp decline. This typically occurs when newly issued tokens flood the market, creating excess supply. Many investors, panicked by the falling prices, sell their holdings, causing further declines, The result is a collapse in market capitalization due to bad inflation and selling pressure.

Token Emission and Selling Pressure

Another critical issue for crypto projects is to take emission the scheduled release of tokens into the market. Even if inflation levels are moderate and tokens are distributed gradually (e.g., over 40 years), there remains the challenge of early investors who received large token allocations during the initial coin offering (ICO). These tokens are often locked in smart contracts and released periodically (monthly or quarterly).

If these early investors choose to sell their holdings as soon as new tokens are unlocked, this leads to negative inflationary pressure, causing excess supply relative to demand and ultimately, a steep decline in market prices.

Some studies examining virtual currencies have addressed the negative impacts that may arise from their use, including the crime of tax evasion. Countries with legislative frameworks that allow the imposition of taxes on virtual currencies and other digital economy activities are at risk of losing significant tax revenues due to manipulation of the tax system. Although there is agreement with the previous viewpoint regarding the tax evasion of many platforms operating in the digital economy, it is preferable to address this issue under the term “digital currencies and tax avoidance” rather than labeling it as tax evasion for several reasons among them: the instability of most tax legislations regarding the mechanisms for taxing digital economy activities let alone imposing taxes on a digital sector that represents a technological leap in business practices, the difficulties tax authorities face in dealing with non-physical entities, and absence of a unified international agreement regarding virtual currency activities.

There are three categories: the first includes countries that impose income tax on profits earned by individuals or companies from digital currency activities, such as Argentina and Belgium. The second includes countries that tax these activities as assets or commodities acquired for ownership or trading purposes, taxing them when the value of the returns exceeds the original value of the cryptocurrency, as seen in Australia and Brazil. The third category considers digital currencies as private money not subject to taxation, as in Italy and South Korea.

U.S. federal authorities have managed to crack down on several virtual currency trading platforms involved in criminal activities, such as Mt. Gox and Silk Road. In July 2014, during the trial of Silk Road founder Ross Ulbricht on money laundering charges, Ulbricht argued that the U.S. Internal Revenue Service (IRS) did not recognize virtual currencies as money but as commodities. Therefore, transactions conducted using these currencies should not be considered financial transactions under anti-money laundering regulations.The U.S. court rejected this argument, affirming that the IRS's classification of virtual currencies would not apply to other government agencies and that their non-recognition as money did not exempt them from existing anti-money laundering regulations. Several countries, including Canada, the U.S., and the European Union, have classified these currencies as commodities and subjected them to value-added tax (VAT). Concerning, the Canada Revenue Agency, it has classified virtual currencies as commodities and subjected all related crypto transactions to the Income Tax Act. Under these laws, merchants who accept these currencies as a means of payment and individuals who invest in them are subject to income tax on the profit margin between the purchase and sale price, as well as value-added tax, considering them as goods or services.

The Position of the United Arab Emirates on Virtual Currencies:

The UAE imposed a 5% value-added tax (VAT) on digital currency transactions, like other commercial transactions. This created a barrier for companies and individuals seeking to enter the digital currency market, especially since taxing cryptocurrencies posed challenges due to their decentralized and anonymous nature. However, the UAE has recently adopted a more open and proactive approach in this field. It introduced a new tax exemption policy aimed at fostering growth and attracting investments in the digital currency sector. As part of this policy, certain activities related to cryptocurrencies and virtual assets have been exempted from VAT, benefiting both individuals and companies. This exemption took effect on November 15, 2024, following the latest amendments to the executive regulations approved by the UAE Cabinet.

The UAE Federal Tax Authority has issued a new public clarification regarding the 5% value-added tax (VAT) on cryptocurrency mining, specifically concerning individuals. It confirmed that a person (individual) can mine digital currency for their own account, which is not considered a taxable supply subject to the 5% VAT but rather falls outside the scope of taxation.

Cryptocurrency mining on behalf of another party:

In contrast, cryptocurrency mining on behalf of another party, which involves the provision of computing power, is considered a taxable service supply. The input tax incurred by an individual on expenses related to mining for their own account is not recoverable, as the individual has not incurred such expenses to make a taxable supply. However, input tax incurred by a registered entity conducting mining on behalf of another party may be recoverable to the extent that the input tax is incurred in making a taxable supply.

An individual engaged in mining for their own account contributes their computing power to the network without providing this computing power to a specific recipient.

This contribution involves validating blockchain transactions, and the individual is rewarded only if they are the first to successfully solve the cryptographic equation. Receiving a reward for solving the cryptographic equation is not guaranteed, as the reward depends not only on solving the equation but also on being the first to do so.

As such, there is no direct link between the mining activity conducted by the miner and the reward received (such as the mined tokens). Furthermore, there is no specific recipient to whom the mining activities are provided. Consequently, an individual who mines cryptocurrencies for their own account is not considered to be making a taxable supply, and the reward received is not regarded as consideration. Therefore, such activities fall outside the scope of value-added tax (VAT).

Supplied Mining Services:

A person who mines cryptocurrencies on behalf of another party in exchange for a fee is making a supply of services. Since there is a specific recipient for the activity and the person conducting the mining on behalf of another receives compensation from their client, the mining activities constitute a taxable supply of services. If the service is supplied by a taxable person to a client within the state, it will be subject to the standard VAT rate. However, the supply may be subject to the zero rate if it is provided to a non-resident and all the conditions for applying the zero rate are met. (Article (31) of Cabinet Decision No. (52) of 2017 on the Executive Regulations of Federal Decree-Law No. (8) of 2017 on Value Added Tax, and its Amendments ("Executive Regulations")

Received Mining Services:

If a business resident in the UAE receives mining services from a non-resident, this supply is subject to value-added tax (VAT). If the recipient of these services is registered for VAT in the UAE, they must account for the VAT due on the relevant services using the reverse charge mechanism, Conversely, if the client is a business resident in the UAE but is not VAT-registered, the non-resident supplier must register for VAT in the UAE and charge VAT on the services provided.

Consumer Protection for Virtual Currency Users in the United Arab Emirates:

Regarding consumer protection methods for those dealing with virtual currencies in the UAE, Federal Law No. 15 of 2020 on Consumer Protection regulates this matter. Under Article (22) of the law, the Ministry of Economy is authorized to receive consumer complaints, along with the Consumer Protection Association, and take the necessary actions. The executive regulations of this law outline the system for receiving complaints, the required procedures, and the coordination between the Ministry and the relevant authority.

Article of the same law defines the consumer as: "Any natural or legal person who obtains a good or service—whether for a price or free of charge to satisfy their needs or those of others, or who enters into a transaction or contract regarding it". The term "good" is defined as: "Any natural material or industrial, agricultural, animal, transformative, intellectual, or technological product, including raw materials and components used in the product". Meanwhile, a goods provider is defined as: "Any legal person who provides a service, manufactures a good, distributes, trades, sells, supplies, exports, imports, or participates in its production, circulation, or storage, with the aim of offering it to the consumer or engaging in a transaction or contract regarding it".

By linking and applying these provisions to consumer transactions involving the buying or selling of virtual currencies through trading platforms, it becomes evident that consumers in the UAE are entitled to seek protection from the Consumer Protection Department in cases of fraud or harm, provided that virtual currencies are classified as goods. Furthermore, even if virtual currencies are classified as investment contracts, consumers will still be protected under the financial regulations of the UAE Securities and Commodities Authority. Consumer protection is thus guaranteed in dealings with virtual currency trading platforms such as goods providers.

Cases involving virtual currencies typically depend on digital evidence, including blockchain transaction histories, wallet identifiers, exchange and custodian records (KYC/AML files), device forensics from wallet applications, and communications supporting intent and knowledge. To support admissibility and reliability, investigators should apply reproducible acquisition methods, preserve integrity through hashing where applicable, maintain a documented chain of custody, and rely on expert reports to explain how addresses, keys, and transaction graphs connect the parties to specific acts. These procedural safeguards are increasingly important in the UAE as virtual-asset activity becomes regulated and subject to compliance requirements.

DIGITAL EVIDENCE AND PROCEDURAL CONSIDERATIONS IN VIRTUAL-CURRENCY CASES

Additionally, comparative and regional legal scholarship on virtual-asset regulation and enforcement supports this discussion (Obeidat et al., 2024; Aldabousi, 2023; Awad et al., 2024, 2025; Ramadan et al., 2025; Al-Tawil, 2023; Othman & ElDosh, 2024; Sayedahmed & Anwar, 2025; Kumar et al., 2025; Al Badawi & Al-Haija, 2021; Nekit, 2023).

CONCLUSION

Amid the challenges posed by the growing virtual currency market, it has become essential to explore legal frameworks to regulate this sector, not only to capitalize on its profits but also to establish a tax system for the revenues it generates. This humble study aimed to address this issue and examine the foundations of the tax treatment for virtual currency activities.

Recommendations:

1. International Cooperation and Regulatory Frameworks: International institutions such as the International Monetary Fund, the Bank for International Settlements, and the Financial Action Task Force should collaborate to establish regulatory standards for virtual currencies.
2. Taxation Frameworks: It is crucial to develop clear tax guidelines for profits generated by virtual currency providers. This should involve coordination between tax authorities and licensing bodies overseeing virtual currency platforms, addressing tax declarations and taxable transactions.
3. Tax Incentives for Compliance: Legislators should consider offering tax incentives to virtual currency users to accurately gauge the volume of transactions and integrate them into the formal economy, thus promoting voluntary tax compliance within this sector.

REFERENCES

Ahmed Qasim Farah. (2019). Virtual currencies in the United Arab Emirates: The need for a legal framework to address their risks—A comparative study. *University of Sharjah Journal of Legal Sciences, 16*(2). https://old.sharjah.ac.ae/ar/Research/spu/Journallaw/Pages/V16.aspx

Al-Sherman, N., & Aldabousi, A. M. (2024). The complementary penalties enforced to combat corporate crimes in UAE law. *Pakistan Journal of Criminology*, *16*(3), 635–648. DOI: 10.62271/pjc.16.3.635.648

Al-Tawil, T. N. (2023). Anti-money laundering regulation of cryptocurrency: UAE and global approaches. *Journal of Money Laundering Control*. https://www.scopus.com/pages/publications/85137537374

Aldabousi, A. M. (2022). Legal problems of conclusion of intelligent software agent for smart commercial contracts in the era of blockchain: U.A.E as a model. *Universidad y Sociedad*, *14*(S3), 713–728. https://rus.ucf.edu.cu/index.php/rus/article/view/3005

Aldabousi, A. M. (2022). Legal problems of electronic pollution according to UAE and Egyptian law. *Arab World Geographer*, *25*(2–3), 154–168. DOI: 10.64903/1480-6800-25.2.154

Aldabousi, A. M. (2023). The legal problems facing the conclusion of cloud computing contracts. *Universidad y Sociedad*, *15*(3), 602–611. https://rus.ucf.edu.cu/index.php/rus/article/view/3815

Awad, A., & Aldabousi, A. M. (2024). Analyzing the impact of viral marketing on brand equity dimensions in Egypt's home appliances sector: A customer and legal perspective. *Innovative Marketing, 20*(4), 100–111. https://www.businessperspectives.org/images/pdf/applications/publishing/templates/article/assets/21026/IM_2024_04_Awad.pdf

Awad, A., Aldabousi, A. M., & Albatal, S. (2025). The influence of social media marketing on customer knowledge management: The role of confidentiality in UAE public banks. *Banks and Bank Systems*, *20*(1), 1–10. Advance online publication. DOI: 10.21511/bbs.20(1).2025.01

Badawi, A., & Al-Haija, Q. A. (2021). Detection of money laundering in Bitcoin transactions. *IET Conference Proceedings*. https://www.scopus.com/pages/publications/85139870704

European Parliament. (2018, July). *Cryptocurrencies and blockchain: Legal context and implications for financial crime, money laundering, and tax evasion.* https://www.europarl.europa.eu/cmsdata/150761/TAX3%20Study%20on%20cryptocurrencies%20and%20blockchain

Kumar, S. G. K., Shreenidhi, P. L., Rahman, S. Z., & Munagalachetty, C. (2025). Secure AI frameworks for detecting cross-border tax fraud. *Industry Applications.* https://www.scopus.com/pages/publications/105021944630

Nekit, K. (2023). Legal nature and types of digital assets in the activities of technology-oriented startups. *Juridical Tribune.* https://www.scopus.com/pages/publications/85167466698

Obeidat, M. A., Alfil, N. Z., Aldabousi, A. M., & Dganni, K. M. (2024). Criminal protection for the merchants from the crimes of electronic publishing about invasion of privacy in UAE legislation. *Pakistan Journal of Criminology*, *16*(3), 779–792. DOI: 10.62271/pjc.16.3.779.792

Othman, A. M., & ElDosh, E. M. E. (2024). Regulating digital currencies in the Emirate of Dubai: A comparative legislative review. *International Journal of Public Law and Policy.* https://www.scopus.com/pages/publications/85190089767

Ramadan, S. A., Abdelsalam, T., Qasim, A., & Aldabousi, A. M. (2025). The role and impact of legal legislation in achieving sustainable development goals: An applied study on UAE legislation. In *Studies in Systems, Decision and Control.* Springer., DOI: 10.1007/978-3-031-96641-5_4

Sayedahmed, N. Y., & Anwar, S. (2025). AI adoption in tax fraud detection in Palestine: Insights from Arab countries on public policy and sustainable governance. *Engineering, and Sustainable Business.* https://www.scopus.com/pages/publications/105013207035

KEY TERMS AND DEFINITIONS

AML/CFT: Anti-Money Laundering and Counter-Terrorism Financing obligations applicable to regulated virtual asset activities.

Asset Tracing: Techniques used to follow transaction flows and connect addresses to entities, typically requiring corroboration.

Blockchain: A distributed ledger recording transactions in blocks linked cryptographically, supporting traceability and integrity.

Cryptocurrency: A form of virtual currency using cryptography and distributed ledger technology for issuance and transaction validation.

Electronic Money (E-Money): Stored monetary value issued by an identifiable entity and typically regulated as a payment instrument.

Off-Chain Evidence: Evidence from exchanges/platforms (KYC files, IP logs, device logs, withdrawal records) used for attribution.

On-Chain Evidence: Evidence from blockchain data (transaction hash, block time, address flows).

Private Key: A cryptographic secret enabling control over a wallet; key compromise can equate to loss of assets.

VASP (Virtual Asset Service Provider): An entity providing exchange, custody, transfer, or related services for virtual assets, often subject to licensing/AML rules.

Virtual Asset: A broader regulatory category covering certain digital representations of value that can be traded/transferred digitally.

Virtual Currency: A digitally represented value used as a medium of exchange and stored/transferred electronically, typically without legal tender status.

Wallet: A software/hardware tool that stores keys enabling control over virtual assets and signing of transactions.

Chapter 4
The Use of Technology in Compulsory Enforcement:
A Comparative Study in Emirati and French Law

Mhd Samer Al Kattan
http://orcid.org/0000-0003-2095-4090
Umm Al Quwain University, UAE

ABSTRACT

This research provides a descriptive and analytical study of the use of technology in compulsory enforcement procedures by outlining the legal framework and the most prominent digital applications, and platforms implemented within the legal system of the United Arab Emirates, in a comparative context with the French legal system. The study is divided into two main parts: the first examines the conceptual and regulatory framework governing the use of technology in compulsory enforcement, while the second addresses the principal forms of its practical application. The research concludes that the use of technological tools in compulsory enforcement has become an established judicial practice in both legal systems, albeit with variations in the level of regulation and the breadth of application. It further recommends extending the experience applied in the Emirate of Dubai to the other Emirates and strengthening institutional digital integration between the relevant judicial and enforcement authorities.

1. INTRODUCTION

Compulsory the final stage of judicial proceedings and the mechanism through which judicial judgments and enforceable instruments are transformed from mere

DOI: 10.4018/979-8-3373-7961-6.ch004

legal determinations into practical reality. As such, it represents a fundamental pillar in ensuring the effectiveness of judicial protection.

In light of rapid technological advancement, compulsory enforcement procedures have undergone notable development in several modern legal systems through the integration of digital applications and electronic platforms into the regulation of certain stages thereof. This is particularly evident in the field of enforcement notifications, the electronic management of enforcement files, as well as certain forms of attachment and the sale of attached assets.

The significance of this research lies in its focus on the stage of compulsory enforcement, as one of the phases of judicial proceedings most closely connected to practical reality, and in its examination of the extent to which technological means have been integrated into the regulation of this stage. This is achieved by clarifying how the procedural legislation under consideration addresses the use of technology and the legal basis upon which such use is founded.

The importance of the research is further underscored by its emphasis on the various forms of employing digital applications and platforms in compulsory enforcement, particularly in the areas of electronic notifications, electronic attachment, electronic auctions, and other related mechanisms, thereby illustrating the features of the procedural transformation experienced by this stage.

The academic significance of the research is further enhanced by the fact that it addresses compulsory enforcement as a field that has not received sufficient attention in legal studies concerning the use of technology, in comparison with other stages of litigation.

The research problem centres on the extent to which the use of technology in compulsory enforcement procedures is regulated under procedural legislation, and the limits of such regulation, within the framework of a comparison between UAE law and French law.

This problem further extends to examining the manner in which digital applications and electronic platforms have been integrated into certain stages of compulsory enforcement, and the extent to which such use is consistent with the traditional procedural rules governing enforcement, in addition to clarifying the scope of such use and its legal limits.

The research problem is also connected to examining the extent to which the use of technology in compulsory enforcement is linked to the concept of expeditious justice, in terms of accelerating and simplifying procedures, without engaging in a comprehensive assessment or an in-depth critique of such use.

2. THE CONCEPTUAL AND REGULATORY FRAMEWORK GOVERNING THE USE OF TECHNOLOGY IN COMPULSORY ENFORCEMENT

Compulsory enforcement constitutes the stage at which the legal rule moves from the sphere of theoretical recognition to the sphere of practical application and thus represents the true test of the effectiveness of the judicial system and its capacity to protect rights.

With the rapid technological development witnessed by contemporary judicial systems, compulsory enforcement procedures have not remained immune from this transformation, as the use of technological means has become one of the most prominent manifestations of modernising enforcement mechanisms and enhancing their efficiency.

The economic development and the growing complexity of financial transactions, as previously noted by the French scholar of civil procedural law Jean Vincent, make it necessary to modernise the rules governing compulsory enforcement. The effectiveness of judicial decisions can no longer be achieved solely through traditional means, which necessitates legislative intervention to adopt modern mechanisms, including technological tools, to ensure that rights are enforced practically and effectively. *(*Vincent & Prévault, 1999*)*

However, the integration of technology into this sensitive field raises a number of conceptual and regulatory issues relating to the nature of such means and the limits of their impact, as well as the extent to which they are compatible with the legal rules and procedural safeguards governing compulsory enforcement. Accordingly, this chapter aims to establish a conceptual and regulatory framework for the use of technology in compulsory enforcement, by distinguishing between traditional means and technological means, and by clarifying the legal and technical controls governing their use, ultimately leading to an examination of the legal permissibility of such use, its safeguards, and its limits, which will be addressed successively in what follows.

2.1. Distinguishing Between Traditional Means and Technological Means in Compulsory Enforcement

2.1.1. The Nature of Traditional Means in Compulsory Enforcement

As a general principle, contracting parties are required to perform their obligations voluntarily and by mutual consent, within the prescribed time limits and in good faith. This is known as voluntary or consensual performance, a principle enshrined in most civil laws, including the UAE Civil Transactions Law, which dictates that:

"A contract must be performed in accordance with its contents and in a manner consistent with the requirements of good faith" (Article 246(1)).

However, where the debtor refrains from performing his obligation voluntarily, the creditor may then resort to the competent public authority in order to compel performance in accordance with the methods prescribed by law. In such a case, this constitutes what is known as "compulsory enforcement", which may be defined as the set of procedures undertaken by the competent authority in the State whether a court or an enforcement department, as the case may be upon the request of a creditor holding an enforceable instrument that satisfies the substantive and formal conditions prescribed by law, with the aim of satisfying the right established therein, even if this requires the use of coercive measures permitted by law. *(Al-Motawalli* Qandil, 2024)

Prior to the emergence and dissemination of technology in the fields of law and the judiciary, compulsory enforcement was undertaken through traditional means of a material and procedurally direct nature, relying primarily on the physical presence of the parties and the intervention of the competent officer at the various stages of enforcement. Such means included the submission of enforcement applications in paper form, the service of notices through traditional methods, the manual drafting of enforcement records, as well as the execution of attachment and enforcement measures against the debtor's assets through in-person procedures, as a general rule, with reliance on paper records for the monitoring and follow-up of enforcement proceedings.

These traditional means were characterised by relative slowness, difficulty in obtaining accurate information regarding the debtor's assets, high procedural costs, and substantial reliance on the human element, which often resulted in prolonged enforcement proceedings and an increase in disputes relating to enforcement procedures.

Such traditional means constituted the framework upon which national legislations relied for many years, until rapid technological development necessitated a reconsideration of compulsory enforcement mechanisms and the pursuit of more effective and flexible means based on the utilisation of technological tools in this field.

2.1.2. The Nature of Technological Means in Compulsory Enforcement

The term "Technology" is derived from the ancient Greek language and is composed of two parts: the first, "Techno", denotes art, craft, performance, skill, or technique, while the second, "Logia", denotes study or science. Accordingly, the term “Technology” refers, in its general sense, to the study or science of skills or techniques. (Schatzberg, 2018)

In a specific sense, technology refers to the practical application of scientific knowledge to solve problems and achieve objectives efficiently and within shorter timeframes, and it encompasses various aspects, including automation, digitalisation, artificial intelligence, software systems, and related technological applications. (Arthur, 2009)

On the basis of this concept, technological means in the field of compulsory enforcement may be defined as the digital tools and systems utilised in the initiation and completion of enforcement procedures, in whole or in part, in lieu of exclusive reliance on traditional methods. This is achieved through the deployment of information systems, digital platforms, and electronic applications, thereby enabling the parties to enforcement proceedings to exercise their rights and allowing the competent authorities to administer and monitor enforcement procedures with efficiency and effectiveness.

This transformation necessitates the conversion of paper-based or in-person procedures into digital processes, permitting the electronic submission of enforcement applications, the service of notices through approved electronic means, and the exchange of data and documents via secure systems, in addition to the tracking and regulation of enforcement procedures through interconnected digital databases.

The use of technological means should not, however, result in any infringement of the essence of compulsory enforcement or its legal nature, as it remains subject to the same rules and safeguards governing traditional enforcement. The impact of such use should be confined to the modernisation of enforcement tools and methods in a manner that achieves greater speed, efficiency, and accuracy, contributes to the reduction of procedural disputes, and enhances confidence in the enforcement system.

In this regard, a report issued by the European Union Agency for Fundamental Rights highlights the importance of ensuring digital access to judicial information and enabling electronic interaction with the justice system as essential elements in achieving effective compulsory enforcement. This is subject to the condition that digitalisation does not become an obstacle for the parties to enforcement proceedings, particularly vulnerable groups, which necessitates accompanying this transformation with legal and technical safeguards to ensure the protection of rights and the attainment of procedural equality.

2.1.3. The Difference Between Traditional Means and Technological Means in Compulsory Enforcement

The foregoing demonstrates that the difference between traditional means and technological means in the field of compulsory enforcement does not affect the essence of enforcement or its legal nature; rather, it is confined to the nature of the procedural tools and methods adopted in carrying it out.

Traditional means were based on paper-based and in-person procedures, with extensive reliance on human intervention at the various stages of enforcement. This, in many cases, resulted in procedural delays, increased costs, and difficulties in accurately tracing the debtor's assets and controlling the stages of enforcement.

By contrast, technological means rely on the utilisation of digital systems and electronic platforms in the administration and monitoring of enforcement procedures. This enables a significant portion of paper-based and in-person procedures to be converted into faster and more flexible electronic processes based on remote interaction, facilitates the exercise of rights by the parties to enforcement proceedings, improves the efficiency of enforcement management, enhances transparency, and reduces procedural disputes associated with the conduct of enforcement.

Nevertheless, the adoption of technological means should not lead to any breach of the legal safeguards afforded to the parties or to a departure from the principle of procedural legality. Compulsory enforcement, whether carried out by traditional or technological means, remains subject to the same legal framework.

2.2. Legal and Technical Controls Governing the Use of Technology in Compulsory Enforcement Procedures

Technology in the field of compulsory enforcement is no longer merely an auxiliary organisational tool; rather, it has become a substantive factor influencing the course of procedures and their legal effects. Despite the speed and simplification it offers, its use remains conditional upon compliance with legal and technical controls. The most important of which include:

2.2.1. The Legal Control governing the probative validity of Electronic Documents and Records in Enforcement Procedures

The use of technological means in compulsory enforcement necessitates the recognition of the legal validity of electronic documents and records produced via digital platforms, whether they relate to enforcement applications, attachment records, sale orders, or other enforcement acts.

Such validity is achieved only when the electronic document satisfies technical reliability requirements, foremost among which are the integrity of the content, the ability to attribute it to its originator, and the inability to modify it without detectable evidence.

In this context, the UAE legislator has stipulated that an electronic document shall have the same evidentiary value as a paper document, provided it meets the legally prescribed conditions, particularly regarding electronic signatures and trust services.

The French legislator has adopted a similar approach, recognising the legal validity of electronic writing when the identity of its author can be verified, and its integrity is ensured through reliable technical means. (Arts. 1366-1367, French Civil Code), (United Nations Commission on International Trade Law, 1996)

2.2.2. The Legal Control of Electronic Signatures, Authentication, and Timestamping

The electronic signature constitutes one of the most important technical controls related to the evidentiary validity of compulsory enforcement procedures carried out electronically, as it serves to evidence consent and attribute the procedure to its originator, whether the enforcement judge, the competent authority, the executing officer, or others.

It is not sufficient merely to have an electronic signature; rather, it must be a reliable or accredited signature, issued within a technical framework that allows verification of the signer's identity and is linked to a valid electronic certification, thereby ensuring the integrity of the procedure and preventing denial or tampering. (Arts. 8 et seq. of UAE Federal Decree-Law No. 46 of 2021), (European Union Regulation, 2014)

Electronic timestamping also acquires particular importance in the field of compulsory enforcement, as many legal effects depend on precise chronological order, such as the priority of attachment or compliance with procedural deadlines. The timestamp must be issued by a trusted authority to ensure that the date and time of the procedure cannot be manipulated. (Arts. 41-42 of European Union Regulation,2014), (European Commission for the Efficiency of Justice [CEPEJ], 2016)

2.2.3. The Legal Control of Electronic Notification in Compulsory Enforcement Procedures

Notification during the stage of compulsory enforcement constitutes a fundamental procedure, upon which the validity of many enforcement acts depends, as it serves as the means by which the party against whom enforcement is directed becomes aware of the measures taken against them. The adoption of electronic notification requires adherence to precise controls that ensure actual knowledge, or at least the reliable possibility of acquiring such knowledge, thereby achieving a balance between enforcement effectiveness and the protection of the right of defence.

By way of example, the French legislator has regulated service of process by electronic means, permitting it to be effected through the transmission of documents in accordance with the rules governing electronic communications, as set out in Book Twenty-One of the French Code of Civil Procedure, subject to the prior consent of the person to be served to this method. The legislation further requires clarification as to whether such service constitutes personal service or service at the place of residence, and obliges the judicial officer (process server) to dispatch the requisite notification in compliance with the legally prescribed formalities. (Art. 662-1 and Arts. 748-1-748-9 of the French Code of Civil Procedure)

2.2.4. The Legal Control of Personal Data Protection in Digital Enforcement Procedures

The digitisation of compulsory enforcement procedures necessitates the processing of a large volume of personal and financial data of a sensitive nature, which requires the application of strict controls to ensure the privacy of the parties to enforcement and to prevent misuse of data or use beyond the purpose for which it was collected. (Regulation (EU) 2016/679 [GDPR], arts. 5, 6, & 9)

This includes adherence to the principle of data minimisation to the extent necessary to achieve the enforcement purpose, limiting its use strictly within the framework of enforcement procedures, and implementing the necessary technical and organisational measures to protect it against unauthorised access, loss, or leakage. (Federal Decree-Law No. 45 of 2021, arts. 5 & 10)

Within this framework, the UAE legislator has established a general regime for personal data protection, imposing clear obligations on data controllers, whereas the French system, as part of the European framework, is subject to the GDPR, which similarly governs digital platforms used in compulsory enforcement.

2.2.5. The Legal Control of Cybersecurity and Continuity of Enforcement Systems

The digitisation of compulsory enforcement procedures cannot be considered complete without ensuring a high level of cybersecurity, given the serious consequences that may arise from breaches or technical failures, such as disruption of enforcement procedures, compromise of data confidentiality, or loss of trust in the digital enforcement system. (CEPEJ, 2018)

This control requires the adoption of appropriate technical and organisational measures, such as data encryption, access authorisation management, creation of digital audit logs, and the establishment of clear business continuity and system recovery plans in emergencies, thereby ensuring that enforcement procedures are not halted and their integrity is preserved. (OECD, 2020)

Accordingly, it is evident that the successful use of technology in compulsory enforcement procedures remains dependent on compliance with a series of legal and technical controls that ensure procedural integrity and evidentiary validity. These controls also pave the way for an examination of the legal permissibility of such use, its safeguards, and its limits, which will be addressed in the following requirement.

2.3. The Legality of Using Technology in Compulsory Enforcement

2.3.1. The Concept of Legality and Its Importance in the Context of Compulsory Enforcement

Examining the legality of using technology in compulsory enforcement constitutes a pivotal issue arising from the digital transformation in the judicial field, particularly because compulsory enforcement represents a sensitive stage that directly affects the rights of the parties to enforcement proceedings. Consequently, strict adherence to the principle of procedural legality is required. In this context, the legality of using technology refers to the extent to which the deployment of technological means in enforcement procedures complies with the applicable legal rules, ensuring respect for the safeguards established to protect the rights of both the creditor and the debtor. Technology, regardless of its level of sophistication, is not an end in itself but rather a procedural tool that must be subject to the requirements of legal legitimacy.

The principle of legality in compulsory enforcement is founded on the subjection of all enforcement procedures to the provisions of the law, whether carried out using traditional or technological means, such that no enforcement measure may be taken except on the basis of a legal provision authorising it or a general principle permitting it. On this basis, the use of technology in compulsory enforcement is considered lawful when it is founded on explicit legislative provisions recognising electronic means, or based on general procedural rules permitting the use of modern means in carrying out procedural acts, provided that no specific provision prohibits it.

2.3.2. The Legal Basis for Using Technology in Enforcement Procedures

Chronologically, it can be said that legislators in most countries initially adopted technological means within a limited scope of litigation procedures, such as electronic filing of claims, conducting judicial notifications via digital means, and holding remote hearings. Over time, this reliance gradually expanded to later stages of proceedings, ultimately reaching the stage of compulsory enforcement.

This expansion materialised in the availability of an increasing number of enforcement procedures using technological means, including some attachment and execution procedures carried out remotely. This indicates that the integration of technology in compulsory enforcement was not a departure from the existing procedural system, but rather a natural result of a gradual legislative process aimed at modernising the justice system and enhancing its efficiency.

For example, in France, provisions regulating electronic communication in court proceedings, particularly Articles 748-1 to 748-9, allow for electronic communications while establishing safeguards for the identity of the parties and the integrity of documents exchanged via digital systems.

Furthermore, the *Arrêté* issued on 9 April 2019 permits commercial courts to sign their judgments electronically in accordance with European regulations on qualified electronic signatures. This reflects the integration of technological means into the French judicial procedural system, both in terms of regulation and legal recognition, paving the way for the digitisation of certain compulsory enforcement procedures. (Arrêté du 9 avril 2019, arts. 2–5)

The UAE model provides a clear example of gradual legislative development in integrating technological means into the judicial field. The UAE legislator initially permitted judicial notification through electronic means at an early stage, via the amendment introduced by Federal Law No. 10 of 2017 to the Civil Procedure Law, which allowed the use of modern communication tools in notifications and regulated their procedures. This approach was subsequently articulated in a clearer and more comprehensive manner in the Civil Procedure Law promulgated by Federal Decree-Law No. (42) of 2022, particularly Article (9) thereof.

Subsequently, the use of electronic evidence was recognised under the Law of Evidence in Civil and Commercial Transactions (Articles 4, 5, and 7 of Federal Decree-Law No. 35 of 2022), alongside the general framework established by the Federal Law on Electronic Transactions and Trust Services regarding the legal validity of electronic records and signatures (Articles 17, 18, and 21 of Federal Decree-Law No. 46 of 2021).

After establishing these foundations, the scope of technological use expanded to include all stages of litigation, culminating in the stage of compulsory enforcement, where technological means were employed in accordance with the general rules provided by the Civil Procedure Law. This confirms that the digitisation of enforcement in the UAE constitutes a natural extension of an organised legislative trajectory, without affecting the essence of enforcement or its legal safeguards.

From this development, it is understood that the legality of using technology in compulsory enforcement derives its basis not only from specific legal provisions but also from the broader legislative trend towards digitising judicial procedures. Technology is thus recognised as a lawful procedural tool when integrated within the legal framework governing enforcement, serving as a means to achieve speed and efficiency without compromising the fundamental principles underpinning the enforcement system.

2.3.3. Safeguards of Legality in the Use of Technology in Compulsory Enforcement and Their Limits

The legality of using technological means in compulsory enforcement is not complete unless it is accompanied by respect for the fundamental procedural safeguards guaranteed by law to the parties to enforcement proceedings. Chief among these are the right of defence, the right to be informed of all procedures as a general principle, and the ability to challenge them in accordance with the prescribed legal rules.

This principle finds its foundation in comparative constitutional systems. For instance, Article 16 of the 1789 French Declaration of the Rights of Man and of the Citizen preserves the principle of guaranteeing rights and the separation of powers as a prerequisite for the rule of law. Similarly, Articles 34 and 66 of the 1958 French Constitution establish that all measures affecting rights and freedoms, including technically mediated enforcement procedures, are subject to the principle of legality, while safeguarding individual liberty and procedural guarantees under judicial authority.

Likewise, the UAE Constitution guarantees personal freedom under Article 26 and ensures the right to access justice for all under Article 41, from which it follows that the use of technological means in compulsory enforcement must comply with the principle of legality, and may not be employed in a manner that undermines these safeguards, except to the extent permitted by law and without prejudicing the rights of the parties to enforcement proceedings.

Therefore, the transition from traditional to technological means is lawful only if it provides an equivalent level of legal protection, and may, in some cases, enhance it by documenting and controlling procedures electronically. This aligns with the provisions of the French *Informatique et Libertés* Law of 6 January 1978, particularly Article 1, which stipulates that information technology must not infringe human identity, human rights, or privacy, as well as *Décret n°2019-1333* relating to the digitisation of judicial procedures, which requires respect for the rights of defence and the principle of adversarial proceedings.

This approach is also consistent with modern UAE legislation, notably Federal Decree-Law No. 45 of 2021 on the Protection of Personal Data, which, in Articles 4 and 5, emphasises the legality of processing, the definition of purpose, and the prohibition of exceeding what is necessary under legal procedures.

It is therefore evident that the use of technology in compulsory enforcement does not affect the essence or legal nature of enforcement but is limited to modernising its tools and mechanisms to achieve greater speed and efficiency.

Accordingly, it becomes evident that the use of technology in compulsory enforcement does not affect its essence or legal nature but is limited to the modernisation of its means and mechanisms in a manner that achieves greater speed and effectiveness. However, despite the positive impact of this development on the administration of justice, it may, conversely, give rise to potential risks, particularly in cases of misuse of technological means, in a manner that may threaten public security, including certain forms of cybercrime. *(Aldabousi et al., 2024, pp. 785-787)*

Technology contributes to serving individuals and advancing their interests when it is properly and effectively utilised; nevertheless, it may conversely become a source of harm when it is misused or improperly applied. *(*Ramey, 2013*)*

Based on the foregoing, the use of technology in the field of compulsory enforcement remains conditional upon compliance with legal and technical controls, adherence to the principle of procedural legality, and the safeguarding of the rights of the parties to enforcement proceedings. Accordingly.

In this context, a report issued by the European Union Agency for Fundamental Rights on the digitalisation of justice indicates that the adoption of case management systems and electronic filing constitutes one of the most significant tools for enhancing the effectiveness of justice, provided that such systems are accompanied by safeguards ensuring the protection of the fundamental rights of the parties, particularly at the post-judgment and enforcement stages. *(*European Union Agency for Fundamental Rights, 2023*, pp. 21–33)*

3. PRINCIPAL FORMS OF TECHNOLOGY USE IN COMPULSORY ENFORCEMENT

Based on the foregoing, the deployment of technology in the field of compulsory enforcement remains conditional upon compliance with legal and technical safeguards, adherence to the principle of procedural legality, and the protection of the rights of the parties to enforcement proceedings. Accordingly, this previous section has established the necessary conceptual and regulatory framework for proceeding to examine the principal forms of technological use in compulsory enforcement through the digital applications, platforms, and systems adopted in practice.

3.1. Digital Applications in Compulsory Enforcement

3.1.1. Definition

By digital applications in the context of compulsory enforcement is meant the set of tools, software, and technical solutions adopted within the justice system or by the authorities responsible for compulsory enforcement, which are used to carry out, manage, document, or exchange the data of this enforcement by electronic means, instead of paper-based or traditional procedures, within the limits permitted by law and in a manner that preserves the procedural guarantees of the parties to the enforcement dispute. *(Riffard, 2019, p. 45;* Al-Aboudi, 2020, *p. 87)*

Accordingly, the concept of digital applications here refers to the functional tools that facilitate or carry out procedural steps in the enforcement process, such as electronic filing, digital notification, electronic tracking of the procedure, and electronic documentation, without extending to digital platforms as comprehensive organisational frameworks for these applications.

3.1.2. Characteristics

Digital applications in compulsory enforcement are characterised by a number of features that distinguish them from traditional means, most notably:

- These applications are based on a functional procedural nature, as they do not create new rules for enforcement, but rather contribute to the execution of legally established procedural rules by electronic means, ensuring the continuity of the procedural system despite the different enforcement tools. *(Riffard, 2019, p. 52)*
- They aim to enhance procedural speed and efficiency by reducing the time required to carry out enforcement procedures and limiting the formal complexities associated with paper-based means, which aligns with the main purpose of the compulsory enforcement system, namely the rapid realisation of rights without prejudice to procedural guarantees. *(Guinchard et al., 2022, p. 315)*
- According to established French procedural doctrine, the function of the judiciary is not fulfilled merely by the issuance of a judicial decision; rather, it is realised in concrete terms through ensuring that the holder of a right is able to obtain it by way of enforcement. This understanding makes the effectiveness of justice directly dependent on the speed and efficiency with which judicial decisions are enforced, within the framework of the theory of effective judicial protection developed by the jurist Henri Motulsky. (Motulsky, 1973, *p. 30 ff.)*

- They rely on the traceability and electronic documentation of procedures, allowing the recording of every stage of enforcement and preserving it in the form of digital data, which enhances transparency, facilitates judicial oversight, and supports the right to appeal enforcement procedures when applicable. (Cadiet, 2020, *p. 98)*
- They are built on integration with traditional procedural guarantees, particularly the right of defence and the right to be informed of the procedure, as their use is assumed not to diminish these guarantees but to reactivate them through technical means equivalent to what is provided in the traditional environment. (Al-Aboudi, 2020, *p. 94)*
- They are subject to the principle of legality and judicial oversight; they are not inherently lawful, but derive their legitimacy from the legal provisions permitting their use and from being subject to judicial control, whether in terms of procedural integrity or respect for the rights of the parties to the enforcement dispute. (Al-Shehi, 2021)

3.1.3. Distinction between Digital Applications and Digital Platforms

A digital application is a technical tool with a specific function, designed to perform a particular purpose or a limited set of purposes, and its use is directed directly to the end-user, whether an individual or a specific entity. These applications often operate within a relatively closed technical framework and are managed by a single authority that controls their structure and functions. (Laudon & Laudon, 2020, *pp. 42–44)*

As for a digital platform, it is a broader technical architecture that provides an interactive environment bringing together multiple parties (users, service providers, or governmental entities), and allows the creation, operation, or hosting of various digital applications and services within it, making it a comprehensive framework in which multiple functions are integrated, beyond merely providing a single service. (European Commission, 2016)

Accordingly, the fundamental difference between digital applications and digital platforms lies in that the former represents a direct enforcement tool to perform a specific function, whereas the latter constitutes an organisational and interactive structure hosting multiple functions and services, and may contain one or more applications within it, without being limited to a single function. (Tiwana, 2014)

This distinction, from a legal perspective, is useful in determining the scope of responsibilities, the nature of obligations, and the effects arising from the use of either digital applications or platforms, particularly in the field of the legal regulation of digital procedures and services, in terms of identifying the operating authority, the limits of oversight, responsibility for data protection, and ensuring service continuity. *(Organisation for Economic Co-operation and Development [OECD], 2020)*

3.1.4. Key Examples of Digital Applications in Compulsory Enforcement in the UAE

Within the framework of the trend towards digitising the justice system, the judicial authorities in the United Arab Emirates have adopted a set of specialised digital applications to contribute to the development of compulsory enforcement procedures, the most important of which are as follows:

Digital applications for registering and following up on execution requests:

The judicial authorities in the UAE have enabled the registration of execution requests electronically through approved digital applications, allowing the applicant to submit their request, attach the enforceable instrument, and follow up on enforcement procedures without the need for personal attendance. These applications also provide access to the decisions issued in the enforcement file and allow real-time monitoring of actions taken, which is expected to contribute to reducing the time required to register requests and to ease the administrative burden on enforcement departments. *(*Ministry of Justice, United Arab Emirates, n.d.*)*

Digital applications for notification and enforcement procedures:

These are specialised digital applications for notification and enforcement procedures, including electronic notification and informing enforcement parties of the procedures and issued decisions. This is expected to overcome issues associated with traditional notifications, particularly regarding delays or difficulties in notification, in addition to digitally documenting notification procedures, which enhances their evidentiary value and ensures greater procedural discipline. *(MOJ, UAE, n.d)*

Digital applications for attachment, travel bans, and enforcement on assets:

These applications are used to issue and execute orders of attachment on assets and travel bans through electronic linkage between judicial authorities, relevant governmental entities, and banks. This linkage allows for the execution of such orders electronically and immediately, and for direct monitoring of their effects, thereby enhancing the efficiency of compulsory enforcement and reducing opportunities for manipulation or delay. *(MOJ, UAE, n.d)*

Digital applications for monitoring enforcement and recovering rights:

These applications provide advanced mechanisms to follow up on compulsory enforcement procedures and recover rights, whether through submitting interim requests, paying fees, or receiving adjudicated amounts electronically. This contributes to enhancing transparency, facilitating communication between enforcement parties and enforcement departments, and reducing direct interaction, in line with the requirements of digital transformation in the justice system. *(MOJ, UAE, n.d)*

Electronic enforcement of dishonoured cheques:

The legislator, at both the federal judiciary level and the local judicial systems in the United Arab Emirates, has established a dedicated electronic service for the enforcement of dishonoured cheques. This service enables the beneficiary of a dishonoured cheque to initiate enforcement proceedings electronically in cases where the drawee bank refuses to honour the cheque, whether in whole or in part. (Al-Kattan, 2024)

3.1.5. Key Examples of Digital Applications in Compulsory Enforcement in France

The judicial and professional authorities in France have adopted a set of digital applications that are practically used in various stages of compulsory enforcement, particularly by judicial officers (**Commissaires de justice**), with the aim of facilitating enforcement procedures, organising the exchange of information, and monitoring enforcement stages quickly and efficiently. Among the most important of these applications are:

Digital applications for registering execution requests and following up on procedures:

In France, specialised digital applications are used to enable the concerned parties, particularly judicial officers, to register requests for compulsory enforcement, manage enforcement files, monitor developments in the procedures, and track issued decisions or orders, in addition to documenting the enforcement acts carried out. This contributes to organising the course of compulsory enforcement and regulating its procedures. *(Ministère de la Justice, n.d.) (Chambre nationale des commissaires de justice, n.d.)*

Digital applications for notification and enforcement procedures:

Practical experience in France relies on digital applications used to carry out notification and enforcement procedures, particularly those related to informing the parties of enforcement, notifying them of procedures and related decisions, and digitally documenting notification operations. This is expected to overcome some practical difficulties associated with traditional notifications and to enhance the reliability of notification procedures. *(Ministère de la Justice, n.d.) (Commissaires de justice, n.d.)*

Digital applications for attachment and enforcement on assets:

Specialised digital applications are used to carry out attachment procedures on assets, whether movable or immovable, and to monitor the execution of attachment orders through digital linkage with the relevant authorities and departments. This allows the exchange of necessary information for enforcement and supports the effectiveness of compulsory enforcement. *(Ministère de la Justice, n.d.) (Direction générale des Finances publiques, n.d.)*

Digital applications for monitoring enforcement and recovering rights:

Some approved digital applications in France enable monitoring of the stages of compulsory enforcement, documenting executed procedures, following up on the collection of due amounts, and verifying the completion or failure of enforcement. This contributes to tightening oversight of the enforcement process and organising the relationship between its parties. *(Commissaires de justice, n.d.) (Ministère de la Justice, n.d.)*

3.2. Digital Platforms in the Field of Enforcement

3.2.1. Definition

A digital platform is an integrated digital infrastructure that provides a unified regulatory and technical framework for the management and coordination of a set of digital operations and services related to a specific activity. It enables the relevant stakeholders to interact within a single system and in accordance with predefined rules and procedures, as is the case with platforms adopted for the management of government services or legal procedures.

The function of a digital platform is not limited to performing a single task; rather, it encompasses the hosting of multiple functions, the organisation of relationships among its users, and the assurance of role integration within the digital environment. This is particularly evident in platforms used for the administration of judicial procedures, through which diverse processes are managed within a unified digital framework. (Parker et al., 2016, *pp. 5–12)*

3.2.2. Its Characteristics

Digital platforms, as compared to digital applications, are distinguished by the breadth of their functional scope. They are not used merely as tools for carrying out a specific procedure; rather, they constitute a structural framework through which the various procedures and operations relating to a particular field are administered. They function as a digital intermediary linking relevant actors, systems, and databases, thereby enabling the integrated exchange of information and coordination of procedures.

In the legal context, digital platforms serve as organisational instruments used to manage legal or judicial procedures within a unified environment that allows for the registration of data, the exchange of documents, the tracking of procedures, and the interconnection of competent authorities. This assumes particular significance in the field of compulsory enforcement, which requires precise coordination between the judiciary and enforcement, administrative, and banking authorities.

In this field, digital platforms perform a central role by unifying the course of enforcement procedures and regulating their sequence, and by providing a single digital channel for the management of the various stages of enforcement, without replacing the legally established authorities or competences. They therefore function as supportive organisational tools for enforcement activity, rather than constituting enforcement measures in and of themselves.

Accordingly, digital platforms in compulsory enforcement embody a transition from the logic of isolated digital tools to that of integrated digital systems, which explains the growing reliance on such platforms in modern legal systems to restructure enforcement mechanisms within an organised digital framework. *(CEPEJ, 2021, pp. 18–23)*

3.2.3. Most Important Examples of Digital Platforms and Systems in Compulsory Enforcement in the United Arab Emirates

Within the framework of the digital transformation being undertaken by the justice sector in the United Arab Emirates, a number of digital platforms and systems have been adopted as organisational frameworks for the management and coordination of compulsory enforcement procedures. These platforms enable the interconnection of judicial authorities with the relevant enforcement, professional, and administrative entities within a unified digital environment.

The significance of these platforms lies in their organisational role in regulating the course of enforcement and ensuring the integration of their various stages, without prejudice to the legally prescribed competences of the competent authorities. This is reflected in the principal platforms adopted in this field, most notably the following:

EFSAAH Platform (Disclosure Platform): The EFSAAH Platform is regarded as one of the most prominent digital platforms adopted in the United Arab Emirates in the field of compulsory enforcement. It was launched by Dubai Courts as part of the broader move towards the digitalisation of justice, with the aim of enhancing the effectiveness of the enforcement of judicial judgments and enforceable instruments, particularly at the stage of disclosure of the financial and legal status of the enforcement debtor.

The platform is not limited to being a technical tool for data collection; rather, it constitutes an organisational framework through which the disclosure procedure, considered a pivotal stage of compulsory enforcement, is administered. This is achieved by linking the Enforcement Court with the parties to enforcement and the relevant governmental and banking entities within a unified digital environment, without encroaching upon the judicial competences conferred by law.

Access to the EFSAAH Platform is provided through the official website of Dubai Courts, by registration via UAE Pass, thereby ensuring secure access in accordance with the legal authorisations granted to each user.

The EFSAAH Platform contributes to strengthening the organisational function of compulsory enforcement, in particular through:

- **Enhancing transparency**, by enabling the court and the parties to enforcement to obtain structured access to financial and legal information relating to the enforcement debtor;
- **Accelerating enforcement procedures** by allowing immediate digital disclosure, which supports the prompt issuance of enforcement decisions and orders;
- **Optimising time and procedural effort** by reducing reliance on paper-based correspondence and replacing it with a unified digital workflow.

The platform also performs a number of core functions that highlight its nature as an organisational digital platform, most notably financial disclosure of the enforcement debtor's assets, legal disclosure of the debtor's legal status, institutional connectivity with governmental and banking entities, as well as monitoring and regulating the disclosure process.

From a legal perspective, the EFSAAH Platform embodies the transition from the logic of isolated digital tools to that of integrated digital platforms, as it organises a coherent set of interrelated procedures connected to compulsory enforcement. It thus constitutes an auxiliary organisational tool supporting the judiciary by contributing to the structuring and integration of enforcement procedures, without itself exercising any judicial authority.

The platform's receipt of the International Innovation Award 2024 reflects the advanced role that digital platforms have come to play in modernising compulsory enforcement mechanisms and enhancing their effectiveness. (Dubai Courts, n.d.)

"Tanfidh +" Program: This program constitutes an integrated digital platform, launched by Dubai Courts on 30 May 2024, representing a qualitative leap in the field of executing judicial judgments and enforcement instruments, through adopting digital integration and enhancing the efficiency and transparency of enforcement procedures. The program's launch comes in the implementation of the strategic plan to develop the system for executing civil judgments and enforcement instruments in the Emirate of Dubai, and within the framework of Dubai Courts' commitment to developing and improving judicial services, in alignment with government directives aiming to achieve prompt justice and expedite adjudication and enforcement in judicial disputes. (Al-Kattan, 2024)

The Execution Plus (Tanfeeth+) Programme is distinguished by core characteristics that reflect its nature as an advanced digital platform. Most notably, it achieves digital integration between Dubai Courts and the entities involved in the enforcement process, thereby reducing duplication of procedures and limiting reliance on traditional transactions. It further enables clear and flexible tracking of enforcement applications, enhances procedural transparency, and improves the user experience by shortening enforcement timelines and reducing delays.

The programme aims to elevate the system for the enforcement of judicial judgments in the Emirate of Dubai in line with international best practices, to accelerate enforcement procedures in furtherance of expeditious justice, to address the practical challenges associated with the execution of judgments, and to strengthen litigants' confidence in the judicial system.

In achieving the digital transformation of enforcement procedures, the programme is structured around five principal pillars: efficiency and digitalisation; speed and flexibility; transparency and information exchange; enhanced cooperation with partners; and ensuring legal compliance throughout all stages of enforcement. (Emarat Al Youm, 2024)

The Automated Disbursement System is one of the intelligent digital systems developed by Dubai Courts to support the framework of compulsory enforcement. It operates as an integrated automated programme responsible for the disbursement of funds deposited in enforcement files without direct human intervention, based on self-verification mechanisms that ensure procedural integrity and compliance with the legal rules governing enforcement.

The system automatically verifies that the enforcement file satisfies the conditions for disbursement, including confirmation that no legal impediments exist and that any outstanding fees or fines have been settled. Such amounts are deducted automatically prior to disbursement, thereby ensuring the accuracy of financial settlements and safeguarding the rights of the parties to enforcement. For files that meet the required conditions, the system completes the disbursement process within a period not exceeding forty-eight (48) hours, reflecting its efficiency in accelerating financial enforcement procedures.

The system is linked to the virtual bank account framework dedicated to enforcement files, enabling funds to be credited directly and disbursed automatically to each entitled party in accordance with the terms of the judicial judgment, while ensuring full traceability of financial transactions and enhanced financial transparency. It is also integrated with the sale notification system to regulate the disposal of attached assets, as well as with the automatic cancellation system for enforcement measures, which lifts attachments immediately upon full settlement without the need for a request by the enforcement debtor.

Accordingly, the Automated Disbursement System represents an advanced model for the automation of the compulsory enforcement stage, by reducing procedural timeframes, limiting human intervention, and enhancing transparency and legal certainty in the execution of judgments and the disbursement of funds. (Emarat Al Youm, 2024)

It should be noted that access to this system and the use of its services are available exclusively through the electronic services portal of Dubai Courts, following authentication via the approved digital identity (UAE Pass). Such access is granted strictly in accordance with the legal authorisations linked to the enforcement file, in order to safeguard judicial and financial data and to ensure the integrity of enforcement procedures.

- **Electronic Auction for the Sale of Attached Assets:** The electronic auction for the sale of attached assets constitutes one of the digital mechanisms adopted within the framework of compulsory enforcement in the United Arab Emirates. It aims to regulate the procedures for the sale of attached property, whether immovable or movable, through an electronic environment that ensures transparency, efficiency, and equality of opportunity among participants, in accordance with specific legal rules and procedures that achieve lawful publicity and limit the issues associated with traditional sale mechanisms.

In implementing electronic auction sale procedures, the courts in the United Arab Emirates rely on cooperation with specialised entities responsible for the management and organisation of auctions, foremost among which is Emirates Auction. Such entities operate the electronic auction platforms, organise public announcements, receive participation applications, and manage the electronic bidding process, all under judicial supervision and in accordance with the determinations of the competent judicial authorities.

This cooperative model contributes to enhancing the efficiency of compulsory sale procedures and ensuring professionalism and transparency in the disposal of attached assets. It also broadens participation in auctions, thereby helping to achieve the best possible value for the attached assets, in a manner that serves the interests of the parties to enforcement.

Practical experience adopted by judicial authorities in the State, including the Abu Dhabi Judicial Department, further demonstrates that the use of specialised digital platforms for auction management contributes to expediting sale procedures, reducing the procedural timeframe of the post-attachment stage, and enhancing confidence in the integrity of compulsory enforcement procedures.

Accordingly, the electronic auction for the sale of attached assets represents an advanced model of digital transformation at the post-attachment stage, based on integration between the judiciary, digital technologies, and specialised entities, thereby enhancing the efficiency of the enforcement of judicial judgments and serving the requirements of expeditious justice. (Emarat Al Youm, 2024) (Abu Dhabi Judicial Department, n.d.)

3.2.4. Key Examples of Digital Platforms and Systems in Compulsory Enforcement in France

Portalis Platform: This platform constitutes one of the fundamental pillars of digital transformation in the French justice system, provided by the Ministry of Justice in France. It represents the technical framework through which civil judicial files are managed electronically.

The importance of this platform in the context of compulsory enforcement lies in its role in the pre-enforcement phase, enabling the digitisation of the civil case process from filing through to the issuance of the judgment, transforming it into a digitally certified enforceable instrument.

This platform contributes to narrowing the temporal gap between the issuance of the judgment and the commencement of enforcement procedures by facilitating electronic access to judgments and enforceable instruments, thereby supporting the effectiveness of compulsory enforcement and reducing procedural complexities. *(.justice/donnees-personnelles portalis, n.d.)*

e-Barreau Platform: This platform represents a professional digital tool approved for use by lawyers in France to manage the electronic exchange of correspondence and documents with judicial authorities. Its importance in the context of compulsory enforcement lies in its role as a digital link between the judicial adjudication phase and the enforcement phase. It enables lawyers to monitor enforceable judgments, prepare requests, and manage procedures associated with initiating or following up on enforcement, thereby contributing to the expedited transition from judgment to actual enforcement and reducing delays associated with traditional methods. (Conseil national des barreaux, n.d.)

SECURACT-HUISSIER Platform: This platform is considered one of the digital systems most closely associated with the compulsory enforcement phase in France, as it is used to organise the electronic service of enforcement acts and procedures conducted by judicial officers. Its practical benefit lies in enabling legally recognised service to be carried out electronically, with the date of service recorded and certified digitally, thereby reducing formal disputes concerning the validity of service and expediting the legal deadlines associated with compulsory enforcement procedures. (Securact-huissier, n.d.)

Accordingly, it is evident from the foregoing discussion that the use of technology in compulsory enforcement has moved beyond the mere deployment of limited digital tools to encompass an integrated system of digital applications and platforms. These have contributed to the reorganisation of enforcement procedures, facilitated their implementation, and enhanced their overall effectiveness.

The review of the models adopted in both the United Arab Emirates and France has demonstrated the practical role of these tools in expediting procedures, improving coordination among the relevant authorities, and strengthening transparency and traceability throughout the enforcement stages.

At the same time, it is apparent that the effectiveness of such applications and platforms remains contingent upon their sound design, their integration with the legal framework governing compulsory enforcement, and the extent to which they respect the prescribed procedural safeguards. In this respect, this section constitutes an applied extension of the theoretical foundations established in the first section and paves the way for the formulation of the study's general conclusions in its final chapter.

4. CONCLUSION

4.1. Research Findings

Through this study, we have arrived at a series of findings that highlight the features of using technology in compulsory enforcement procedures, in light of the descriptive comparative analysis conducted between the UAE and French legal systems. The key findings can be summarised as follows:

It has been established that the integration of technology into compulsory enforcement procedures is no longer an exceptional trend, but has become an established legislative option in both legal systems, notwithstanding differences in the degree of regulation and the scope of applications.

The research demonstrates that the use of digital applications and platforms extends to several stages of compulsory enforcement, particularly enforcement notifications, the management of enforcement files, and certain forms of attachment and the sale of attached assets, reflecting a notable evolution in procedural mechanisms.

The UAE legislator has moved towards the adoption of digital solutions in compulsory enforcement within the framework of a broader public policy of judicial digital transformation, granting judicial and enforcement authorities a central role in activating and implementing these tools.

By contrast, the French legal system has adopted a more detailed regulatory approach in certain aspects of electronic compulsory enforcement, drawing on well-established procedural traditions while gradually integrating digital tools.

The use of technology in compulsory enforcement is closely linked to the concept of expeditious justice, insofar as it contributes to accelerating procedures, simplifying them, and improving their organisation, within the limits of the scope of this study.

4.2. Recommendations

In light of the findings reached, a set of recommendations may be proposed to contribute to the development of the regulation governing the use of technology in compulsory enforcement procedures, as follows:

Enhance legislative clarity in regulating the use of digital applications and platforms in compulsory enforcement procedures, by specifying the scope of such use and its guarantees, thereby contributing to legal certainty for enforcement parties.

Benefit from the experience of the enforcement platforms and applications adopted in Dubai, and work towards generalising and adapting them to the other enforcement courts in the Emirates, alongside expanding digital connectivity with all relevant authorities involved in compulsory enforcement, particularly land and financial departments and other related entities, thereby enhancing procedural integration and the speed of execution.

Pay particular attention to procedural aspects related to the protection of the rights of enforcement parties when using technological means, ensuring a balance between the requirements of procedural efficiency and respect for legal safeguards.

Encourage specialised legal studies addressing the challenges and risks associated with the use of technology in compulsory enforcement, particularly with regard to data protection and cybercrime, matters that this study only addressed in a limited scope.

Emphasis is placed on the need to accompany the adoption of digital tools in compulsory enforcement procedures with practical safeguards that ensure digital access to judicial information and enable electronic interaction with the enforcement system. At the same time, due care must be taken to prevent this digital transition from becoming an obstacle for the parties to enforcement, particularly vulnerable groups. This can be achieved by providing non-digital alternatives, along with mechanisms for technical assistance and guidance, thereby safeguarding their rights, ensuring procedural equality, and enhancing the overall effectiveness of compulsory enforcement.

Expand comparative studies in this field to include other legal systems, thereby facilitating the exchange of experiences and the identification of diverse regulatory models for electronic compulsory enforcement.

AI USE DECLARATION

The authors used an artificial intelligence–assisted writing tool (QuillBot) solely for language editing, including rephrasing sentences for clarity and improving grammar and readability. No AI tools were used for study design, data collection, statistical analysis, interpretation of results, or generation of scientific content. The authors reviewed and verified all revisions and take full responsibility for the accuracy and integrity of the manuscript.

REFERENCES

Abu Dhabi Judicial Department. (n.d.). Auctions. Retrieved February 20, 2026, from https://www.adjd.gov.ae/ar/pages/auctions.aspx

Al-Aboudi, A. R. (2020). *E-litigation and its impact on judicial procedures*. Dar Al Nahda Al Arabiya.

Al-Kattan, M. S. (2024). Bounced cheque as an enforceable instrument: A comparative study between the United Arab Emirates (UAE) & French legislations, (SSRN Scholarly Paper No. 5159907). Social Science Research Network. DOI: 10.24857/rgsa.v18n1-198

Al-Kattan, M. S. (2024). *Digital justice "model of the United Arab Emirates", 6-9 (SSRN Scholarly Paper No. 5159911)*. Social Science Research Network., DOI: 10.2139/ssrn.5159911

Al-Motawalli Qandil, M. (2024). *A concise treatise on forced enforcement in accordance with the UAE Civil Procedure Law* (7th ed.). Al-Afaq Publishing.

Al-Shehi, M. A. (2021). Digital transformation in the UAE judiciary. University of Sharjah Journal of Legal Sciences Aldabousi, A. M., Obeidat, M. A., Alfil, N. Z. & Dganni, K. M. (2024). Criminal protection for the merchants from the crimes of electronic publishing about invasion of privacy in the UAE legislation. *Pakistan Journal of Criminology*, *16*(3), 779–792. DOI: 10.62271/pjc.16.3.779.792

Arthur, W. B. (2009). *The nature of technology: What it is and how it evolves*. Free Press.

Cadiet, L. (2020). *Le procès civil à l'ère numérique*. LGDJ.

Chambre nationale des commissaires de justice. (n.d.). Outils numériques professionnels. https://commissaire-justice.fr

Commissaires de justice. (n.d.). Gestion numérique des dossiers d'exécution. https://commissaire-justice.fr

Commissaires de justice. (n.d.). Signification électronique des actes. https://commissaire-justice.fr

Conseil national des barreaux. (n.d.). e-Barreau. https://www.cnb.avocat.fr/fr/webinaire-e-barreau

Direction générale des Finances publiques. (n.d.). Échanges numériques avec les commissaires de justice. https://www.impots.gouv.fr

Dubai Courts. (n.d.). Official website of Dubai Courts. Retrieved February 20, 2026, from https://www.dc.gov.ae

Emarat Al Youm. (2024). https://www.emaratalyoum.com/local-section/other/2024-10-18-1.1890425

Emirates Auction. (n.d.). Emirates Auction. Retrieved February 20, 2026, from https://www.emiratesauction.com/ar

European Commission. (2016). Online platforms and the digital single market: Opportunities and challenges for Europe. Publications Office of the European Union. https://eur-lex.europa.eu/legal-content/EN/TXT/?uri=celex:52016DC0288

European Commission for the Efficiency of Justice. (2016). Guidelines on how to drive change towards cyberjustice. Council of Europe. https://rm.coe.int/16807482de

European Commission for the Efficiency of Justice. (2018). European ethical charter on the use of artificial intelligence in judicial systems and their environment, 59 Council of Europe.

European Union. (2014). Regulation (EU) No 910/2014 of the European Parliament and of the Council of 23 July 2014 on electronic identification and trust services for electronic transactions in the internal market (eIDAS). Official Journal of the European Union, L 257, 73-114.

European Union. (2016). Regulation (EU) 2016/679 of the European Parliament and of the Council of 27 April 2016 (General Data Protection Regulation – GDPR). Official Journal of the European Union, L 119, 1-88.

European Union Agency for Fundamental Rights. (2023). *Digitalising justice: A fundamental rights-based approach*. Publications Office of the European Union.

France. Code civil [Civil Code], arts. 1366-1367. France. Code de procédure civile [Code of Civil Procedure], art. 662-1; arts. 748-1–748-9.

Laudon, K. C., & Laudon, J. P. (2020). *Management information systems: Managing the digital firm* (16th ed.). Pearson.

Ministère de la Justice. (n.d.). Dématérialisation des actes judiciaires. https://www.justice.gouv.fr

Ministère de la Justice. (n.d.). Exécution des décisions de justice. https://www.justice.gouv.fr

Ministère de la Justice. (n.d.). La transformation numérique de la justice. https://www.justice.gouv.fr

Ministère de la Justice. (n.d.). Services numériques judiciaires. https://www.justice.gouv.fr

Ministère de la Justice (France). (n.d.). Portail du justiciable https://www.justice.fr/donnees-personnelles/portalis

Ministry of Justice, United Arab Emirates. (n.d.). Digital and smart judicial services. Retrieved February 20, 2026, from https://www.moj.gov.ae

Motulsky, H. (1973). *Droit judiciaire privé* (2nd ed.). Dalloz.

Organisation for Economic Co-operation and Development. (2020). *Digital government policy framework: Six dimensions of a digital government*. OECD Publishing., DOI: 10.1787/f64fed2a-

Organisation for Economic Co-operation and Development. (2020). *Regulatory approaches to the digital economy*. OECD Publishing., DOI: 10.1787/bb167041-

Parker, G. G., Van Alstyne, M. W., & Choudary, S. P. (2016). *Platform revolution: How networked markets are transforming the economy and how to make them work for you*. W. W. Norton & Company.

Ramey, K. (2013, December 12). What is technology – Meaning of technology and its use. Use of Technology. https://www.useoftechnology.com/what-is-technology/

Schatzberg, E. (2018). *Technology: A critical history of a concept*. University of Chicago Press. DOI: 10.7208/chicago/9780226584027.001.0001

Securact. (n.d.). SECURACT – Signification électronique des actes. https://www.securact-huissier.fr

Tiwana, A. (2014). *Platform ecosystems: Aligning architecture, governance, and strategy*. Morgan Kaufmann. DOI: 10.1016/B978-0-12-408066-9.00001-1

United Arab Emirates. (2021). Federal Decree-Law No. 45 of 2021 concerning the protection of personal data.

United Nations Commission on International Trade Law. (1996). UNCITRAL Model Law on Electronic Commerce.

Vincent, J., & Prévault, J. (1999). Voies d'exécution et procédures de distribution (19e éd.). Dalloz.

ADDITIONAL READING

CEPEJ – European Commission for the Efficiency of Justice. (digital justice resources). https://www.coe.int/en/web/cepej

Civil Procedure Law, U. A. E. (Federal Decree-Law No. 42 of 2022) – official portal. https://uaelegislation.gov.ae/en/legislations

EU eIDAS Regulation (Regulation (EU) No 910/2014) – EUR-Lex. https://eur-lex.europa.eu/eli/reg/2014/910/oj

Evidence Law, U. A. E. (Federal Decree-Law No. 35 of 2022) – official portal. https://uaelegislation.gov.ae/en/legislations

GDPR. (Regulation (EU) 2016/679) – EUR-Lex. https://eur-lex.europa.eu/eli/reg/2016/679/oj

OECD – Digital Government & justice-related resources (gateway). https://www.oecd.org/governance/digital-government/

UAE Electronic Transactions & Trust Services (Federal Decree-Law No. 46 of 2021) – official portal. https://uaelegislation.gov.ae/en/legislations

KEY TERMS AND DEFINITIONS

Compulsory Enforcement: Procedures that transform judgments and enforceable instruments into practical recovery (attachment, sale, payment).

Cybersecurity: Controls to protect enforcement platforms from tampering, leakage, or disruption.

Data Minimisation: Limiting personal data processing to what is necessary for enforcement purposes.

Electronic Attachment: Digitally initiated measures to freeze or seize assets (e.g., bank accounts) through interoperable systems.

Electronic Auction: Sale of seized assets via digital platforms, requiring transparency, auditability, and bidder integrity controls.

Electronic Document: A digital record with evidentiary value if integrity and attribution requirements are satisfied.

Electronic Notification (Service): Notifying parties using approved electronic means, subject to rules ensuring reliable delivery/knowledge.

Electronic Signature: A signature in electronic form used to attribute intent and authenticate enforcement acts where legally recognised.

Enforcement File: The case record containing enforceable title, notices, attachments, and procedural steps taken by enforcement authorities.

Interoperability: Secure data exchange between courts/enforcement bodies and registries/banks enabling fast enforcement.

Procedural Legality: Requirement that every enforcement act is grounded in law and respects due process safeguards.

Trusted Timestamp: A verifiable time-stamp issued by a trusted service supporting procedural deadlines and priority disputes.

Chapter 5

Legal Provisions for Contracts During Pandemics:

A Practical Study on the COVID-19 Pandemic According to UAE Legislation

Fouad Al Shaibi
http://orcid.org/0009-0005-7122-150X
College of Law, Umm Al Quwain University, UAE

Abdulla Ali Binmalek
Umm Al Quwain University, UAE

Akmal Ramadan Ramdan
City University, UAE

Khulood Eid Abdulaziz
Umm Al Quwain University, UAE

ABSTRACT

This study examines the impact of the COVID-19 pandemic on contractual obligations within the labor market. It posits that the pandemic qualifies as a force majeure event, potentially suspending or limiting contractual obligations due to its unforeseen nature. The study also identifies obligations that remain unaffected by the pandemic, thereby precluding parties from using it as a pretext to evade their commitments. It recommends seeking amicable solutions and establishing specialized committees, particularly for minor cases that cannot sustain litigation. Additionally, it suggests

DOI: 10.4018/979-8-3373-7961-6.ch005

legislative reform in the Civil Transactions Law to clarify the definition and scope of force majeure, thereby preventing judicial confusion and ensuring that it is not limited to natural calamities, as some rulings by the Dubai Court of Cassation have relied on their interpretation of the explanatory memorandum of the Federal Civil Transactions Law.

1. INTRODUCTION

Pandemics are not "ordinary" commercial risks. They are public events with multi-layered effects: health impacts on labor availability, disruptions to supply chains, sudden policy restrictions, and a shifting regulatory landscape that can vary by sector and emirate. These features make pandemics doctrinally and evidentially complex. Doctrinally, the legal system must decide whether the crisis triggers termination, suspension, adjustment, or no relief at all. Evidentially, parties must show more than the existence of a pandemic; they must show the causal pathway from the crisis to the specific obligation that was not performed.

The World Health Organization announced that COVID-19 could be characterized as a pandemic on 11 March 2020 (World Health Organization, 2020). The declaration was rapidly followed by governmental measures around the world and within the UAE, including restrictions on movement, capacity limitations, remote work directives, and various public health requirements. Commercial parties then faced a practical dilemma: performance might be restricted, delayed, or rendered financially oppressive, yet many contracts continued to require strict compliance with time, cost, and quality obligations. Unsurprisingly, disputes followed. Parties invoked force majeure clauses, sought judicial adjustment, requested extensions of time, or claimed exemption from damages.

For an edited volume on digital evidence and procedural law, a purely doctrinal account is incomplete. Pandemic disputes are heavily evidence-driven and increasingly data-driven. The "facts" of disruption are often stored in digital form: emails and electronic letters, workflow approvals in contract management systems, supplier communications in procurement platforms, shipment histories in logistics portals, and official announcements on government websites. In a typical pandemic dispute, the judge or arbitrator is not asked to accept that "COVID-19 caused delays" in the abstract; the judge or arbitrator is asked to evaluate a chain of digital artifacts and decide whether the legal threshold is met.

COVID-19 also accelerated digital procedure. UAE institutions expanded remote hearings and electronic filing to maintain access to justice. The Official Portal of the UAE Government describes "virtual litigation" as an official litigation channel, enabling remote sessions and electronic procedures (UAE Government, 2025). The

Abu Dhabi Judicial Department likewise provides guidance for remote hearings and requests that parties prepare identification and authority documentation in digital format (Abu Dhabi Judicial Department, n.d.). These procedural shifts are significant for evidentiary practice: electronic bundles must be indexed, searchable, readable on-screen, and suitable for screen-sharing in remote hearings.

The objective of this chapter is therefore practical as well as analytical. It explains the UAE legal framework for pandemic disruption, with emphasis on Articles 273 and 249 of the Civil Transactions Law, and translates those doctrines into an evidence-centered method for dispute assessment. It then addresses how digital evidence is collected, preserved, and presented in a remote or hybrid procedural environment. Finally, it offers drafting and dispute-management recommendations designed to reduce future disputes and improve adjudicative clarity in crises.

2. UAE LEGAL FRAMEWORK FOR PANDEMIC DISRUPTION IN CONTRACTING

UAE contract relations are primarily governed by the Civil Transactions Law (United Arab Emirates, 1985). The law is built on party autonomy, the binding force of contract, and good-faith performance. At the same time, it recognizes that exceptional public events can distort the contractual equilibrium or make performance impossible. Pandemic disputes therefore occupy the space where contractual risk allocation meets statutory intervention.

2.1 Contractual Allocation Of Risk

Commercial contracts often contain force majeure clauses, sometimes with non-exhaustive lists that include epidemics or "governmental action." Many contracts also contain price adjustment clauses, notice and documentation requirements, "change in law" provisions, and termination rights triggered by prolonged disruption. In UAE practice, careful drafting matters because statutory rules operate as defaults, and because the contract may define consequences that differ from the statutory baseline. For example, Article 273 tends toward cancellation in cases of impossibility, while many contracts prefer suspension and extension.

2.2 Force Majeure Under Article 273 (Impossibility)

Article 273 provides that in bilateral contracts, if force majeure occurs making performance of an obligation impossible, the corresponding obligation ceases and the contract is automatically cancelled (United Arab Emirates, 1985). The text also recognizes partial impossibility: if only part of the contract becomes impossible, that part may be extinguished with corresponding consequences for the counter-obligation. For continuing contracts, temporary impossibility can justify temporary suspension. In pandemic contexts, this doctrine is most plausible where a legal prohibition or physical impossibility prevents performance, such as a closure order affecting a specific activity that cannot be substituted.

The central conceptual feature of force majeure is impossibility, not inconvenience or reduced profitability. The party invoking Article 273 must show that performance could not be achieved by reasonable means. This is why causation and mitigation evidence are central. A party that could have performed through alternative sourcing, alternative routing, or regulatory exemption may struggle to show impossibility, even if disruption existed.

2.3 Exceptional Circumstances Under Article 249 (Hardship/Oppressive Performance)

Article 249 empowers the judge to reduce an oppressive obligation to a reasonable level when exceptional circumstances of a public nature, unforeseeable at the time of contracting, make performance oppressive though not impossible. The doctrine thus aims to preserve the contract while restoring balance. Pandemic conditions often fit the "public nature" element because they are widespread and linked to public policy measures. However, not every cost increase qualifies as oppressive. Parties must show a level of burden that undermines the contractual equilibrium in a manner that exceeds normal market fluctuations.

Hardship is therefore a doctrine of quantified imbalance. Evidence of cost escalation, scarcity, compliance expense, or risk amplification must be documented and contextualized. The judge's role is discretionary and involves balancing interests, which makes the credibility of documentation and the reasonableness of mitigation highly influential.

2.4 Overlap, Sequencing, And Pleading Strategy

In practice, parties may plead force majeure and hardship in the alternative. The dispute then becomes a classification exercise: do the facts support impossibility (Article 273), oppressive performance (Article 249), or neither? A sophisticated pleading strategy aligns legal labels with specific time periods. For example, a short period of total shutdown may support temporary impossibility, while later phases of partial restriction may support hardship, delay, or contractually agreed adjustments.

2.5 The Digital Infrastructure Of Contracting And Evidence

Pandemic contracting was often executed remotely. UAE law recognizes the legal force of electronic documents and electronic signatures through the Electronic Transactions and Trust Services framework (United Arab Emirates, 2021) and its executive regulations (United Arab Emirates, 2023). Practical commentary emphasizes that electronic signatures can be binding but that parties should pay attention to form, authority, and evidentiary readiness (Charles Russell Speechlys, 2026). As a result, evidentiary disputes increasingly focus on audit trails, timestamps, and digital integrity rather than traditional wet-ink disputes.

UAE-focused legal guidance during COVID-19 emphasized that force majeure analysis in the UAE is fact-dependent and that documentation and notice can be decisive (K&L Gates, 2020; Baker McKenzie, 2020). This chapter builds on that guidance by translating the legal framework into a structured approach to digital proof.

3. ANALYTICAL THRESHOLDS IN PANDEMIC CLAIMS: FORESEEABILITY, CONTROL, CAUSATION, AND MITIGATION

Pandemic claims are often emotionally compelling, yet adjudicators must apply legal thresholds. Four thresholds dominate the analysis: foreseeability, control, causation, and mitigation. These thresholds are interdependent; weaknesses in one often undermine the entire claim.

3.1 Foreseeability

Foreseeability is not assessed abstractly ("pandemics are foreseeable in the modern world") but concretely ("was this impediment and its effect on this obligation foreseeable at the time of contracting?"). For contracts executed before widespread warnings or before the pandemic declaration, parties can plausibly argue that the scale and timing of disruption were not reasonably contemplated. For contracts executed after public warnings, or after the relevant sector had already experienced disruptions (for example, shipping congestion or supply shortages), the foreseeability argument may weaken. Foreseeability also depends on what the contract says. If a contract executed post-declaration includes explicit risk clauses, a judge or arbitrator may treat the risk as assumed and therefore not "exceptional" for Article 249 purposes.

Digital evidence can establish foreseeability and knowledge. Draft histories, negotiation emails, internal approvals, meeting minutes, and the time-stamped execution of the contract all help identify what the parties knew and what they assumed. The practical lesson is that contracting metadata and negotiation archives can become central in later disputes, especially for contracts signed after early pandemic indicators.

3.2 Control And Allocation Of Risk

A party seeking relief must show that the impediment was beyond its control and not caused by its own conduct. This requirement limits opportunistic claims. For example, if a supplier claims inability to deliver due to shipping restrictions, the counterparty may argue that the supplier could have reserved shipping slots earlier, sourced from alternative suppliers, or shipped through alternative routes. Control is therefore a factual inquiry into operational choices. It also intersects with contractual allocation of risk: if the contract places the risk of procurement delays on the supplier, a hardship claim may face additional hurdles unless the burden becomes truly oppressive and public in nature.

Operational systems generate the evidence of control. Procurement logs show when orders were placed and which suppliers were approached. Logistics dashboards show when shipments were booked and rerouted. Internal decision records show whether management prioritized the contract or diverted resources. These digital records can therefore either substantiate or defeat claims.

3.3 Causation

Causation is often the most difficult element. A pandemic is a background condition; the legal question is whether a pandemic-related event caused the specific breach. To prove causation, the claimant should construct a credible timeline connecting (a) the event or measure, (b) its operational impact, and (c) the contractual obligation. Consider a construction dispute: a party claiming delay should show how a restriction affected labor availability or site access and how that affected critical path activities. Consider a supply dispute: a party claiming inability to deliver should show supplier unavailability, export restrictions, shipping cancellations, or customs delays and explain why alternatives were not feasible.

In evidentiary terms, causation is best demonstrated through contemporaneous documents rather than retrospective narratives. Emails sent at the time of disruption, weekly progress reports, shipping cancellation notices, and revised schedules are more persuasive than after-the-fact summaries. Digital evidence also enables quantification, which supports causation: if the claimant can show that a specific measure reduced capacity by a measured percentage or increased lead times by documented intervals, the causal story becomes stronger.

3.4 Mitigation And Good Faith

Mitigation is both a substantive and a credibility factor. Many force majeure and hardship clauses require mitigation explicitly, and international standard clauses highlight mitigation as a core element (International Chamber of Commerce, 2020). Even where mitigation is not explicit, adjudicators often expect parties to take reasonable steps to reduce harm. Mitigation can include seeking alternative suppliers, negotiating revised delivery schedules, applying for exemptions, reorganizing workflows, or proposing partial performance.

The evidentiary value of mitigation is substantial. It shows contemporaneous effort and good faith, reduces suspicion of opportunism, and helps the adjudicator balance fairness. The practical lesson is that parties should document mitigation in real time: alternative quotations, internal approvals, and correspondence showing proposals and responses. In digital disputes, "silence" can be fatal; if there is no documented attempt to mitigate, the claim may appear opportunistic even if disruption existed.

4. DIGITAL EVIDENCE: WHAT MUST BE PROVED AND HOW TO PROVE IT RELIABLY

Digital evidence is the backbone of modern pandemic disputes. Yet digital evidence does not speak for itself. It must be collected, preserved, and presented in a way that demonstrates authenticity, integrity, and relevance. This section maps the legal thresholds to the most probative categories of digital evidence and explains how to strengthen evidentiary credibility.

4.1 Contract Formation And Variations: Electronic Signatures, Audit Trails, And Authority

Pandemic restrictions increased reliance on remote execution. Under the UAE Electronic Transactions and Trust Services framework, electronic documents and electronic signatures are recognized as legally effective (United Arab Emirates, 2021), and executive regulations provide additional structure (United Arab Emirates, 2023). Practical legal guidance emphasizes that electronic signatures can be binding and enforceable, while also highlighting the importance of understanding statutory exclusions and ensuring proper authority (Charles Russell Speechlys, 2026).

In disputes, the question is rarely "Is an electronic signature valid in principle?" and more often "Was this particular execution valid and authorized?" Accordingly, the best evidentiary package includes: the executed document in its original electronic form; the full signature audit trail (including date, time, IP addresses where available, and platform identifiers); certificate information if a qualified trust service was used; and evidence of corporate authority (board resolutions, POAs, delegation matrices). For contract variations, the evidentiary focus includes version history and proof of acceptance. In digital practice, a revised PDF attached to an email may be a binding variation if the parties clearly agreed, but disputes arise where acceptance is ambiguous. Preserving the entire negotiation chain is therefore critical.

4.2 Notice Requirements: Proof Of Sending, Receipt, And Content

Force majeure and hardship clauses commonly require notice within a set period and may specify delivery methods (registered mail, email to a specific address, or platform notice). Even where the contract is silent, notice is relevant to good faith and mitigation. Digital notice evidence includes: email headers showing transmission and routing; delivery receipts; read confirmations where used; and responses acknowledging receipt. The content of the notice matters too. A minimal statement that "COVID-19 affects us" is usually weak; a persuasive notice identifies the specific measure, explains its impact, provides preliminary mitigation steps, and commits to updates.

For messaging platforms, evidentiary challenges increase. Screenshots are easy to manipulate and often lack metadata. Parties should preserve verifiable exports and, where the dispute is serious, consider preserving device-level metadata or obtaining platform confirmation through permissible procedural routes. The more important the dispute, the more important the method of preservation.

4.3 Proof Of The External Event: Official Measures And Stable Preservation

Pandemic disruption is often linked to government measures. The evidentiary goal is to show the exact measure, its effective date, and its legal relevance. Parties should preserve official documents (circulars, resolutions, directives) from official sources, including government portals. Where a measure is published online, parties should preserve a copy (PDF) and a dated screenshot, because web pages can change. A robust practice is to store official documents in a dedicated evidence folder with date-stamped filenames and a brief note describing relevance.

4.4 Causation And Impact: Operational Data That Connects Event To Obligation

The central evidentiary question is causation. Therefore, the best digital evidence is the evidence that connects the external event to the specific obligation. Typical categories include:

(a) Supply and logistics data: bills of lading, airway bills, container tracking histories, carrier cancellation notices, customs clearance logs, warehouse inventory reports, and supplier correspondence explaining production stoppages or export restrictions.
(b) Project and construction data: baseline schedules, updated schedules, critical-path analyses, daily progress logs, workforce counts, procurement lead-time records, inspection reports, and site access permits.
(c) Financial data: invoices, quotations for alternative sourcing, cost breakdowns showing increases attributable to pandemic measures, bank payment evidence, and budget or cashflow reports demonstrating the magnitude of burden.
(d) Workforce and compliance data: attendance logs, quarantine notices, remote work policies, permit records, and compliance cost documentation (e.g., required protective measures that increase cost or reduce productivity).

Evidence should be organized into a timeline and accompanied by explanation. Raw data dumps are rarely persuasive. A coherent narrative is typically built by aligning three "timelines": (1) the timeline of measures and restrictions; (2) the operational timeline of the claimant's activities; and (3) the contractual timeline (deadlines, milestones, notice periods). When these timelines align, causation becomes easier to evaluate.

4.5 Authenticity And Integrity: Practical Methods For Strengthening Reliability

Digital evidence can be challenged as altered, incomplete, or taken out of context. For many disputes, authenticity can be strengthened without complex forensic work by following simple rules: preserve originals; preserve metadata; preserve the chain of custody; and avoid "cleaning" documents. For email, preserve in native format or export with headers. For platform logs, export from the platform rather than copying into new spreadsheets. For PDFs, preserve the original file rather than printing and scanning again. For spreadsheets relied upon as evidence, preserve a read-only PDF version and, where appropriate, preserve the native file for verification.

In higher-stakes disputes, forensic readiness may become relevant. Parties may use hashing to demonstrate integrity, and may need to explain how data was extracted from systems. This is especially important where the opposing party argues that the data is self-serving because it originates from the claimant's systems.

4.6 Common Pitfalls And How To Avoid Them

Pandemic disputes reveal repeated evidentiary errors. First, late or inconsistent notices: a claimant that continues performance without complaint and later asserts force majeure may appear opportunistic. Second, reliance on general media reports rather than official measures: courts and tribunals prefer official and verifiable sources. Third, failure to show alternatives: if the claimant does not document efforts to source alternatives or reroute shipments, "impossibility" may not be persuasive. Fourth, loss of digital records: staff turnover and device changes can destroy evidence unless centralized archiving exists. Fifth, disorganized exhibits: in remote procedure, judges and arbitrators are less likely to engage with a chaotic bundle.

A practical solution is to adopt an "evidence-first" approach: at the onset of disruption, create a digital case file, preserve all notices and responses, export key operational logs weekly, and maintain a running timeline memo. This transforms future disputes from reconstruction to verification, which improves efficiency and fairness.

5. PROCEDURAL CONTEXT: REMOTE HEARINGS, E-FILING, AND DIGITAL CASE FILES

Procedural transformation during COVID-19 shaped how disputes were initiated, argued, and decided. Virtual hearings and electronic filing reduced delays but increased the importance of digital case management and exhibit readability.

5.1 Remote Hearings And Identity/Authority Documentation

The Abu Dhabi Judicial Department's guidance on remote court hearings emphasizes that proceedings can be conducted through videoconference applications and that parties should prepare identification documents and powers of attorney in PDF form for review (Abu Dhabi Judicial Department, n.d.). This guidance highlights an important procedural reality: in remote litigation, authority is not presumed.

Counsel must be prepared to prove representation and authorization through digital documents that can be quickly presented and verified.

5.2 E-Filing And The Architecture Of The Evidence Bundle

When filing is electronic, the structure of the bundle becomes part of persuasion. A clear, indexed, and searchable bundle reduces cognitive burden for the decision-maker and improves the likelihood that key documents are read. Good practice includes a consistent exhibit naming system, chronological ordering, and a short index explaining what each exhibit proves. A timeline exhibit is especially useful in pandemic disputes because it can integrate restriction dates, correspondence milestones, and contractual deadlines into a single visual narrative.

5.3 Witness Evidence, Experts, And The Handling Of Data

Remote hearings affect the dynamics of examination. Witnesses may need to view and respond to documents on-screen, which requires exhibit clarity and readability. Where the dispute involves technical data (e.g., scheduling analysis, cost escalation), experts should prepare explanations that can be understood through screen-shared charts and tables. Parties may also need to provide native data files, subject to procedural rules and confidentiality obligations, especially where the opposing party challenges the reliability of system-generated evidence.

5.4 Confidentiality, Privacy, And Non-Recording Norms

UAE procedural guidance emphasizes confidentiality and restricts unauthorized recording of remote sessions (Ministry of Justice, n.d.). These norms support the integrity of remote adjudication but also require careful internal practice. Parties should use secure communications for team coordination, store evidence in controlled-access repositories, and avoid unnecessary dissemination of sensitive documents.

5.5 Procedural Consequences For Settlement And Dispute Avoidance

Digital procedure can reduce transaction costs, enabling earlier settlement. At the same time, it can accelerate timelines, making early evidence preservation essential. Parties that implement early case assessment—based on documented mitigation, quantified impacts, and a credible timeline—are better positioned to negotiate rational settlements or to litigate efficiently if settlement fails.

6. APPLICATION BY CONTRACT TYPE: TYPICAL PANDEMIC DISPUTES AND EVIDENCE PATTERNS

Pandemic disruption affects different contract types in different ways. The legal doctrine may be the same, but the evidentiary pattern varies.

6.1 Continuing Performance Contracts

Leases, managed services, and long-term supply agreements involve continuing obligations. A temporary restriction may support temporary impossibility or hardship rather than cancellation. Evidence in such disputes focuses on duration and functional impairment: occupancy restrictions, access logs, service-level dashboards, and correspondence about temporary alternatives. Claims that a party could not use premises or could not deliver services must be linked to specific restrictions and to the contract's usage assumptions.

6.2 Construction And Infrastructure Projects

Construction disputes often involve time and cost. Parties may seek extensions, claim additional costs, or argue for termination. Evidence typically includes baseline schedules, revisions, daily reports, procurement records, and correspondence with project managers or engineers. Because construction projects have many concurrent causes of delay, causation analysis is complex. Parties must demonstrate whether delays were on the critical path and whether they are attributable to pandemic measures. UAE practice guidance during COVID-19 highlighted that Article 249 may be invoked where performance becomes oppressive due to exceptional public circumstances, while Article 273 remains relevant in genuine impossibility scenarios (Baker McKenzie, 2020).

6.3 Shipping, Logistics, And Cross-Border Supply

Logistics disputes are often document-heavy, and digital logs are central. Bills of lading, vessel tracking, port notices, carrier booking histories, customs logs, and supplier communications can establish whether a delay was caused by pandemic measures or by poor planning. These disputes also raise issues of risk allocation under shipping terms and insurance coverage, which makes contract drafting and documentary alignment critical.

6.4 Service Delivery Tied To Staffing

Many service obligations depend on the availability of skilled staff. Pandemic quarantine or health requirements may reduce staff levels or limit deployment. Evidence may include HR attendance logs, quarantine notices, remote work directives, and regulatory permits. However, staffing issues are often contestable: the counterparty may argue that the service provider could have reorganized staffing, subcontracted, or used remote tools. Mitigation evidence becomes central.

6.5 Cross-Border Sales And The Role Of International Standards

In international sales, the CISG may apply, and Article 79 provides exemption from damages where an impediment beyond control prevents performance (UNCITRAL, 1980). Even when UAE law governs, CISG and UNIDROIT concepts can inform best practice, especially regarding notice and avoidance/overcoming of impediments. Cross-border disputes also underscore the importance of digital trade documents, electronic bills of lading where used, and secure evidence preservation across jurisdictions.

7. COMPARATIVE NOTES: UNIDROIT, CISG, AND ICC CLAUSES

Comparative frameworks do not replace UAE law, but they sharpen analysis and assist drafting. Pandemic disputes are increasingly transnational, and comparative standards provide a common language for risk management.

7.1 UNIDROIT Principles (PICC)

The UNIDROIT Principles excuse non-performance where an impediment beyond the party's control prevents performance and could not reasonably have been taken into account or avoided or overcome (UNIDROIT, 2016). The Principles also contain a hardship framework that encourages renegotiation and enables adaptation or termination in certain circumstances. For UAE disputes, the value of PICC is structural: it reinforces that impossibility and hardship analysis depends on control, foreseeability, and the possibility of overcoming the impediment. This maps closely onto Articles 273 and 249 and provides a coherent template for evidence-based reasoning.

7.2 CISG Article 79 And Proof Of Impediment

CISG Article 79 provides a limited exemption from damages where the party proves an impediment beyond control that could not reasonably have been foreseen or avoided or overcome (UNCITRAL, 1980). The focus on proof and overcoming is instructive. It pushes parties to document not only the existence of restrictions but also the unavailability of reasonable alternatives. This is valuable in UAE practice because many pandemic disputes turn on whether performance was truly impossible or merely more difficult.

7.3 ICC Force Majeure And Hardship Clauses As Drafting Models

The ICC published updated force majeure and hardship clauses that provide both long and short forms, designed to improve predictability and reduce disputes (International Chamber of Commerce, 2020). The ICC approach is operational: it specifies notification, evidence expectations, the effect of temporary impediment, obligations to mitigate, and termination rights after prolonged disruption. For UAE-governed contracts, the ICC clauses offer a drafting blueprint that aligns with UAE statutory themes while clarifying procedure and evidence.

7.4 Digital Evidence In International Practice

International contracting increasingly integrates evidence mechanisms: defined notice channels, agreed formats for digital records, and obligations to preserve audit trails. These mechanisms become critical during crises when business shifts to remote mode and recordkeeping can fragment. The UAE's digital contracting and digital justice frameworks make such drafting feasible and encourage parties to treat evidence preservation as a contractual duty rather than a litigation afterthought.

8. DRAFTING AND DISPUTE-MANAGEMENT RECOMMENDATIONS

The best pandemic dispute is the dispute that never occurs. Because pandemics are evidence-intensive, the most effective risk reduction combines drafting clarity with operational preparedness.

Once the obligation is clear, evidence can be collected to show how the pandemic-related event affected that obligation.

10.3 Step Three: Create A Three-Layer Timeline

Pandemic disputes are timeline disputes. A practical method is to create three parallel timelines in a single document. The first timeline is the "measure timeline," listing relevant governmental measures or public restrictions and their effective dates. The second timeline is the "operational timeline," recording internal operational events such as supplier shutdown notices, shipment cancellations, workforce quarantines, or site access restrictions. The third timeline is the "contract timeline," listing deadlines, milestones, notice dates, and any contractual extension mechanisms. The evidentiary goal is to demonstrate alignment: the measure affected operations during the period relevant to the obligation, and the party took timely steps under the contract.

10.4 Step Four: Quantify Impact And Separate Categories Of Loss

Hardship claims under Article 249 depend on proof of oppressive burden. Oppressive burden is not established by general statements that "costs increased." The party should quantify the increase and show that it is exceptional relative to the contract's expected baseline. A useful method is to separate categories of cost into: direct cost of performance (inputs, transport, labor), compliance cost (protective measures, testing requirements), and financing or delay cost (idle resources, extended overhead). Each category should be supported by primary digital evidence such as invoices, quotations, payment records, and internal cost ledgers. Where a party relies on data exported from an ERP system, it should preserve the export in its native form and be prepared to explain extraction methods.

10.5 Step Five: Document Alternatives And Explain Why They Were Not Feasible

The "avoidance/overcoming" concept appears in comparative frameworks and is implicitly relevant in UAE analysis. Adjudicators will often ask whether performance could have been achieved through alternatives, even at higher cost. Mitigation evidence therefore has two functions: it demonstrates good faith and it answers the "why not" question. The party should document alternatives considered, including alternative suppliers, alternative shipping routes, alternative work sequences, and alternative modes of delivery. If alternatives were rejected, the party should preserve

8.1 Draft With Evidentiary Foresight

Force majeure and hardship clauses should define triggering events (including epidemics/pandemics and government measures), require timely notice, and specify what evidence must accompany notice. This might include official circulars, supplier notices, shipping cancellations, or platform dashboards. Clauses should also define consequences: suspension with extension, renegotiation steps, partial performance options, and termination thresholds after prolonged disruption. Where parties prefer continuity, the clause should state that temporary impediment results in suspension rather than cancellation.

8.2 Integrate Electronic Signature And Authority Protocols

Remote execution should be anticipated. Parties should use e-signature solutions that provide verifiable audit trails and that align with the UAE trust services framework (United Arab Emirates, 2021; United Arab Emirates, 2023). Parties should also document internal authorization matrices and delegation rules for emergency contracting. Practical guidance emphasizes that electronic signatures can be enforceable, but authority and proper process remain essential (Charles Russell Speechlys, 2026).

8.3 Build An Evidence Preservation Protocol

Evidence is often lost in the first weeks of disruption. Organizations should establish a simple protocol: create a crisis contract folder; centralize communications to a dedicated contract email; preserve emails in native format; export key operational logs on a recurring basis; and store official announcements as dated PDFs. This protocol can be implemented without complex technology and can significantly improve future dispute outcomes.

8.4 Quantify Impact And Classify Claims Correctly

Parties should distinguish impossibility from hardship. If performance is prohibited or physically impossible, the evidence should show why and for how long. If performance is possible but oppressive, the evidence should quantify cost escalation or risk amplification and show that the burden exceeds ordinary market fluctuations. Quantification also supports fair renegotiation, reducing the need for adjudication.

8.5 Document Mitigation As A Workflow

Mitigation should be systematic and documented. Evidence should show alternative sourcing efforts, exemption applications, scheduling revisions, and negotiation proposals. Mitigation records not only support legal relief but also demonstrate good faith and may improve the probability of judicial adjustment under Article 249.

8.6 Prepare For Remote Procedure

Evidence bundles should be designed for screen review: searchable PDFs, clear indexing, and exhibits that are readable when shared on a video platform. Teams should also prepare digital authority documents and secure channels for hearing coordination, consistent with guidance on remote hearings and non-recording norms (Abu Dhabi Judicial Department, n.d.; Ministry of Justice, n.d.).

UAE practice guidance during COVID-19 emphasized the importance of factual documentation and notice in force majeure analysis (K&L Gates, 2020; Baker McKenzie, 2020). The recommendations above operationalize that guidance in a digital evidence context.

9. CONCLUSION

Pandemic-related contract disputes in the UAE demonstrate that legal doctrine operates through evidence. Force majeure under Article 273 requires proof of impossibility caused by an external event; exceptional circumstances under Article 249 require proof of oppressive burden and invite judicial balancing to restore contractual equilibrium. In both settings, the most persuasive proof is usually digital: electronic contract versions, e-signature audit trails, time-stamped notices, platform logs, project records, financial documents, and official government measures preserved from reliable sources.

Procedurally, the move toward remote hearings and e-litigation makes evidence organization and digital integrity even more important. Digital procedure can increase efficiency and access, but it demands disciplined evidence management and secure handling of sensitive documents. The central lesson for parties is simple: preserve early, preserve natively, quantify impacts, and document mitigation. The central lesson for institutions is that continued investment in digital justice should be matched by practical guidance on electronic evidence reliability and secure remote adjudication. By integrating substantive doctrines with digital evidentiary practice, the UAE can handle future crises with greater predictability, fairness, and commercial stability.

Declaration of AI-Assisted Language Editing

The authors used artificial intelligence tools (QuillBot and Grammarly) solely to support language editing, grammar checking, and stylistic improvement of the manuscript. All substantive legal analysis, interpretations, and conclusions are the authors' own. The authors reviewed, verified, and take full responsibility for the final content.

10. EVIDENCE TOOLKIT FOR PANDEMIC-RELATED CONTRACT CLAIMS

The preceding sections emphasized that pandemic disputes are decided through proof. This section offers a practical toolkit that parties, counsel, and adjudicators can apply to organize proof in a consistent manner. The toolkit is written as a workflow and is designed to be compatible with electronic filing and remote hearings.

10.1 Step One: Build A Dated "Event File" At The First Sign Of Disruption

The most common evidentiary weakness in pandemic disputes is reconstruction. When a crisis unfolds, teams focus on operations and delay legal documentation until later. By the time a dispute arises, key emails, platform logs, and internal decisions may be scattered across devices, accounts, and personnel. A simple solution is to create a dedicated digital folder for each affected contract and to preserve records from the first day the impediment is noticed. The folder should store the contract and all amendments, the notice history, and a running timeline memo that is updated weekly.

10.2 Step Two: Map The Obligation Structure Before Collecting Proof

Evidence should not be collected "by category" alone (e.g., collect all emails, collect all invoices). It should be collected in relation to the obligation structure. The party should identify the specific obligation that is allegedly affected, the date and manner of performance, and any contractual prerequisites such as notice or certification. For example, in a supply contract the obligation may be delivery of specified goods by a specified date at a specified location; in a construction contract the obligation may be completion of a milestone and certification by an engineer

evidence of the reason: legal prohibitions, unavailability confirmed by suppliers, or cost that would be truly ruinous relative to the contractual equilibrium.

10.6 Step Six: Preserve Authenticity And Chain Of Custody

Digital evidence can be challenged. The party should preserve originals and metadata where possible. For email, the best practice is to preserve messages in a format that retains headers. For platform logs, the best practice is to export directly from the platform with timestamps. For documents, the party should preserve the original file, not only a printed PDF. In high-stakes disputes, the party may record an internal chain-of-custody note: who collected each record, from what system, on what date, and where it is stored. This is not an onerous requirement; a simple spreadsheet or memo can strengthen credibility and reduce authenticity disputes.

10.7 Step Seven: Present Evidence As A Narrative, Not A Dump

Many disputes fail because parties submit large amounts of data without explanation. The decision-maker's task is to decide whether legal thresholds are met; therefore, each key threshold should be matched to exhibits. A simple structure is to use short "proof maps" within the pleading or witness statement. For example, under the heading "External event," the party cites the official measure exhibits. Under "Causation," the party cites operational logs and correspondence. Under "Mitigation," the party cites alternative quotations and negotiation emails. This approach reduces confusion and supports fair adjudication.

10.8 Step Eight: Align The Bundle To Remote Procedure

In remote hearings, exhibit usability is central. Evidence should be readable on screen and searchable. Documents should have consistent page numbering. Complex data should be summarized with clear tables or charts in the body of pleadings and supported by underlying native files where procedural rules allow. The party should also prepare a short set of "hearing exhibits" for screen sharing, containing only the most decisive documents: the contract, the notice, the key governmental measure, the key causation log, and the mitigation correspondence. This improves efficiency and reduces the risk that critical evidence is overlooked.

10.9 Step Nine: Use Early Case Assessment To Support Settlement

The toolkit also supports rational negotiation. Once the party has a coherent timeline, quantified impact, and mitigation record, it can evaluate the realistic strength of a force majeure or hardship claim and can negotiate adjustments that reflect evidence rather than positions. This is consistent with the policy objective of maintaining commercial stability during emergencies and can reduce unnecessary litigation costs.

11. DRAFTING MODELS FOR PANDEMIC READINESS AND DIGITAL EVIDENCE

Experience from COVID-19 suggests that many disputes could be reduced through targeted drafting. The purpose of this section is not to impose one model clause but to provide drafting "modules" that can be adapted to the sector and transaction.

11.1 A Pandemic And Government Measures Definition

Parties often disagree about whether an event is within scope. A clause may define "pandemic event" as an epidemic or pandemic declared by the World Health Organization or a competent governmental authority, and may define "government measure" as any law, regulation, circular, directive, or order that restricts movement, capacity, or operations. The drafting benefit is that it ties the contractual trigger to verifiable sources, improving evidentiary clarity.

11.2 Notice And Evidence Requirements

Many disputes arise from late or vague notices. A clause may require the affected party to provide written notice within a defined period and to attach primary evidence, such as an official measure, a supplier shutdown notice, or a carrier cancellation notice. The clause may also require periodic updates and a description of mitigation steps. This is not merely procedural; it shapes behavior during the crisis and creates a contemporaneous evidentiary record that supports later adjudication.

11.3 Temporary Impediment And Suspension Mechanism

Article 273 tends toward termination when impossibility is established, but commercial parties often prefer temporary suspension and extension for temporary impediments. A clause can provide that where performance is prevented for a temporary period, obligations are suspended and deadlines extended for the duration of the impediment plus a reasonable restart period. The clause can also define a maximum suspension period after which either party may terminate. The benefit is predictability and reduced pressure for immediate termination litigation.

11.4 Hardship Adjustment Mechanism Linked To Measurable Indices

Hardship disputes are driven by disagreement about whether cost increases are "exceptional." A clause can provide an adjustment mechanism based on measurable changes in certain input costs, such as freight indices or commodity price references, subject to caps or sharing formulas. Even where parties do not want automatic price changes, a clause can define a renegotiation trigger and a structured negotiation period, after which an expert or arbitral tribunal may adapt the contract. This aligns with the spirit of Article 249 by seeking a balanced adjustment rather than binary termination.

11.5 Digital Evidence And Audit Trail Obligations

Because digital proof is decisive, parties may impose mutual obligations to preserve records. For example, the clause may require each party to preserve relevant digital records in their original formats and to provide reasonable exports of platform logs, procurement records, or shipping records where those records are necessary to verify causation and impact. The clause may also define acceptable electronic signature methods and require preservation of audit trails. Such drafting aligns with the UAE electronic transactions framework and reduces authenticity disputes.

11.6 Dispute Resolution And Remote Procedure Readiness

Parties may include provisions allowing notices and submissions to be delivered electronically and may designate specific email addresses or contract management portals as authoritative channels. They may also confirm that hearings may be conducted remotely and that electronic bundles will be used. While procedural rules ultimately depend on the forum, this drafting supports efficiency and matches the reality of remote litigation described in UAE practice (UAE Government, 2025; Abu Dhabi Judicial Department, n.d.).

11.7 A Caution On Over-Drafting

Excessively rigid clauses can backfire. The objective is to create predictable triggers and evidence expectations without removing flexibility needed in emergencies. Therefore, the best drafting uses modular components and preserves room for good-faith renegotiation, consistent with the policy objectives of commercial stability and fairness.

DECLARATION

Declaration of AI-Assisted Language Editing

The authors confirm that AI-assisted tools were used solely for language editing purposes (improving clarity, grammar, and academic style) and not for generating original legal analysis, research data, or substantive conclusions. Specifically, QuillBot and Grammarly were used to refine English language expression, correct grammatical errors, and enhance readability. The authors reviewed, verified, and take full responsibility for the final content.

REFERENCES

Abu Dhabi Judicial Department. (n.d.). Remote Court Hearings. Retrieved February 22, 2026, from https://www.adjd.gov.ae/en/Pages/RemoteCourtHearings.aspx

Baker McKenzie. (2020, March 30). COVID-19 in the UAE: Overview and FAQs (client alert). https://www.bakermckenzie.com/-/media/files/insight/publications/2020/03/bmham-client-alert--covid19-in-the-uae--overview-and-faqs--30-mar-2020_final_v3.pdf

Charles Russell Speechlys. (2026, January 27). An overview of electronic signatures in the UAE. https://www.charlesrussellspeechlys.com/en/insights/expert-insights/corporate/2026/an-overview-of-electronic-signatures-in-the-uae/

Dubai Court of Cassation. (2011, September 18). Rights guaranteed by the Dubai Court of Cassation ruling in Case No. 2011/119 (Real Estate Appeal) [Legal rule]. Retrieved March 10, 2020, from https://www.dc.gov.ae/SubscribedServices/LegalRule

Dubai Court of Cassation. (2016, November 27). Rule derived from judgment in Appeal No. 2016/453 (Commercial Appeal) [Legal rule]. Retrieved March 25, 2020, from https://www.dc.gov.ae/SubscribedServices/LegalRule

Dubai Court of Cassation. (2017, May 10). Rights guaranteed by the Dubai Court of Cassation ruling in Case No. 2016/496 (Real Estate Appeal) [Legal rule]. Retrieved March 20, 2020, from https://www.dc.gov.ae/SubscribedServices/LegalRule

. Dubai Court—Seventh Primary Committee. (2020, June 7). *Judgment in the original case* [Court judgment].

Financial Action Task Force (FATF). (2020). *Mutual evaluation report.*

Government, U. A. E. (2025, November 19). Virtual litigation. The Official Portal of the UAE Government. https://u.ae/en/information-and-services/justice-safety-and-the-law/litigation-procedures/virtual-litigation

International Chamber of Commerce. (2020, March 24). ICC Force Majeure and Hardship Clauses. https://iccwbo.org/news-publications/icc-rules-guidelines/icc-force-majeure-and-hardship-clauses/

International Chamber of Commerce. (2020). ICC Force Majeure and Hardship Clauses (PDF). https://iccwbo.org/wp-content/uploads/sites/3/2020/03/icc-forcemajeure-hardship-clauses-march2020.pdf

K&L Gates. (2020, March 11). COVID-19: Force majeure in the United Arab Emirates. https://www.klgates.com/COVID-19-Force-Majeure-in-the-United-Arab-Emirates-03-11-2020

Ministry of Justice (UAE). (n.d.). The guideline for using remote trials (English). Retrieved February 22, 2026, from https://www.moj.gov.ae/assets/remote-trial-advisory-guide-in-english-638793604613261872

UAE Ministry of Health and Prevention. (2020). *COVID-19 information center.* Retrieved April 24, 2020, from https://www.mohap.gov.ae/ar/AwarenessCenter/Pages/COVID19-Information-Center.aspx

UNCITRAL. (1980). United Nations Convention on Contracts for the International Sale of Goods (CISG). https://uncitral.un.org/en/texts/salegoods/conventions/sale_of_goods/cisg

UNIDROIT. (2016). UNIDROIT Principles of International Commercial Contracts 2016. https://www.unidroit.org/english/principles/contracts/principles2016/principles2016-e.pdf

United Arab Emirates. (1985). *Federal Law No. 5 of 1985 (Civil Transactions Law). Official Gazette, 15*(158), December 29, 1985. (Amended by Federal Law No. 1 of 1987, *Official Gazette*, Issue 173; effective March 29, 1987).

United Arab Emirates. (1985). Federal Law No. (5) of 1985 concerning the issuance of the Civil Transactions Law of the United Arab Emirates. https://uaelegislation.gov.ae/en/legislations/1025/download

United Arab Emirates. (2021). Electronic Transactions and Trust Services law (Federal Decree-Law No. 46 of 2021) (webpage and PDF). The Official Portal of the UAE Government. https://u.ae/en/about-the-uae/digital-uae/regulatory-framework/electronic-transactions-and-trust-services-law

United Arab Emirates. (2023). Cabinet Resolution No. (28) of 2023 on the executive regulations of Federal Decree-Law on Electronic Transactions and Trust Services (English). https://uaelegislation.gov.ae/en/legislations/2199/download

United Arab Emirates Ministry of Justice. (n.d.). *Federal Civil Transactions Law (Federal Law No. 5 of 1985): Article 273* [Webpage]. Retrieved from https://elaws.moj.gov.ae/UAE-MOJ_LC-En/00_CIVIL%20TRANSACTIONS%20AND%20PROCEDURES/UAE-LC-En_1985-12-15_00005_Kait.html

World Health Organization. (2020, March 11). WHO Director-General's opening remarks at the media briefing on COVID-19 – 11 March 2020. https://www.who.int/news-room/speeches/item/who-director-general-s-opening-remarks-at-the-media-briefing-on-covid-19---11-march-2020

ADDITIONAL READING

Civil Transactions Law, U. A. E. (Federal Law No. 5 of 1985) – official portal. https://uaelegislation.gov.ae/en/legislations

ICC Force Majeure and Hardship Clauses. (2020) – ICC resource page. https://iccwbo.org/publication/icc-force-majeure-and-hardship-clauses/

NIST SP 800-86 (forensic techniques for incident/evidence preservation). https://csrc.nist.gov/publications/detail/sp/800-86/final

UAE Government Portal – Virtual litigation (procedural context). https://u.ae/en/information-and-services/justice-safety-and-the-law/litigation-procedures/virtual-litigation

UNCITRAL Model Law on Electronic Commerce. (1996). https://uncitral.un.org/en/texts/ecommerce/modellaw/electronic_commerce

UNIDROIT Principles of International Commercial Contracts (Hardship). https://www.unidroit.org/instruments/commercial-contracts/unidroit-principles-2016/

WHO – Timeline and public health communications (COVID-19). https://www.who.int/emergencies/diseases/novel-coronavirus-2019

KEY TERMS AND DEFINITIONS

Audit Trail: System-generated logs documenting decisions, approvals, and changes relevant to performance claims.

Causation: The demonstrated causal link between the pandemic measure and the specific non-performance or delay.

Change in Law / Government Measures: Regulatory actions (closures, capacity limits) that can trigger contractual relief depending on drafting.

Contemporaneous Records: Time-stamped emails, logs, and notices created at the time of disruption, typically more persuasive than later summaries.

Electronic Contract: A contract formed and stored electronically, including via e-signature, if recognised by applicable law.

Electronic Evidence Bundle: Organised, searchable compilation of digital exhibits for e-litigation/arbitration.

Force Majeure: An extraordinary event beyond a party's control that can excuse performance when it renders performance impossible under law/contract.

Foreseeability: Assessment of whether the risk was reasonably foreseeable at contract formation, impacting availability of relief.

Hardship (Exceptional Circumstances): A public, unforeseeable event making performance excessively onerous, allowing judicial adjustment in some systems.

Mitigation: Reasonable steps to reduce impact and attempt performance; evidence of mitigation strengthens credibility.

Notice Requirement: Contractual or legal duty to notify the counterparty of force majeure/hardship within specified timelines.

Remote Hearing: Hearing conducted via digital platforms, requiring clear exhibit management and identity/authority proof.

Chapter 6 Procedural and Evidentiary Safeguards for Corporal Punishments in Islamic Law: Implications for Digital Evidence Under UAE Criminal Procedure

Mohammed Ibrahim Sarhan
http://orcid.org/0000-0001-8020-588X
Umm Al-Quwain University, UAE

Emad Ibrahim
http://orcid.org/0009-0009-8571-315X
Umm Al-Quwain University, UAE

Ehab Alrousan
Umm Al-Quwain University, UAE

Amira Badr
http://orcid.org/0009-0005-6245-5806
Umm Al-Quwain University, UAE

ABSTRACT

The study aims to provide a clear understanding and a general overview of corporal punishment in Islam compared to corporal punishment in other legal systems. It sheds light on the key regulations governing the implementation of corporal punishment in Islam in contrast to modern criminal policies. The two researchers

DOI: 10.4018/979-8-3373-7961-6.ch006

seek to refute the criticisms raised about this form of punishment that are based on personal biases rather than solid evidence and reasoning. Their objective is to clarify for contemporary scholars that corporal punishments in Islam are not merely a continuation of ancient punitive practices. Instead, Islamic punishments are unique because they are governed by strict regulations that ensure they are fair and just, while also respecting human dignity and showing mercy, even during the execution of such punishments. This principle was exemplified by the Prophet of Mercy (peace be upon him) in both word and deed, as reflected in the Quranic verse: "And We have not sent you except as a mercy to the worlds." (Surah Al-Anbiya, 107).

1. INTRODUCTION

Scope and rationale (edited-book alignment): this chapter fits a book on procedural law and evidence by focusing on how corporal punishments are regulated, proven, reviewed, and executed under lawful process. It argues that contemporary debates are incomplete when they ignore the practical fact that most miscarriages of justice arise from weak evidence governance (coerced confessions, unreliable witnesses, contaminated forensic traces, or unauthenticated digital artifacts). For that reason, the chapter links Sharia-based principles (legality, shubha, and protection of dignity) with modern criminal policy (legitimacy, deterrence through certainty, and rights-respecting procedure), and translates those norms into institutional controls that can be audited by courts and editors alike (Peters, 2006; Penal Reform International, 2015; Stoykova, 2023).

Research questions (review-friendly): (i) Which Islamic principles constrain implementation and prevent error? (ii) How do modern criminal-policy goals reshape regulatory choices within ta'zir and procedural governance? (iii) What proof thresholds and evidentiary rules should apply when digital evidence is central? (iv) What severity-sensitive safeguards are suitable for the UAE context and similar jurisdictions?

comparative doctrinal analysis (fiqh + statutory procedural logics + policy literature), organized as a control-matrix mapping offense category to proof standards, admissibility tests, evidence types, and mandatory review layers. The analysis is normative and procedural; it avoids empirical claims that would require datasets unless directly supported by cited sources.

2. KEY CONCEPTS AND JURISPRUDENTIAL TAXONOMY

bodily sanctions associated with criminal enforcement. The chapter focuses on the regulatory conditions that make such sanctions lawful and defensible: competence, proof, fairness, documentation, and oversight. It distinguishes corporal sanctions from imprisonment and fines, and highlights that ta'zir permits policy substitution and mitigation in a way fixed hudud sanctions do not. fixed sanctions for specific offenses with strict evidentiary thresholds and narrow construction. In governance terms, hudud function as a 'high reliability / low discretion' domain: the state must accept that many cases will be reclassified or dismissed when proof is not exceptionally strong. This conservatism is not a weakness; it is the system's built-in error-prevention feature.

retaliation and compensation mechanisms for homicide and bodily harm. Qisas governance requires careful proof of identity, causation, intent, and proportionality, plus documented victim/family choices. Modern medical evidence and forensic reconstruction are often decisive here, and procedural safeguards are essential to prevent coerced waivers or coerced retaliation claims. discretionary sanctions that allow policy tailoring (rehabilitation programs, restorative measures, fines, community supervision, treatment). Ta'zir is also the space where uncertainty can be managed: when evidence strongly suggests wrongdoing but does not meet hudud-level reliability, ta'zir can preserve public interest while avoiding irreversible error.

3. NORMATIVE FOUNDATIONS AND THE LOGIC OF ERROR AVOIDANCE

protection of religion, life, intellect, lineage, and property. Procedural safeguards support maqasid by preventing wrongful punishment, discouraging coercion, and sustaining public trust. A maqasid reading treats institutional reliability (trained judges, accredited labs, and transparent records) as a modern instrument for protecting these objectives. the legal system must clearly define offenses, elements, defenses, and proof conditions. Unclear elements invite arbitrary enforcement, which undermines both Sharia legitimacy and modern rule-of-law expectations. Therefore, codified checklists and written reasoning are not bureaucratic add-ons; they are legality instruments.

proportionality applies most directly in ta'zir but also matters procedurally in hudud and qisas because proportionality shapes classification, evidentiary caution, and review thresholds. A proportionality-informed procedure demands that courts explain why evidence reaches the required standard and why alternative interpretations were rejected. the avoidance of hudud in doubt is a procedural doctrine that can be operationalized today as a reliability screen. Shubha can arise from contradictions, weak attribution, illegal searches, chain-of-custody gaps, questionable confession voluntariness, or plausible alternative explanations supported by digital or forensic inconsistencies. The practical implication is that the system should prefer non-irreversible outcomes when doubt is reasonable, even if moral suspicion remains.

4. OFFENSE-BY-OFFENSE PROCEDURAL AND EVIDENTIARY MAPPING

Theft (sariqa) in hudud logic is governed by strict proof conditions. implementation rules typically require clear proof of taking, qualifying property, protected custody conditions, and absence of shubha (e.g., ownership dispute, necessity, consent ambiguity). Modern evidence often includes CCTV, access logs, telecom location, and payment traces. Governance implication: digital artifacts must be authenticated; unclear attribution should create doubt. Where proof is strong but custody/qualification conditions are disputed, reclassification to ta'zir is a legally conservative resolution that preserves justice while avoiding irreversible sanction.

Digital evidence controls for theft allegations: require original video files (not edited clips), camera system logs, time synchronization checks, and chain-of-custody from DVR extraction to court. For device-based evidence (e.g., phone showing coordination), require forensic images and hash values. Screenshots without provenance should be treated as weak corroboration only (Peters, 2006).

Zina and related sexual offenses in hudud logic: classical proof is highly restrictive and designed to protect dignity and prevent false accusations. Modern states also require strong protections against coercion and misuse. Governance implication: investigators must avoid invasive digital fishing, must document consent and context, and must treat privacy and dignity as procedural values. Where evidence is circumstantial or digitally ambiguous, the conservative procedural choice is to avoid irreversible sanctions and, where justified, address harm through ta'zir or protective measures rather than fixed hudud enforcement.

Digital evidence controls for intimate-content cases: require legality of acquisition (no unlawful hacking), authenticated provenance, and expert examination to detect editing, coercion, or synthetic manipulation. Courts should be skeptical of forwarded messages, cropped screenshots, and non-original media. The risk of deepfakes and coerced sharing makes independent forensic validation essential.

False accusation (qadhf) and reputational harms: governance must balance protecting honor with protecting speech from misuse. Implementation requires careful proof of the accusation content, intent, and publicity. Digital evidence (posts, messages, platform logs) is common. Procedural safeguards should require reliable attribution (account ownership, device linkage) and allow defenses such as truth or mistake where applicable under the jurisdiction's rules. The chapter emphasizes that qadhf-type cases illustrate why authenticity and attribution standards are decisive in digital environments (Aykul & Uddin, 2025; Zahid et al., 2015; Aldabousi et al., 2025).

Platform evidence for qadhf-type allegations is governed by strict proof conditions. require archived URLs, platform data where available, and forensic capture methods (e.g., timestamped preservation) rather than informal screenshots. Courts should document why attribution is accepted, especially when accounts can be spoofed or shared.

Alcohol or intoxication-related offenses is governed by strict proof conditions. proof can involve witness observations, medical tests, or possession evidence. Modern criminal policy stresses public safety and harm prevention. Governance implication: procedural fairness requires validated testing methods, documented sampling, and safeguards against false positives/contamination. Where intoxication evidence is weak or collection violated rights, the resulting doubt should prevent severe sanction choices and shift the response to proportional ta'zir measures or public-safety interventions.

Forensic controls is governed by strict proof conditions. chain of custody for biological samples; lab accreditation; disclosure of method sensitivity/specificity; and recording of officer observations. Digital evidence such as venue CCTV should be synchronized with test times to reduce misidentification. Violent crimes and bodily harm under qisas/diyya: implementation focuses on identity, causation, intent, and proportionality. Modern evidence is often medical (injury documentation), forensic (DNA, tool marks), and digital (CCTV, location). Governance implication: expert evidence must be validated and contestable; victim/family decisions regarding retaliation or compensation must be documented as voluntary and informed. This domain shows how procedural law and evidence management directly shape justice outcomes.

Medical evidence controls is governed by strict proof conditions. standardized injury documentation, imaging retention, expert independence, and disclosure. Digital reconstruction tools (e.g., timeline analysis from devices) should be explained to the court in plain language, with limitations and error sources stated.

5. MODERN CRIMINAL-POLICY OBJECTIVES AND REGULATORY IMPLICATIONS

deterrence is driven more by certainty, swiftness, and fairness than by severity alone. Severe corporal punishments with weak evidence governance can be counterproductive: they increase incentives to tamper with evidence, pressure witnesses, or coerce confessions, and they reduce public cooperation. Therefore, deterrence arguments support stricter admissibility standards, robust chain-of-custody discipline, and transparent appellate review. modern policy recognizes that many offenders can be reintegrated. Ta'zir can incorporate education, addiction treatment, mental health support, vocational programs, and supervised community measures. Regulations should specify eligibility criteria and ensure sanctions are not merely symbolic but linked to risk reduction. A rehabilitation lens also supports procedural protections: unfair processes increase resentment and reduce compliance (United Arab Emirates, 2021a; United Arab Emirates, 2022a).

especially relevant in qisas/diyya and some ta'zir contexts. Restorative options require procedures that protect victims from coercion, ensure informed consent, and document agreements. When well-governed, restorative outcomes can reduce conflict escalation and preserve community trust, aligning with maqasid objectives. Legitimacy, dignity, and governance capacity: modern states are evaluated by their institutions. A system that demonstrates conservative proof standards, transparent reasoning, and error correction gains legitimacy even when it maintains traditional sanctions in limited circumstances. Conversely, weak governance erodes legitimacy regardless of substantive doctrine. This is why the chapter prioritizes institutional design (training, accreditation, documentation) as a policy lever.

6. STANDARDS OF PROOF AND EVIDENCE GOVERNANCE

implement a formal ladder of proof thresholds. Level A (irreversible/fixed sanctions): near-certainty with corroborated evidence and zero integrity gaps. Level B (serious discretionary sanctions): high confidence with validated evidence and manageable uncertainty. Level C (preventive/administrative responses): moderate threshold but strong oversight. This structure makes judicial reasoning and appellate review more consistent. confession only if recorded, counsel-assisted, and judicially confirmed; witness testimony only if credible and consistent; forensic reports only from accredited labs with disclosed methods; digital evidence only if authenticated via forensic images, hashes, and attribution analysis; and mandatory appellate review before execution (United Arab Emirates, 2021a; United Arab Emirates, 2022a).

implement structured credibility assessment (opportunity to observe, consistency, motive, corroboration). Require contemporaneous recording of interviews, disclosure of prior statements, and documented reasons for accepting or rejecting testimony. In high-severity cases, allow expert testimony on memory fallibility or perception limitations where relevant. treat confession as high-risk. Require: (i) clear rights notification, (ii) access to counsel, (iii) audiovisual recording, (iv) judicial confirmation of voluntariness and comprehension, (v) medical/psychological screening when coercion is alleged, and (vi) documentation of any retraction with reasons. A retracted confession should trigger a reliability review and may constitute shubha in hudud-level decisions.

labs should be accredited; analysts should document methods, tools, validation status, and limitations. Reports should separate observed facts from interpretation, and should disclose any uncertainty (e.g., partial profiles, low-quality traces). Courts should allow defense cross-examination of experts and, where needed, independent re-testing. fairness requires timely disclosure of inculpatory and exculpatory evidence, including forensic notes, tool logs, and chain-of-custody forms. Delayed or selective disclosure increases wrongful punishment risk and undermines legitimacy. A disclosure schedule should be mandatory in serious cases.

7. DIGITAL EVIDENCE: AUTHENTICATION, INTEGRITY, AND CHAIN OF CUSTODY

seize devices lawfully, isolate them from networks to prevent remote wiping, and document the device state (on/off, lock status, visible notifications). Create forensic images using write blockers, compute hashes, and store originals securely. Any bypass method (e.g., password extraction) must be documented and legally authorized. maintain secure storage with role-based access control, audit logs, and environmental protections. For cloud data, use lawful requests to providers where possible and preserve server-side logs. Preservation should capture both content and metadata because metadata is central to authenticity.

use validated forensic tools, document tool versions, settings, and steps, and preserve analysis logs. Where AI tools assist (e.g., video enhancement), document the method and avoid presenting enhanced outputs as raw evidence; provide original files and explain transformations. forensic reports should explain methods in plain language, state limitations, and show how attribution was established. Courts should ask: Who controlled the account/device? Could someone else have sent the message? Are timestamps reliable? Was the content edited? Is there corroboration? These questions should be recorded in the judgment reasoning.

screenshots can be fabricated; videos can be edited; chats can be spoofed; accounts can be hijacked; timestamps can be altered; and synthetic media can be generated. Countermeasures include provider logs, forensic imaging, hash verification, and expert analysis. In severe-sanction contexts, any unresolved manipulation risk should be treated as shubha.

7A. Integrative Discussion: Proof Ladders, Digital Artefacts, and Review

Digital evidence intensifies the need for severity-sensitive proof governance because it can appear persuasive while remaining fragile. Screenshots, forwarded messages, and short video clips often reach investigators already filtered, compressed, and detached from reliable provenance. As a result, a court that treats such artefacts as self-authenticating risks shifting the burden of proof to the accused, especially in socially sensitive cases. A defensible approach is to operationalize a "proof ladder" tied to sanction severity: the closer a case moves toward a fixed or irreversible outcome, the more the fact-finder should require (i) original data sources, (ii) validated extraction methods, (iii) documented integrity controls, and (iv) adversarial testing opportunities. This logic is compatible with the Sharia principle of shubha (doubt) because it treats uncertainty not as a mere rhetorical argument, but as a recordable procedural state that triggers higher safeguards (Soltan, 2025; Granja, 2017; Garrie & Morrissy, 2014).

In practice, courts can require that digital evidence be presented as a traceable package rather than as isolated content. A complete package typically includes the original device or a forensic image, a hash list, extraction logs, tool versions, a short expert explanation of error rates and limitations, and a disclosure record showing what was provided to the defense and when. Where remote procedures are used (e.g., remote hearing, electronic records, or electronic signatures), the system should demonstrate that it complied with the information-security policies governing remote communication and electronic documentation. Such requirements do not impose an unrealistic "perfect evidence" threshold; rather, they help the court distinguish between content that is merely plausible and content that is procedurally reliable.

A key institutional safeguard is to treat coercion and integrity breaches as admissibility problems, not only as credibility issues. Modern procedural law in the UAE emphasizes preservation of personal freedom and prohibits physical or moral harm and degrading treatment, treating evidence obtained by such methods as null. Translating this rule into day-to-day practice means: (i) mandatory audio-visual recording of interrogations in serious cases; (ii) a clear protocol for handling retractions; (iii) judicial reasoning that explicitly separates corroborated facts from confession-derived facts; and (iv) a remedy framework that incentivizes compliance (exclusion, adjournment for defense testing, or adverse inferences against sloppy handling) (United Arab Emirates, 2022a; Soltan, 2025).

Finally, the chapter's approach encourages transparent reasoning as a legitimacy tool. In disputes involving corporal sanctions or related enforcement, written reasons should explain: (i) the applicable standard of proof; (ii) the evidentiary chain for each essential element; (iii) why digital artefacts were accepted or rejected; and (iv) how doubt was assessed and resolved. This "reason-giving" discipline supports appellate review, allows policymakers to audit error patterns, and helps reconcile doctrinal commitments with modern expectations of due process. Over time, publishing anonymized procedural statistics (e.g., disclosure timeliness, integrity-incident rates, and exclusion decisions) can create feedback loops that improve both accuracy and public trust without requiring the legal system to abandon its substantive foundations.

This model also helps reviewers verify consistency between legal claims, evidentiary thresholds, and the chapter's implementation recommendations across cases.

Where regulatory drafting is needed, a useful technique is to separate "general admissibility rules" from "offense-specific proof rules." General rules codify baseline requirements for collection, documentation, storage, expert qualification, and defense access across all cases. Offense-specific rules can then raise the threshold in high-stakes contexts by requiring corroboration, independent evidence sources, and senior review before charges proceed. This separation avoids overbreadth: routine cases remain workable, while catastrophic error risk is reduced in severe cases. For the UAE context, it also supports consistent electronic workflows because judges can cite stable general rules while explaining why a higher ladder applies in a given file.

8. UAE IMPLEMENTATION ARCHITECTURE AND PRACTICAL CONTROLS

adopt a national or inter-emirate protocol for digital evidence that standardizes evidence IDs, handover forms, hash verification checkpoints, and disclosure packages. Standardization reduces variance and improves appellate consistency, which is critical when sanctions are severe. invest in cross-training where prosecutors and judges understand core digital forensic concepts (imaging, hashing, metadata, attribution), and forensic analysts understand evidentiary standards and courtroom communication. Capacity gaps are a root cause of evidence misuse; training is therefore a procedural safeguard. This is especially important in investigations that involve online conduct and platform-derived records under the UAE cybercrime framework (United Arab Emirates, 2021b). (UNODC, n.d.; ISO/IEC, 2012; NIST, 2006; SWGDE, 2025; United Arab Emirates, 2022a; United Arab Emirates, 2022b).

require courts to document admissibility, authenticity, integrity, and doubt analysis for each key evidence item. Templates should include a section explicitly addressing shubha triggers and explaining why they do or do not apply. This increases transparency and makes editorial and appellate review easier. require supervisory prosecutorial review and independent forensic quality review before seeking any irreversible sanction. Require mandatory appeal/cassation review prior to execution.

These rules institutionalize conservative error-avoidance consistent with Sharia and modern policy.

9. COMPARATIVE NOTES FOR SIMILAR JURISDICTIONS

adopt internationally recognized lab quality systems and regular blind proficiency tests. Publish aggregated error-correction statistics. This transforms reliability from a personal virtue into an institutional property. establish oversight units that audit chain-of-custody logs, review random case files, and investigate allegations of evidence tampering or coercion. Oversight reduces corruption risk and strengthens legitimacy, especially where sanctions are socially sensitive. introduce clear consequences for unlawful searches, coerced confessions, or integrity breaches. Consequences may include exclusion, weight reduction, or mandatory reclassification to ta'zir. Predictable remedies deter misconduct and protect system credibility.

10. COMPLIANCE MATRIX FOR COURTS AND INVESTIGATORS

list offense category, elements, possible defenses, and required proof standard. Document why hudud classification is justified (if claimed) and identify any shubha indicators at the element level. verify lawful authority for arrest, search, seizure, digital extraction, medical testing, and data requests. Record document IDs, dates, scopes, and any deviations. Any unauthorized intrusion should be treated as a major doubt flag in severe-sanction pathways. for each evidence item, confirm chain of custody with timestamps, handlers, storage location, and access logs. For digital items, confirm forensic imaging and hash verification, and ensure originals are preserved. Unexplained gaps should be escalated for investigation.

examine witness consistency; confession voluntariness; forensic validation; and digital attribution. Require corroboration for any single-source evidence in serious cases. Document contradictions and how they were resolved. confirm disclosure completeness, defense access, translation needs, and time to prepare. Confirm that the court recorded reasons for accepting evidence and addressed defense challenges. A fairness failure is a legitimacy failure and must be corrected before enforcement.

11. POLICY RECOMMENDATIONS

Adopt a unified digital-evidence standard operating procedure (SOP) and require certification for investigators and analysts. Make SOP compliance auditable through mandatory logs and periodic inspections. require written proportionality reasoning and supervisory approval for seeking severe outcomes; publish internal guidelines to reduce arbitrary variance. Institutionalize audiovisual recording of interrogations and courtroom proceedings in serious cases; integrate automated log retention; and define retention periods that support appeal without compromising privacy. Strengthen defense resources through expert rosters and controlled access to forensic images; establish rules for protective orders and redaction to balance privacy with equality of arms. anonymized reporting, procedural statistics, and an internal misconduct reporting channel for evidence manipulation or coercion.

12. LIMITATIONS AND FUTURE RESEARCH

The chapter is doctrinal and procedural. Future studies should analyze appellate decisions, forensic error rates, and case-file audits to empirically test whether the proposed compliance matrix reduces wrongful punishment and increases legitimacy perceptions. Rapid technology change requires periodic protocol updates, especially for encrypted messaging, cloud-first evidence, and AI-generated content. Comparative research across GCC jurisdictions can identify best practices for harmonized admissibility standards (Wan Ismail et al., 2021; Hussin & Majdah, 2013; Korbatieh, 2018, 2020).

13. CONCLUSION

Islamic jurisprudence contains a conservative error-avoidance logic; modern criminal policy can strengthen this logic by investing in institutions that make evidence reliability auditable. Digital evidence can either protect justice by clarifying facts or undermine justice if mishandled. Therefore, authentication, integrity controls, and defense access are essential safeguards, particularly in any case where a bodily sanction is contemplated. A UAE-focused integration approach based on standardized workflows, severity-sensitive review, and transparent judicial reasoning can preserve public interest and dignity while reducing wrongful punishment risk.

14. REGULATORY DRAFTING BLUEPRINT

Define a severity-based decision rule in the procedural code or in binding judicial guidance: when the prosecutor seeks a sanction that is fixed, bodily, or otherwise difficult to reverse, the court must apply a heightened reliability threshold and must document, item-by-item, how authenticity, integrity, and attribution were proven. This drafting move is crucial because it turns an abstract commitment to fairness into a justiciable requirement that appellate courts can enforce. The rule can be framed neutrally—without naming any specific punishment—by linking it to the general concept of 'irreversible consequences' and by requiring 'enhanced evidentiary justification' in such cases.

Create an explicit 'doubt management' provision: if material doubt exists about any essential element, the court must (i) record the doubt, (ii) specify which evidence could not resolve it and why, and (iii) select the legally available path that avoids irreversible outcomes. This provision operationalizes the classical shubha doctrine in a modern, record-based form. It also improves consistency because different judges are less likely to treat doubt informally or inconsistently. Importantly, the provision should clarify that doubt may arise from evidentiary uncertainty, procedural violations, or integrity gaps—so that rights violations have structured legal consequences.

Set minimum documentation requirements for every evidence item. For physical evidence, this includes a chain-of-custody form with timestamps, handler names, storage locations, seal status, and transfer signatures. For digital evidence, it additionally includes the forensic imaging certificate, hash values computed at acquisition and at each later access, tool logs, and a clear description of how data was extracted and parsed. Documentation must be standardized (templates) so that courts and defense counsel can compare cases and spot anomalies. In an edited-book context, a standardized documentation model strengthens the chapter's practical value and its alignment with procedural-evidence themes.

Clarify institutional roles and accountability. Regulations should separate (a) investigative collection, (b) forensic analysis, (c) prosecutorial evaluation, and (d) judicial admissibility determinations. Each role should have an obligation to record actions and to report suspected integrity violations. A practical accountability mechanism is a 'two-person integrity rule' for key digital steps (imaging, hashing, exporting reports), where a second qualified person signs off on the process. This reduces single-point-of-failure risks and is especially valuable in serious cases.

Codify disclosure obligations and timelines. The prosecution should disclose the full digital-evidence package (forensic image inventory, hash list, extraction logs, and analyst notes) early enough for the defense to prepare. The rule should explicitly include exculpatory material and alternative leads. Where privacy is an issue, disclosure can be managed through protective orders, redactions, and controlled viewing environments, but it should not be avoided. A disclosure rule is a procedural safeguard that directly reduces wrongful punishment risk and increases the legitimacy of outcomes (Antwi-Boasiako & Venter, 2017; SWGDE, 2025).

Introduce expert evidence standards. Expert reports must state qualifications, methods, tools, validation status, and limitations. Courts should be empowered to order an independent expert review when the sanction sought is severe or when the defense raises a credible integrity challenge. Experts should distinguish between raw observations (e.g., recovered file hashes, GPS coordinates) and interpretive conclusions (e.g., intent, identity). This structure helps judges avoid over-weighting speculative expert interpretation.

Add a confession reliability protocol. A confession should be admissible only if the interrogation was recorded, the accused had meaningful access to counsel, and the judge confirmed voluntariness and comprehension in open court. The protocol should require the court to inquire about the circumstances of interrogation, duration, deprivation, threats, promises, or inducements. If any coercion indicator exists, the confession should be treated as unreliable and should trigger a broader doubt assessment across the case file. This protocol is consistent with both modern due process and the conservative Islamic emphasis on avoiding irreversible error.

Embed a privacy-and-proportionality filter for digital searches. Warrants or authorizations should specify scope: offense type, time window, data categories, and accounts/devices. Investigators should document minimization steps (excluding irrelevant private content) and should preserve only relevant extracts where permissible. A proportionality filter protects dignity and reduces the risk that investigations become intrusive fishing expeditions, which can undermine public trust and generate legal challenges that weaken the legitimacy of outcomes.

Define remedies for procedural violations. Remedies should be predictable and severity-sensitive: unlawful collection or integrity breaches may lead to exclusion, reduced evidentiary weight, mandatory reclassification to a discretionary track (ta'zir), or dismissal depending on the violation and the remaining evidence. A remedy framework deters misconduct and makes the system auditable. In a serious-sanction context, even if evidence is not fully excluded, the existence of a violation should be treated as a shubha factor unless convincingly cured.

Create implementation KPIs and audit routines. KPIs can include: percentage of serious cases with complete chain-of-custody packets, percentage of interrogations recorded, time-to-disclosure compliance, frequency of hash verification, and number of integrity incidents detected and resolved. Independent audits (internal inspection units or external oversight) should review random case files. KPI-driven governance moves procedural fairness from aspiration to measurable practice, which strengthens policy legitimacy and professionalization.

Address AI-assisted analysis explicitly. Where AI tools are used for triage (e.g., searching large chat logs) or enhancement (e.g., video deblurring), regulations should require logging of the tool, version, settings, and outputs, and should preserve original data. Courts should treat AI outputs as investigative aids unless validated as forensic evidence through transparent methods and error characterization. This prevents over-reliance on opaque algorithms and keeps the evidentiary process aligned with reliability principles.

Provide a concise 'courtroom admissibility checklist' as an annex or internal bench card: legality of collection; scope and proportionality; authenticity; integrity; attribution; corroboration; disclosure; and defense opportunity to challenge. The checklist should be used in hearings and referenced in written judgments. This ensures that the court's reasoning covers the full admissibility logic rather than focusing only on content. For edited-book readership, such a checklist demonstrates practical usefulness and strengthens acceptance (Stoykova, 2023; Granja, 2017).

15. GLOSSARY OF KEY TERMS

Admissibility refers to the legal decision that an evidence item may be considered by the court. Admissibility is distinct from weight; even admissible evidence may be weak if it lacks corroboration or has reliability issues.

Authentication refers to the process of showing that evidence is what it claims to be. For digital evidence, authentication usually requires provenance documentation, metadata coherence, and forensic extraction records.

Chain of custody refers to the documented history of evidence handling from collection to court. A complete chain includes timestamps, handlers, storage conditions, and transfer signatures.

Hash value refers to a cryptographic fingerprint of a digital file or forensic image. Matching hashes support integrity by showing data has not changed since the hash was computed.

Shubha (doubt) refers to a legally relevant doubt that prevents applying a fixed or irreversible sanction. In modern governance terms, shubha can be triggered by evidentiary uncertainty, procedural violations, or integrity gaps that prevent near-certainty.

16. OPERATIONAL SOP FOR HANDLING DIGITAL EVIDENCE

Step A - Seizure and isolation: when a device is seized, officers should photograph the device in situ, record its state (powered on/off, network connections, visible notifications), and immediately isolate it from networks using airplane mode or a Faraday bag where appropriate. The goal is to prevent remote wiping and preserve volatile data. Officers must document who seized the device, the exact location, the time, and the legal authorization under which the seizure occurred. Any deviation from the authorized scope should be recorded as it may affect admissibility and weight.

Step B - Imaging and hashing: qualified forensic personnel should create a bit-for-bit image using validated tools and write blockers. Hash values (e.g., SHA-256) must be computed for the original and the image and recorded in the case file. The imaging report should list tool versions, settings, and any errors encountered. If the device cannot be imaged due to encryption or damage, the report must explain the alternative method used (logical extraction, chip-off, cloud acquisition) and its limitations. This transparency is essential for judicial evaluation and defense challenges.

18. HUMAN-RIGHTS COMPATIBLE SAFEGUARDS

Regardless of substantive doctrine, modern criminal policy must respond to concerns about dignity, coercion, and error. The chapter's approach is not to import external norms mechanically but to show compatibility between conservative Islamic error-avoidance principles and modern safeguards: legality, voluntariness, transparency, and effective remedy. Practical safeguards—recording interrogations, guaranteeing defense access, accrediting forensic labs, and mandating appellate review—directly reduce the risk of wrongful punishment. They also protect the integrity of the justice system, which is itself a public interest recognized in maqasid reasoning.

A key governance principle is reversibility: when outcomes are hard to reverse, the system must invest more in proof reliability and review. This principle is ethically intuitive, procedurally implementable, and consistent with the shubha doctrine. Therefore, human-rights concerns can be addressed through a procedural design that is both Sharia-consistent and institutionally modern. The chapter recommends that policymakers explicitly communicate this design to the public, explaining that strict proof and fairness are not 'leniency' but are necessary to prevent injustice and maintain legitimacy.

19. IMPLEMENTATION GOVERNANCE AND CAPACITY BUILDING

Implementation should prioritize institutional capacity (trained personnel, standardized forms, and quality assurance) and transparent documentation that enables judicial review. At minimum, agencies should adopt a unified digital-evidence SOP with auditable chain-of-custody, hash verification, controlled storage, and disclosure practices proportionate to the gravity of the alleged sanction (ISO/IEC, 2012; NIST, 2006; SWGDE, 2025; United Arab Emirates, 2022a).

AI-ASSISTED LANGUAGE EDITING DECLARATION

The authors used an artificial intelligence–assisted writing tool (QuillBot) solely for language editing, including rephrasing sentences for clarity and improving grammar and readability. No AI tools were used for study design, data collection, statistical analysis, interpretation of results, or generation of scientific content. The authors reviewed and verified all revisions and take full responsibility for the accuracy and integrity of the manuscript.

REFERENCES

Aldabousi, A. M., Awad, A., Hassan, H. E. M., Abdullah, S. S., & Ghonim, A. (2025). Arbitration in Islamic banking: Exploring legal and practical implications for dispute resolution. *Banks and Bank Systems*, *20*(2), 15–26. DOI: 10.21511/bbs.20(2).2025.02

Antwi-Boasiako, A., & Venter, H. S. (2017). A model for digital forensic readiness for cloud computing environments. *Journal of Forensic Sciences*, *62*(6), 1534–1544. DOI: 10.1111/1556-4029.13434 PMID: 28230894

Aykul, A., & Uddin, A. H. M. F. (2025). Evaluating the influence of doubt (shubhah) in the implementation of hudud penalties. Ahkam. *Jurnal Ilmu Syariah*, *25*(1), 87–104. DOI: 10.15408/ajis.v25i1.37953

Garrie, D. B., & Morrissy, D. J. (2014). Digital forensic evidence in the courtroom: Understanding content and quality. *Northwestern Journal of Technology and Intellectual Property*, *12*(2), 122–172. https://scholarlycommons.law.northwestern.edu/njtip/vol12/iss2/5

Granja, F. M., & Rafael, G. D. R. (2017). The preservation of digital evidence and its admissibility in the court. *International Journal of Electronic Security and Digital Forensics*, *9*(1), 1–19. DOI: 10.1504/IJESDF.2017.081749

Hussin, N., & Majdah, M. (2013). The application of the rule of "avoiding hudud due to shubhah" in Islamic criminal law. In Proceedings of the Islamic Law and Contemporary Issues Conference (ISLAC 2013). https://irep.iium.edu.my/34400/1/ISLAC_2013_final_paper-_Dr.Nasimah_%26_Dr.Majdah_%28UIAM%29.pdf

ISO/IEC. (2012). ISO/IEC 27037:2012—Information technology—Security techniques—Guidelines for identification, collection, acquisition and preservation of digital evidence. International Organization for Standardization. https://www.iso.org/standard/44381.html

Korbatieh, S. (2018). The law of evidence in the Islamic criminal justice system: A critical appraisal in the light of modern technology (Doctoral thesis, Macquarie University). *Figshare*. https://figshare.mq.edu.au/articles/thesis/The_law_of_evidence_in_the_Islamic_criminal_justice_system_a_critical_appraisal_in_the_light_of_modern_technology/19440422

Korbatieh, S. (2020). Evidence rules in sharia and the impact of modern technology and DNA testing. *Australian Journal of Islamic Studies*, *5*(3), 4–29. https://ajis.com.au/index.php/ajis/article/view/303. DOI: 10.55831/ajis.v5i3.303

National Institute of Standards and Technology. (2006). Guide to integrating forensic techniques into incident response (NIST Special Publication 800-86). https://csrc.nist.gov/pubs/sp/800/86/final

Penal Reform International. (2015). Sharia law and the death penalty: Would abolition of the death penalty be unfaithful to the message of Islam? https://cdn.penalreform.org/wp-content/uploads/2015/07/Sharia-law-and-the-death-penalty.pdf

Peters, R. (2006). *Crime and punishment in Islamic law: Theory and practice from the sixteenth to the twenty-first century*. Cambridge University Press., https://www.cambridge.org/core/books/crime-and-punishment-in-islamic-law/75C4EBE9B545F4F0FD7F41B62C4B3883 DOI: 10.1017/CBO9780511610677

Scientific Working Group on Digital Evidence. (2025). SWGDE best practices for cloud service providers (Version 1.1). https://www.swgde.org/documents/published/2025-01-15%20SWGDE%20Best%20Practices%20for%20Cloud%20Service%20Providers%20Version%201.1.pdf

Soltan, K. R. (2025). Digital evidence as a means of proof in criminal proceedings in the UAE. Al Dhakheerah (UAE) repository. https://aldhakheerah.ae/handle/123456789/105076

Stoykova, R. (2023). The right to a fair trial as a conceptual framework for digital evidence rules in criminal investigations. *Computer Law & Security Review*, *49*, 105801. DOI: 10.1016/j.clsr.2023.105801

United Arab Emirates. (2021a). Federal Decree-Law No. (31) of 2021 promulgating the crimes and penalties law. UAE Legislation. https://uaelegislation.gov.ae/en/legislations/1529

United Arab Emirates. (2021b). Federal Decree-Law No. (34) of 2021 on combatting rumors and cybercrimes. UAE Legislation. https://uaelegislation.gov.ae/en/legislations/1418

United Arab Emirates. (2022a). Federal Decree-Law No. (38) of 2022 on criminal procedures. UAE Legislation. https://uaelegislation.gov.ae/en/legislations/1609

United Arab Emirates. (2022b). Federal Law by Decree No. (35) of 2022 issuing the law of evidence in civil and commercial transactions. UAE Legislation. https://uaelegislation.gov.ae/en/legislations/1719

United Nations Office on Drugs and Crime. (n.d.). Cybercrime module 6: Handling of digital evidence. https://www.unodc.org/e4j/en/cybercrime/module-6/key-issues/handling-digital-evidence.html

Wan Ismail, W. A. F., Baharuddin, A. S., Mutalib, L. A., & Alias, M. A. A. (2021). An appraisal of digital documents as evidence in Islamic law. *Academic Journal of Interdisciplinary Studies*, *10*(3), 198–206. DOI: 10.36941/ajis-2021-0076

Zahid, A., Shariff, A. A. M., & Zulkifli, A. N. (2015). The use of qarinah in proving hudud and qisas crimes: An analysis of the debate between Islamic schools and the Malaysian syariah courts. *Mediterranean Journal of Social Sciences*, *6*(2), 141–147.

ADDITIONAL READING

Council of Europe – Budapest Convention. (evidence cooperation). https://www.coe.int/en/web/cybercrime/the-budapest-convention

Criminal Procedure Law, U. A. E. (Federal Decree-Law No. 38 of 2022) – official portal. https://uaelegislation.gov.ae/en/legislations

Cybercrimes Law, U. A. E. (Federal Decree-Law No. 34 of 2021) – official portal. https://uaelegislation.gov.ae/en/legislations

Digital Evidence, S. W. G. D. E. Best Practices (forensics). https://www.swgde.org/documents

NIST Computer Forensics Tools & Techniques. https://www.nist.gov/itl/ssd/software-quality-group/computer-forensics-tools-techniques

UN Office on Drugs and Crime (UNODC) – Cybercrime/evidence cooperation (gateway). https://www.unodc.org/unodc/en/cybercrime.html

WHO – Human rights and health governance (gateway for standards context). https://www.who.int/about/governance

KEY TERMS AND DEFINITIONS

Chain of Custody: Continuity documentation for seized devices/data to prevent tampering and contamination claims.

Coerced Confession Risk: Risk that admissions are influenced by pressure; safeguards include recording, counsel access, and judicial review.

Digital Evidence: Electronic traces (CCTV, device data, cloud logs) that can clarify facts but also introduce integrity risks.

Disclosure: Duty to provide sufficient evidentiary material for meaningful challenge and adversarial testing.

Expert Evidence: Forensic/technical testimony explaining methods, limits, and error sources in digital/medical evidence.

Hudud: Fixed-category offences with strict elements and traditionally high proof thresholds to avoid wrongful punishment.

Procedural Legality: Requirement that investigation and evidence collection comply with criminal procedure safeguards.

Proportionality: Matching severity of sanction with reliability of proof and procedural safeguards.

Qisas and Diyya: Retaliation/compensation framework for bodily harm and homicide involving causation and victim-family rights.

Shubha (Doubt): A doctrine requiring restraint where material doubt exists; operationalised as a severity-sensitive reliability standard.

Standard of Proof: The level of certainty required before imposing a sanction; higher for severe/irreversible outcomes.

Ta'zir: Discretionary sanctions enabling policy-adapted responses when strict proof for fixed sanctions is not satisfied.

Chapter 7
The Legal and Technological Challenges of Practicing Law in the Age of Artificial Intelligence (AI): An Analytical Study

Saad Ali Ramadan
http://orcid.org/0000-0003-0043-6982
Umm Al Quwain University, UAE

Naser Al-Sherman
http://orcid.org/0000-0003-4365-842X
American University in the Emirates, UAE

Ahmed Helmy Radwan
Mansoura University, Egypt

ABSTRACT

Undoubtedly, the legal profession, like other fields, is influenced by the rapid developments occurring in society, which require keeping up with these advancements and dealing with them in a positive and realistic manner. This has enhanced the ability of law to adapt to rapid technological changes, especially considering the information revolution and the digital transformation that the world is experiencing today. Technology has become an essential tool in enhancing knowledge and improving the efficiency of legal practice, while maintaining the human and ethical aspects that distinguish this profession. This research reviews the legal and techno-

DOI: 10.4018/979-8-3373-7961-6.ch007

logical challenges facing the legal profession in light of developments in artificial intelligence, with a focus on its impact on legal practice and finding solutions to these challenges.

INTRODUCTION

Research Topic

Undoubtedly, the progress, prosperity, and well-being of societies throughout history have largely depended on the creative ideas developed by humans that align with the changes of life, interact with the needs and desires of individuals, as well as the opportunities available within those societies. Human problems, desires, and needs are an integral part of the continuity of life, and the search for solutions to these challenges requires the generation of innovative ideas capable of providing effective solutions and fulfilling those desires and needs. These ideas form the foundation for new innovations that transform into entrepreneurial projects offering diverse goods and services to communities (Aldabousi, A. M. (2022).

The legal profession is one of the earliest legal fields to benefit from this technology, whether in reviewing and drafting legal briefs. This technology can save lawyers significant time, allowing them to focus on strategic planning, in-depth case analysis, and quick data connection. The UAE Ministry of Justice, in partnership with the Government Development and Future Office, the Artificial Intelligence and Digital Economy Office, and the Remote Work Applications in the UAE Government, announced the "Virtual Lawyer" project during the events of "GITEX 2024." The Virtual Lawyer is the first project of its kind in the UAE and the region. Its goal is to add value by speeding up litigation time and developing its services, making them globally pioneering, as well as simplifying the litigant's journey. The virtual lawyer relies on the "Unified National Legislative Text Database," which will be created by the Ministry of Justice. Law firms wishing to use it will have to feed data into this database after registering the virtual lawyer with the ministry.

At the same time, however, a variety of legal and technological challenges emerge that face the legal profession considering the developments in Artificial Intelligence.

Research Importance

This research addresses a highly significant topic due to the increasing reliance on artificial intelligence in various fields, including the legal sector in general and the legal profession specifically. This transformation is evident in improving the efficiency of legal work through automating routine tasks such as reviewing contracts and drafting briefs. However, with these benefits come new challenges related to the trustworthiness of legal results and the credibility of digital evidence, necessitating a detailed study to determine the boundaries of artificial intelligence usage in this field. Therefore, this research contributes to enhancing the understanding of the relationship between technology and law, offering scientific insights that support innovation in legal practices, while maintaining human oversight to ensure fairness and transparency in the legal system.

Research Problem

The research problem lies in studying the impact of Artificial Intelligence (AI) on the legal profession. Despite the facilitation Artificial Intelligence (AI) provides, such as drafting contracts and writing legal briefs, the increasing reliance on it raises a number of challenges. Among the most prominent of these challenges is the accuracy and credibility of the legal results generated by Artificial Intelligence (AI) systems. Therefore, the research aims to address these issues by examining how to strike a balance between benefiting from Artificial Intelligence (AI) and ensuring the preservation of the core values of the legal system in the legal profession.

Research Methodology

The research adopts an analytical approach, relying on the analysis of evidence and data related to the use of artificial intelligence. It reviews the evolution of Artificial Intelligence (AI) technology in the legal profession and analyzes its impact on legal procedures, while also studying the legal challenges that may arise due to the unchecked use of these tools.

Research Plan

The research consists of an introduction, three main chapters, and a conclusion:

- Introduction: Discusses the research topic, its importance, the research problem, and methodology.
- Chapter One: Conceptual Framework and Technological Developments
    - Section One: Definition of Artificial Intelligence (AI) and its prominent applications in the legal field.
    - Section Two: The historical development of the legal profession in light of technology.
- Chapter Two: Legal and Technological Challenges in Practicing the Legal Profession

- o Section One: Legal challenges in practicing the legal profession.
- o Section Two: Technological challenges in practicing the legal profession.
- Chapter Three: Mechanisms for Addressing the Challenges
  - o Section One: Developing legal regulations to cover the use of Artificial Intelligence (AI)
  - o Section Two: Enhancing training for lawyers on technological tools.
- Conclusion: Includes the research findings and recommendations.

CONCEPTUAL FRAMEWORK AND TECHNOLOGICAL DEVELOPMENTS

Introduction and Division

Artificial intelligence (AI) is increasingly seen as a tool that can help enhance creativity and innovation by analyzing data, predicting trends, and generating new ideas. Modern applications include arts, literature, and design, where Artificial Intelligence (AI) assists in producing new works or inspiring human creators. In light of this, we will divide this chapter into two sections:

Section One: Definition of Artificial Intelligence (AI) and Its Prominent Applications in the Legal Field.

Section Two: The Historical Development of the Legal Profession in Light of Technology.

Section One: Definition of Artificial Intelligence and Its Prominent Applications in the Legal Field

Concept of Artificial Intelligence

Artificial Intelligence (AI) is one of the branches of computer science and a fundamental pillar of the technology industry in the present age. Artificial Intelligence (AI) is described as the science that enables machines to think like humans. Artificial Intelligence (AI) has specific behaviors and characteristics that computer programs exhibit to simulate human mental abilities and patterns of work. Some of the most important characteristics include the ability to learn, reason, and react to situations that the machine was not programmed for Extance, A. (2018). Artificial Intelligence (AI) is based on the assumption that human intelligence can be accurately described to the degree that a machine can mimic it Goltz, N., & Dondoli, G. (2019).

The definitions of Artificial Intelligence (AI) vary, but it is generally defined as the simulation of human intelligence processes by computers. These processes include learning by acquiring information, rules for using that information, reasoning, and using rules to reach specific or approximate results Hosseini, M., Resnik, D., & Holmes, K. (2023).

Artificial Intelligence (AI) is considered a science that combines many disciplines, such as computer science, biology, linguistics, cognitive psychology, mathematics, engineering, and more. It is also a technology aimed at producing systems that rely on knowledge in specific fields, enabling computers to think, see, speak, hear, and move. These systems are called Knowledge-Based Systems, characterized by their ability to perceive reason, infer, and learn.

We support the view that Artificial Intelligence (AI) is a branch of computer science that allows the design and development of computer programs that simulate human intelligence, enabling computers to perform tasks that require thinking, understanding, speaking, and logical movement Extance(Obeidat, M. A., Alfil, N. Z., Aldabousi, A. M., & Dganni, K. M. (2024).

Prominent Applications of Artificial Intelligence (AI) in the Legal Profession

The applications of artificial intelligence in the legal profession in the third millennium are highly diverse. Some of the most prominent applications are Koul, P. (2023).

1. Contract Review and Management

Integrating artificial intelligence into contract review and management can significantly improve workflow efficiency and accuracy. Artificial Intelligence (AI) systems can quickly review and identify relevant information in contracts, such as terms and obligations, and provide insights and recommendations. This not only saves time but also reduces the likelihood of human errors, thus improving accuracy.

2. Legal Summary Analysis and Prediction

Artificial intelligence can analyze vast amounts of legal texts and laws rapidly; extracting relevant information and offering insights and recommendations that can benefit legal strategies. Artificial Intelligence (AI) technologies can analyze legislation, understand its content, assess its impact on society, and provide recommendations for amendments.

3. Developing More Effective and Fair Laws

Artificial Intelligence (AI) technologies are used to develop more effective and fair laws, including timelines, penalties, and violations.

4. Legal Advice and E-Arbitration

Clients of law firms can now access legal advice online, and even e-arbitration services can be provided through modern applications Tripathi, K., & Mubarak, U. (2020).

5. Automated Contract Analysis and Creation

Modern technology and Artificial Intelligence (AI) are used to analyze and create contracts automatically, making it easier for lawyers and legal experts to conduct a comprehensive evaluation of contracts and their details more effectively.

Section Two: The Historical Development of the Legal Profession in Light of Technology

The legal profession has witnessed significant development with technological advancements, as technology has helped speed up procedures and improves the efficiency of lawyers. With the advancement of artificial intelligence, the nature of the profession is likely to change radically; requiring lawyers to adapt to these modern tools and develop their skills to keep up with future challenges. The historical development of the legal profession in light of technology reflects the changes that this sector has experienced over time, and how technological developments have impacted the performance of lawyers and the nature of their work. We will discuss the historical development as follows:

1. In the early days of the legal profession, lawyers relied on primitive methods for legal research, such as manually reviewing legal texts, books, and references. Administrative processes and correspondence were done manually, such as filing complaints, registering lawsuits, and managing execution files, which consumed a lot of time. Cases were resolved in traditional courts that were limited to paper-based transactions, and communication between lawyers and clients took place in person or through appearances in courts, public prosecutors' offices, or police stations.
2. With the advent of computers in the 1970s and 1980s, the legal profession began to witness the introduction of technology in the form of tools for legal research and file management. Lawyers started using software to manage legal documents, records, and the drafting of contracts and legal briefs. During this phase, lawyers began using computers for various tasks, but the tools were limited and relied on static databases.

3. In the 1990s, the legal profession experienced notable progress with the emergence of the internet, where lawyers started using the internet to search for legal information, review case precedents, and engage in legal discussions through online forums and legal groups. The first legal research platforms, such as "Westlaw" and "LexisNexis," were introduced, making it easier to access legal databases and providing advanced tools for searching.

In the last two decades, artificial intelligence has entered the legal field in a more significant way, being used to analyze legal data, extract information from legal documents faster and more accurately. Artificial Intelligence (AI) began being used in specialized areas such as contract review automation and generative legal writing tools, helping lawyers save time and effort.

Innovative platforms for case management and client communication have also emerged, making the legal profession more efficient in delivering legal services.

1- Currently, we can highlight the various forms of artificial intelligence used in the legal profession, which serves the public interest and participates in the judiciary's mission to achieve justice, uphold the rule of law, and ensure the right to defend rights and freedoms, as stated in Article 1 of Federal Law No. (23) Of 1991 regarding the regulation of the legal profession.

Recently, the People's Republic of China has started to make a strong entry into this promising market through some law firms or companies. According to estimates from 2017, the world's top law firm in terms of annual income is the American firm Kirkland & Ellis LLP, with an annual income of (USD 3.165 billion), employing 2,000 lawyers. In second place is the American firm Latham & Watkins LLP, with an annual income of (USD 3.063 billion), employing 2,436 lawyers. In third place is the American firm Baker McKenzie, with an annual income of (USD 2.9 billion), employing 4,723 lawyers (Aldabousi, A. M., & Ali, I. M. S. 2025).

Major Law firms worldwide have begun to heavily utilize artificial intelligence, and the concept of the "robot lawyer," "automated lawyer," or "smart lawyer" has emerged. A "Robot Lawyer" is a software or electronic application that performs many tasks typically carried out by human lawyers.

The United States has launched the so-called "Automated Lawyer," which provides legal information, communicates directly with people, and offers certain legal services through which one can access any legal information, specific court rulings, and case precedents. These services are provided by some private companies that use predictive technologies to forecast the judgments that judges will make, known as predictive justice Şahin, Ş., & Erkmen, B. (2023).

As we are discussing the electronic lawyer or robot lawyer, the conversation shall touch upon the five most famous robots for providing legal services. The first and most well-known application in this field is the "DoNotPay" robot lawyer, an

Artificial Intelligence (AI) -based application that initially aimed— as its name suggests— to help individuals avoid paying unfair parking fines by facilitating and simplifying the procedures for challenging their parking tickets. The credit for the creation of this application goes to British American entrepreneur Joshua Browder, born in London in 1998.

While the initial goal of the application was to assist individuals in contesting their parking tickets, it later expanded into other areas. A new version was released in 2018 to help litigants with small claims cases and other routine legal matters, as some have described it as handling "very routine simple cases."

In one of the reports issued shortly after the launch of the application, Do Not Pay revealed that its software helped people cancel between 160,000 and 250,000 parking tickets since its launch, with a success rate of 64%, which is a result not to be underestimated or undervalued (Al-zaher, 2020, p. 1).

The second most famous application worldwide is the robot lawyer LISA, which is considered the first neutral Artificial Intelligence (AI) lawyer in the world. It is the first two-way application that can be accessed from a computer or smartphone. The first product of the robot lawyer "LISA" was the Non-Disclosure Agreement (NDA), which eliminates the need to hire lawyers during the negotiation process by starting in the middle ground between the two parties. The lawyer "LISA" asks the user a series of questions, and based on these answers, a document is generated and sent to the reviewer. The reviewer uses the "LISA" robot to make any changes.

After the LISA robot lawyer, we move on to discuss the robot lawyer ROSS, which uses the computational power of IBM Watson to scan large data sets. Over time, it learns how to offer the best service to its users. The program can produce a document in seconds, while it would take humans several hours to do the same. BakerHostetler, a global law firm, was one of the first companies to use ROSS, where the program handles bankruptcy cases. Employees enter commands into the program daily, such as the need to find examples of precedents for specific cases, and ROSS then searches through its legal database to produce the relevant information.

In fourth place is the robot lawyer Billy Bot, described as a chatty robot who loves to converse. It helps individuals who need a lawyer or mediator to solve their legal problem but don't know how to choose the right lawyer or what criteria can be used to determine the right one. Thus, "Billy Bot" can be seen as a small assistant programmed to help individuals find the right lawyer or mediator for their legal issues.

Billy Bot also serves as an assistant to human lawyers and provides basic legal information to users online. It was named after the clerk character in the TV series "Silk," and its ultimate goal is to guide users to free online legal resources and assist them in determining whether they need legal help. If they do, Billy Bot helps them find the right lawyer, whether it be a solicitor for procedural matters or a barrister for direct litigation, as well as scheduling appointments and handling all tasks typically performed by a human assistant (Al-zaher, 2020, p. 2).

The robot lawyer "Automio" is a lawyer designed for lawyers who wish to acquire their own Artificial Intelligence (AI) lawyer. Human lawyers can use the "Automio" robot to meet with clients, provide advice, and instantly create contracts and legal documents in a specialized manner. Using the robot technology of "Automio" reduces the time lawyers spend on repetitive and lower-value routine tasks.

Additionally, with this technology, clients of law firms can serve themselves online and instantly obtain the legal documents they need. "Automio" has a marketplace where human lawyers can build, buy, sell, and resell Artificial Intelligence (AI) lawyers.

Chapter Two

LEGAL AND TECHNOLOGICAL CHALLENGES IN PRACTICING LAW

Introduction and Division

With the rapid advancements in technology and the adoption of artificial intelligence across various sectors, the legal profession has not been immune to these transformations. The legal field now faces new legal and technological challenges that affect the nature of legal work, methods of service delivery, and professional ethics. Based on this, this chapter will be divided into two sections:

Section One: Legal Challenges in Practicing Law in the Age of Artificial Intelligence

Section Two: Technological Challenges in Practicing Law in the Age of Artificial Intelligence (AI)

Section One

LEGAL CHALLENGES IN PRACTICING LAW IN THE AGE OF ARTIFICIAL INTELLIGENCE

The legal profession faces numerous challenges in the face of the development of artificial intelligence. These challenges are diverse and range from issues related to professional ethics to concerns regarding data protection and privacy, as well as dealing with decisions that may be difficult to predict or assign responsibility for (Aldabousi, A. M. (2023). Below are some of the key legal challenges:

1. Legal Liability for Artificial Intelligence (AI) Errors

One of the primary challenges is determining legal liability in the event of an error or harm caused using Artificial Intelligence (AI) tools. For example, if artificial intelligence provides incorrect legal advice, who is responsible? Is it the company that developed the technology or the lawyer who used the tool? This question presents a significant challenge in determining legal accountability (Awad et al., 2024).

Additionally, if Artificial Intelligence (AI) is used for illegal purposes, such as manipulating evidence or creating fraudulent documents, should the developers or the lawyers who benefit from this technology be held accountable? This issue requires precise regulation to govern the legal uses of technological tools (Al-Falasi, 2019).

1- Challenges Related to Privacy and Data Protection

- Protection of Personal Data: Artificial intelligence often relies on big data to analyze and provide recommendations. However, this poses numerous risks regarding privacy and the protection of personal data, especially in sensitive cases or those involving trade secrets or medical information (Abdullah, 2020).
- Cybersecurity: Since Artificial Intelligence (AI) heavily depends on the internet and cloud technologies, protecting legal information and the confidential data of lawyers and clients has become more complex. Security breaches could expose data to theft or unauthorized use Allah Rakha, N. (2023).

2. Challenges Related to Professional Ethics (New University, 2023)

- Impact on Lawyer Independence: As lawyers increasingly rely on Artificial Intelligence (AI), the role of the human lawyer in making legal decisions may diminish, which could affect their independence in providing legal advice or taking legal positions.
- Impact on Quality and Justice: Extensive use of Artificial Intelligence (AI) could lead to decisions that lack the necessary human sensitivity in some complex cases, raising concerns about fairness and the quality of legal advice.

3. Challenges Related to Regulation and Legislation

- Lack of Legislative Framework: In many legal systems, there is no clear legal framework regulating the use of Artificial Intelligence (AI) in the legal profession. This ambiguity in legislation opens the door for some technologies to be exploited in an illegal or unethical manner.
- International Regulation: With the development and global spread of Artificial Intelligence (AI), coordinating between countries to establish

unified laws or global standards to protect the legal profession from potential technological risks may become challenging.

4. Challenges Related to Credibility and Transparency

- Dependence on Opaque Algorithms: Some Artificial Intelligence (AI) relies on complex algorithms that are difficult to understand, even by experts. This could lead to a lack of transparency in how legal decisions are made, raising concerns about the integrity of the system.
- Data Manipulation: There is a risk that some may manipulate Artificial Intelligence (AI) to achieve specific goals, such as altering legal outcomes or falsifying documents, which threatens the credibility of legal decisions.

5. Challenges of Interaction between Lawyers and Artificial Intelligence

- Harmony between Humans and Machines: Lawyers may face difficulties adapting to the idea that artificial intelligence may become part of the decision-making process. This challenge is particularly evident when a lawyer shall make a final decision based on Artificial Intelligence (AI) recommendations, raising questions about how to balance human judgment with machines.

6. Employment Issues and the Impact of Artificial Intelligence (AI) on the Labor Market

- Impact on Lawyer Jobs: With the development of artificial intelligence, concerns may arise regarding the replacement of some tasks currently performed by lawyers, especially routine tasks such as legal research or document preparation. This could have negative effects on the Labor Market in the legal profession.

Section 2

6. Technological Challenges in Practicing Law in the Age of Artificial Intelligence

The technological challenges in practicing law with artificial intelligence encompass a wide range of complex issues related to Artificial Intelligence (AI) applications in the legal profession. These challenges range from problems related to dependency on technology to issues concerning training and the ability to handle modern technologies. Below are some of the most significant technological challenges:

1. Complexity and Diversity of Artificial Intelligence (AI) Tools

Many artificial intelligence technologies used in the legal profession, such as legal research tools and contract automation, may not be compatible with each other or with older systems. This creates difficulties in integrating these tools into existing legal work systems (Kahli, 2024).

2. Concerns About the Accuracy of Artificial Intelligence (AI)

Although Artificial Intelligence (AI) may provide fast results, there is concern that some tools may not be accurate enough in certain complex legal cases. These tools may be prone to errors that affect the correct decision-making process.

3. Challenges in Training Lawyers to Use AI

Many lawyers may not have the necessary technical skills to use artificial intelligence tools effectively. Training lawyers on new tools and techniques requires time and resources, which is a significant challenge, particularly for older lawyers or those without a technical background (Joudah, n.d.).

4. Cybersecurity and Data Protection

As lawyers increasingly rely on artificial intelligence technologies; legal data becomes more susceptible to cyber threats such as cyberattacks and unauthorized data breaches. The data lawyers handle often includes personal and sensitive information, making it an attractive target for hackers.

5. Challenges in Relying on Artificial Intelligence for Legal Decision-Making

Despite the ability of artificial intelligence to analyze data and provide recommendations, it may lack the capacity for creative decision-making or a deep understanding of human and ethical values that are often integral to the legal process.

Artificial Intelligence (AI) tools may produce recommendations or decisions based on complex algorithms that are difficult to understand, even by lawyers or judges. This exposes the law to the risk of making decisions that are hard to justify or explain appropriately. (Newiversity, 2023)

6. Challenges Related to the Integration of Legal Systems and Technology

Most traditional legal systems are not designed to work with modern artificial intelligence tools. Adding Artificial Intelligence (AI) to these systems may require significant modifications, both in terms of infrastructure and in terms of training legal personnel.

7. Challenges in Ensuring Transparency

Sometimes, Artificial Intelligence (AI) algorithms may be so complex that lawyers or even judges find it difficult to understand how the system made its recommendations. This can affect the transparency of legal decisions and reduce trust in the system.

Chapter Three

7. Mechanisms for Addressing Challenges

Introduction and Division

Artificial intelligence is one of the modern technologies that is causing a radical change in many fields, including the legal profession. With the increasing use of these technologies in providing legal consultations and analyzing cases, it has become necessary to update and develop legal legislation to cover the growing use of artificial intelligence and ensure its legal and secure use. Below are some proposed mechanisms to address these challenges through the development of legal legislation. Based on this, we will divide this chapter into two sections:

Section One: Developing legal legislation to cover the use of Artificial Intelligence (AI).

Section Two: Enhancing the training of lawyers on technical tools.

Section One

Developing Legal Legislations to Cover the Use of Artificial Intelligence (Shallafa, 2024)

Developing legal legislations to cover the use of artificial intelligence in the legal profession is crucial to ensure the integration of these technologies in a legal and secure manner. This requires continuously updating laws, setting ethical standards, enhancing data protection, and providing a flexible legislative framework to ensure that legislation aligns with technological developments. Furthermore, the presence of regulatory bodies and clear legislation on legal responsibility and the use of artificial intelligence in decision-making will help enhance the reliability of legal justice in the context of these modern technologies.

1. Issuing Specific Legislation for Artificial Intelligence

Legislation shall be established to regulate the use of artificial intelligence in legal fields. This includes defining artificial intelligence and its types, its uses in the legal profession, and how to integrate these tools into the legal process in a legal and secure manner.

2. Setting Ethical Standards for the Use of Artificial Intelligence

Legislation should include ethical standards that define how lawyers should use artificial intelligence tools. Some tools may provide recommendations or legal consultations, but these recommendations may lack the human touch or the ethical perspective that a human lawyer can provide.

3. Developing Legislation for Data Protection and Privacy

As artificial intelligence in the legal profession requires collecting and analyzing vast amounts of sensitive legal data, it is essential to develop legislation to protect this data. Legislation shall ensure the protection of personal data for clients and lawyers, as well as the security of data stored and processed using artificial intelligence.

4. Legislation on Adaptability and Amendments

Legal legislation shall be flexible enough to allow for regular amendments and updates to keep pace with the rapid developments in the field of artificial intelligence. New technologies and evolving legal practices may require continuous changes in legal texts, so that legislation reflects technological realities and changing legal needs.
Section Two

9- Enhancing Lawyers' Training on Technical Tools

Considering the rapid advancements in artificial intelligence and its applications in the legal profession, it becomes essential to enhance lawyers' training on modern technical tools to ensure they can fully benefit from this technology. Training on technical tools is not limited to learning how to use them, but also includes understanding how they work and how to integrate them into daily legal practices in accordance with professional and ethical standards. Below are some mechanisms that can be followed to enhance lawyers' training on technical tools:

INTRODUCING SPECIALIZED TRAINING PROGRAMS

Specialized training programs should be introduced for lawyers, aimed at providing them with the knowledge and skills necessary to use modern technical tools in the legal profession. These programs can range from short courses to advanced training certifications covering topics such as Artificial Intelligence (AI) in legal research, contract automation, and legal data analysis tools (Abdullah, 2020).

PROVIDING ONLINE EDUCATIONAL PLATFORM

Remote learning platforms should be utilized to provide specialized courses on artificial intelligence and legal technology tools. These platforms can offer lawyers the ability to train on technical tools from anywhere and at any time, making it easier for them to stay updated on technological development without affecting their daily schedules Bielova, M., & Byelov, D. (2023).

ENHANCING COLLABORATION WITH LEGAL TECH COMPANIES

Legal institutions and legal tech companies can collaborate to develop training courses specifically aimed at lawyers. These partnerships can provide lawyers with training on the artificial intelligence tools available in the market and offer hands-on experience on how to apply these tools in legal cases (Aldabousi, A. M. 2025).

ENCOURAGING LAWYERS TO ENGAGE IN CONTINUOUS LEARNING

As artificial intelligence and legal technology are constantly evolving, lawyers should be encouraged to adopt a culture of continuous learning. Lawyers can register for ongoing programs to keep up with technological developments, such as regular legal and technological seminars, conferences, and advanced courses in artificial intelligence.

CONCLUSION

In conclusion, this research highlights that artificial intelligence has become a pivotal tool in the development of the legal profession, enhancing efficiency and effectiveness in delivering legal services. Despite the legal and technological challenges faced by lawyers due to this evolving technology, the application of artificial intelligence in the legal field holds great potential to improve work quality and accelerate legal procedures. Many countries, including the UAE, are working towards facilitating this transition by developing tools and technologies that enable lawyers to benefit from this technology, while maintaining the ethical and legal standards that govern judicial work. Ramadan, S. A., Qasim, A., & Raslan, L. (2025).

By considering the challenges faced by the legal profession in this context, whether legal or technological, it is evident that there is a critical need for legislative development and continuous training for lawyers to ensure optimal use of these technological tools. Despite these challenges, overcoming them through legislative innovation and the development of human competencies will enhance the ability of the legal profession to effectively adapt to technological changes.

Results

1. We found that artificial intelligence can significantly contribute to improving legal efficiency by speeding up legal research procedures and automating repetitive tasks, saving time and effort for lawyers.
2. There are legal challenges associated with the use of artificial intelligence in law, such as privacy protection, ensuring the quality of legal analysis, and the potential contradictions in decisions that Artificial Intelligence (AI) might make compared to human judgment.
3. One of the major technological challenges related to the application of Artificial Intelligence (AI) is the need for complex technical tools and their high costs, along with the need for data protection from cyber-attacks.
4. There is still a need for the development of legal legislation to keep pace with the increasing use of technology in law, especially regarding privacy protection and legal rights in the context of artificial intelligence usage.

Recommendations

1. Clear legal regulations should be developed to keep up with technological advancements, especially concerning the use of artificial intelligence in legal proceedings, to ensure the protection of legal rights and privacy.
2. It is essential for lawyer training programs to continuously focus on technological and artificial intelligence skills. Regular training courses should be offered in collaboration with universities and tech companies to enhance lawyers' proficiency in using technical tools.
3. Legal institutions should adopt flexible and user-friendly technologies, which will help reduce the entry barrier for lawyers who do not have a strong technical background.

REFERENCES

Abdullah, F. M. (2020). *Civil liability for damages resulting from the use of artificial intelligence in the medical profession* [Thesis]. United Arab Emirates University. https://scholarworks.uaeu.ac.ae/all_theses/1016

Ahmed Abd El-Zaher. (2020). The road to artificial intelligence in the legal profession. *Egyptian Bar Association*. https://egyls.com/%D8%A7%D9%84%D8%B7%D8%B1%D9%8A%D9%82-%D8%A5%D9%84%D9%89-%D8%A7%D9%84%D8%B0%D9%83%D8%A7%D8%A1

Al-Falasi, A. A. M. (2019). Criminal liability resulting from artificial intelligence errors. *Legal Journal*. https://jlaw.journals.ekb.eg/article_190836_001cd12821ed784ae2d063d3a6832284.pdf

Aldabousi, A. M. (2022). Legal problems of conclusion of intelligent software agent for smart commercial contracts in the era of blockchain: UAE as a model. *Universidad y Sociedad, 14*, 713–728.

Aldabousi, A. M. (2022). Legal problems of electronic pollution according to UAE and Egyptian law. *Arab World Geographer, 25*(2–3), 154–168. DOI: 10.64903/1480-6800-25.2.154

Aldabousi, A. M. (2023). The legal problems facing the conclusion of cloud computing contracts. *Universidad y Sociedad, 15*(3), 602–611.

Aldabousi, A. M. (2025). Governance as a means to protect family businesses from collapse according to the laws of the United Arab Emirates. In *Advances in Science, Technology and Innovation* (pp. 123–138). Springer. DOI: 10.1007/978-3-031-92135-3_13

Aldabousi, A. M., & Ali, I. M. S. (2025). Legal safeguards against market rumors in UAE securities: A comparative commercial law study. *Investment Management and Financial Innovations, 22*(4), 227–236. DOI: 10.21511/imfi.22(4).2025.18

Allah Rakha, N. (2023). Ensuring cyber-security in remote workforce: Legal implications and best international practices. *International Journal of Law and Policy, 1*(3). Advance online publication. https://irshadjournals.com/index.php/ijlp/article/view/43. DOI: 10.59022/ijlp.43

Awad, A., Al-fil, N. Z., Dganni, K. M., Aldabousi, A. M., & Obeidat, M. A. (2024). Optimizing dormant account management in UAE banking: Legal gaps and proposed reforms. *Banks and Bank Systems, 19*(4), 124–135. DOI: 10.21511/bbs.19(4).2024.10

Bielova, M., & Byelov, D. (2023). Challenges and threats of personal data protection in working with artificial intelligence. *Uzhhorod National University Herald. Series: Law*. DOI: 10.24144/2307-3322.2023.79.2.2

Extance, A. (2018). How AI technology can tame the scientific literature. *Nature*, *561*(7722), 273–274. DOI: 10.1038/d41586-018-06617-5 PMID: 30202054

Goltz, N., & Dondoli, G. (2019). A note on science, legal research and artificial intelligence. *Information & Communications Technology Law*, *28*(3), 239–251. DOI: 10.1080/13600834.2019.1644065

Hosseini, M., Resnik, D., & Holmes, K. (2023). The ethics of disclosing the use of artificial intelligence tools in writing scholarly manuscripts. *Research Ethics*, *19*(4), 449–465. DOI: 10.1177/17470161231180449 PMID: 39749232

Koul, P. (2023). Disclosing use of artificial intelligence: Promoting transparency in publishing. *Lung India : Official Organ of Indian Chest Society*, *40*(5), 401–403. DOI: 10.4103/lungindia.lungindia_370_23 PMID: 37787350

Obeidat, M. A., Alfil, N. Z., Aldabousi, A. M., & Dganni, K. M. (2024). Criminal protection for the merchants from the crimes of electronic publishing about invasion of privacy in UAE legislation. *Pakistan Journal of Criminology*, *16*(3), 779–792. https://www.pjcriminology.com/wp-content/uploads/2024/05/49-Criminal-Protection-for-the-Merchants.pdf

Ramadan, S. A., Qasim, A., & Raslan, L. (2025). The impact of scientific and technological advancements on judicial evidence methods: An applied study on UAE law. In *Lecture Notes in Networks and Systems* (Vol. 1575, pp. 187–197). Springer., https://www.springerprofessional.de/en/the-impact-of-scientific-and-technological-advancements-on-judic/51291204

Şahin, Ş., & Erkmen, B. (2023). Navigating the impact of artificial intelligence on scholarly authorship: Transparency and responsibility in the technological era. *European Journal of Therapeutics*, *29*(4), 994–995. Advance online publication. DOI: 10.58600/eurjther1811

Tripathi, K., & Mubarak, U. (2020). Protecting privacy in the era of artificial intelligence.

ADDITIONAL READING

ABA Model Rules of Professional Conduct (competence/confidentiality baseline). https://www.americanbar.org/groups/professional_responsibility/publications/model_rules_of_professional_conduct/

European Commission – Ethics Guidelines for Trustworthy AI. (archival). https://digital-strategy.ec.europa.eu/en/library/ethics-guidelines-trustworthy-ai

International Bar Association – AI and the legal profession resources (gateway). https://www.ibanet.org/

NIST AI Risk Management Framework. (AI RMF 1.0). https://www.nist.gov/itl/ai-risk-management-framework

OECD AI Principles. (2019) – official. https://oecd.ai/en/ai-principles

UAE Personal Data Protection Law. (Federal Decree-Law No. 45 of 2021) – official portal. https://uaelegislation.gov.ae/en/legislations

UNESCO Recommendation on the Ethics of AI. (2021). https://www.unesco.org/en/artificial-intelligence/recommendation-ethics

KEY TERMS AND DEFINITIONS

AI Audit Trail: Documentation of tool use, prompts, versions, and human edits to support accountability and compliance.

Algorithmic Bias: Systematic errors producing unfair outcomes; in law, may affect screening, recommendations, or drafting.

Artificial Intelligence (AI): Computational methods enabling pattern recognition, prediction, and language processing; in law, used for research, drafting, and review.

Confidentiality: Obligation to protect client information; heightened risk when data is uploaded to external AI systems.

Cybersecurity: Security controls preventing leakage of sensitive legal materials processed by digital tools.

Data Protection: Legal rules governing personal data processing (lawful basis, minimisation, security, cross-border transfer).

Disclosure of AI Use: Transparent statements describing AI use where required by policy, court, or publisher standards.

Explainability: Ability to explain the basis of an AI output; supports transparency and error detection.

Generative AI: Models that produce new text content (e.g., summaries, drafts) which require verification in professional settings.

Human-in-the-Loop: Governance model requiring human review/approval before AI outputs are relied upon.

Legal Ethics: Professional duties including competence, confidentiality, independence, and avoidance of misleading representations.

Professional Responsibility: Accountability for advice and filings remains with the lawyer/firm even when AI tools are used.

Chapter 8
The Legal Framework of Blockchain and Smart Contracts in UAE:
A Study Considering the Challenges Facing Blockchain and Smart Contracts in United Arab Emirates

Mohamed Nagib Saleh
Al Nagib Legal Consultancy, UAE

Mohamed Abdulkareem Almenhali
State Litigation Authority, UAE

ABSTRACT

Blockchain technology and smart contracts are revolutionizing legal and commercial transactions worldwide. These innovations enhance efficiency, automation, and security in contract execution while reducing reliance on intermediaries. However, their adoption presents legal challenges related to enforceability, regulatory oversight, and dispute resolution. This research examines the UAE's legal framework governing blockchain and smart contracts, analysing their recognition under contract and commercial law, as well as the roles of key regulatory UAE authorities, including the Securities and Commodities Authority ("SCA") and the Virtual Assets Regulatory Authority ("VARA").

DOI: 10.4018/979-8-3373-7961-6.ch008

INTRODUCTION

Blockchain and smart contracts are transforming the global legal and economic landscape by enabling decentralized, automated, and transparent transactions. The UAE has positioned itself as a regional leader in blockchain adoption, launching the UAE Blockchain Strategy 2021 and pioneering regulatory initiatives such as Dubai's Law No. (4) of 2022 on digital assets. However, the legal framework remains fragmented, with significant challenges in harmonizing federal and emirate-level laws, ensuring data protection, and integrating Islamic legal principles 1 17. Addressing these challenges is critical for fostering innovation, protecting stakeholders, and maintaining the UAE's competitive edge in digital transformation (Aldabousi, A. M. (2022).

Blockchain and smart contract technology are transforming legal and financial transactions globally, offering automation, transparency, and security through decentralized digital agreements. In UAE, the government has embraced blockchain as part of its national digital transformation strategy, integrating the technology into public and private sectors, including real estate, trade, and financial services (Hussein, S., & Serria, E. 2024).

The legal recognition of smart contracts under UAE law, particularly through the Electronic Transactions Law and trust services regulations, has positioned the country as a leader in blockchain adoption. However, the enforceability and interpretation of smart contracts in legal disputes remain evolving areas, requiring further judicial and legislative development (Al Barghuthi, N. B., Ncube, C., & Said, H. (2019).

The legal framework governing blockchain and smart contracts in the UAE is characterized by a mix of progressive initiatives like Dubai's Law No. (4) of 2022 and the UAE Blockchain Strategy, yet it suffers from regulatory fragmentation and significant legal gaps. Key challenges include reconciling blockchain's decentralized nature with traditional data protection and privacy laws, ensuring enforceability in diverse sectors such as construction and healthcare, and integrating Islamic legal principles into modern digital contracts. Comparative insights with international frameworks underscore the need for a harmonized, flexible, and adaptive regulatory framework that not only fosters innovation but also ensures robust legal oversight and compliance

1.1 Research Significance

This research is significant as it addresses the evolving legal landscape of blockchain and smart contracts in the UAE, a jurisdiction actively integrating digital transformation into its legal and financial systems. As blockchain technology gains widespread adoption across real estate, trade finance, and digital assets, ensuring legal clarity and enforceability of smart contracts is crucial for businesses, investors, and regulatory bodies. The study highlights key regulatory challenges, jurisdictional complexities, and enforcement gaps while analysing the roles of SCA, VARA, and UAE courts in governing blockchain-based agreements.

1.2 Research Objectives

This research aims to examine the legal framework governing blockchain technology and smart contracts in the United Arab Emirates (UAE) by analyzing their recognition, enforceability, and challenges under UAE contract and commercial law. It seeks to assess the compatibility of existing legal provisions with blockchain-based transactions, particularly smart contracts, and identify potential gaps in regulation, liability, and dispute resolution. Additionally, the study evaluates the role of UAE regulatory bodies.

1.3 Literature Review

Academic and legal discourse on blockchain has expanded globally in the past decade, but focused studies on the UAE context remain relatively limited. In UAE, much of the analysis to date comes from legal practitioners and regulators who have published guidance notes and commentaries. These writings highlight uncertainty around the enforceability of smart contracts under civil law principles and the need for explicit legal recognition. For example, commentators note that while smart contracts offer automation and efficiency, their legal enforceability remains a grey area in the UAE, since traditional contracts allow human interpretation of terms whereas code does not. *(Muhami, 2024)*

This literature review reveals that, despite growing attention, there is still a lack of clarity in UAE law on several aspects of blockchain and smart contracts – a gap this research aims to address by collating the latest legal developments and proposing reforms.

1.4 Methodology

This study adopts a descriptive and analytical approach to examine the legal framework and technological applications related to blockchain and smart contracts in the UAE. It is structured into three main sections:

- **First section:** General Provisions on Blockchain and Smart Contracts
- **Second section:** The Legitimacy of Smart Contracts and Their Enforceability in UAE Law

- **Third section:** Challenges of enforceability and using Blockchain in Legal Transactions.

2. GENERAL PROVISIONS ON BLOCKCHAIN AND SMART CONTRACTS

2.1 Concept of Blockchain Technology

Blockchain is a decentralized ledger that records transactions in chronological, tamper-proof blocks, validated by a network of nodes rather than a central authority. Its trust architecture ensures data integrity without intermediaries, enhancing authenticity in legal transactions. The UAE government recognizes blockchain's role in securing contracts and asset records, notably in land registries and other legal frameworks *(UAE government, Jun 2024).*

2.2 Legal Concept of Smart Contracts

The term "Smart Contract" is not a traditional contract but rather a self-executing code that performs actions based on predefined conditions. For example, an insurance smart contract could automatically issue payments upon detecting a flight cancellation. Legally, its enforceability depends on fulfilling contractual elements like offer, acceptance, and intent.

While UAE law does not explicitly define "smart contracts (Aldabousi, A. M. 2023)," it recognizes contracts formed via Automated Electronic Information Systems under its Electronic Transactions Laws, allowing agreements to be validly executed without human intervention. This means UAE law already supports blockchain-based contracts, provided they reflect mutual intent and meet legal requirements. Recognizing smart contracts as a new form of agreement, UAE legislation ensures their enforceability alongside traditional contracts *(A Beginner's Guide to Smart Contracts; Al Tamimi & CO, 2021).*

3. Benefits and Risks of Blockchain and Smart Contracts in Legal Transactions

3.1 Benefits of Blockchain and Smart Contracts in Legal Transactions

Blockchain and smart contracts offer several benefits for legal transactions, which is why they are gaining traction in UAE and globally:

a) Trust and Security

Blockchain's cryptographic security ensures tamper-proof records, reducing fraud risks. i.e Dubai Land Department's blockchain system prevents title fraud, ensuring recorded transactions cannot be secretly altered *(Dubai Land Department, 2017)*

b) Automation and Efficiency

Smart contracts self-execute when predefined conditions are met, eliminating manual oversight. This speeds up payments, asset transfers, and trade finance transactions.

c) Transparency and Auditability

Blockchain transactions are time-stamped, traceable, and immutable, aiding compliance and dispute resolution. Regulators and auditors can verify transaction histories, strengthening legal enforceability.

3.2 Risks of Blockchain and Smart Contracts in Legal Transactions

a) Legal Uncertainty

Smart contracts operate as code, which may not fully capture legal nuances. Ambiguities—such as defining "reasonable time" for performance—can lead to disputes. UAE law validates automated contracts, but clarity on contractual intent and essential terms is crucial to avoid misinterpretation (Al Tamimi & Co, 2021).

b) Irreversibility and Mistakes

Blockchain transactions are permanent, making error correction difficult. A flawed smart contract could cause unintended payments that may be legally challenging to reverse *(Securities and Commodities Authority, 2022).*

c) Security and Privacy Concerns

Blockchain is secure, but smart contracts can be hacked if poorly coded. Legal responsibility for breaches—whether falling on developers, users, or no one—remains ambiguous *(HZ Legal, 2023).*

In summary, blockchain and smart contracts enhance efficiency and trust but introduce new legal complexities. UAE is actively integrating these technologies into its legal framework while refining safeguards to address emerging risks.

4. RECOGNITION AND ENFORCEABILITY UNDER UAE LAW

4.1 Legal Basis

- As stipulated in Federal Law No. 5 of 1985 (Civil Transactions Law) and its amendments, valid agreement requires offer and acceptance, a lawful subject matter, and clear intent between the parties, as UAE law generally allows contracts in any form—written, oral, or electronic—unless specific formalities apply *(Article no. 125, 132 of Federal Law No. 5 of 1985 (Civil Transactions Law).*
- The recognition of smart contracts in the UAE is further established under Federal Decree-Law No. 46 of 2021 on Electronic Transactions and Trust Services (ETTSL). This legislation affirms the legal validity of electronic transactions and automated agreements, ensuring that contracts executed via electronic means—including blockchain-based smart contracts—are legally binding and enforceable.

4.2 Smart Contract Formation and Legal Validity

- Under Article 10(1) of ETTSL, contracts can be formed through electronic means, and an offer and acceptance expressed electronically are deemed legally valid. Furthermore, Article 10(2) explicitly states that a contract does not lose its validity, enforceability, or evidentiary weight solely because it was concluded via an electronic document.
- Additionally, Article 11(1) allows contracts to be executed through fully automated electronic information systems, even in the absence of direct human

intervention. This provision confirms that smart contracts—where obligations are self-executed based on predefined conditions—are legally recognized, provided they meet the fundamental contract formation principles under Federal Law No. 5 of 1985 on Civil Transactions (UAE Civil Code), which requires offer, acceptance, legal capacity, and a legitimate cause.

4.3 Authentication and Evidence of Smart Contracts

- The enforceability of smart contracts is further strengthened by ETTSL Article 18(1), which states that an electronic document, electronic signature, or electronic seal shall not be denied legal effect or evidentiary value merely because it exists in electronic form. .
- Article 18(3) of the said law equates certified electronic signatures to handwritten signatures, ensuring that transactions authenticated through blockchain or cryptographic mechanisms are recognized as legally binding.

4.4 Judicial Recognition of Blockchain Transactions

- Recent UAE court rulings have begun to recognize blockchain-based transactions, strengthening the enforceability of smart contracts. A 2024 Dubai Court decision affirmed that salaries could be legally paid in cryptocurrency, acknowledging digital assets as a legitimate form of contractual remuneration *(Wasel & Wasel, 2024).*
- Such rulings indicate a growing judicial acceptance of blockchain-based transactions, including smart contracts, within the UAE's legal framework.

4.5 Challenges in Enforcement and Blockchain Legal Framework

Despite the formal validity of smart contracts in the UAE, multiple challenges can arise when enforcing or interpreting them in disputes:

a) Intent and "Meeting of Minds"

A fundamental issue is whether parties fully understood and consented to the terms encoded in a smart contract. If a party claims they did not anticipate a specific outcome due to programming nuances, courts must determine whether true consent existed. The UAE Civil Code allows courts to consider surrounding circumstances, so parties should document their intent through written protocols or whitepapers to minimize disputes.

b) Immutability vs. Equitable Relief

Blockchain's irreversibility makes it difficult to rectify errors or unjust outcomes. In traditional contracts, courts can grant rescission or amendments for mistakes or misrepresentation. However, smart contracts may have already executed transactions before an issue arises. For example, if a coding flaw causes double payment, recovering funds can be challenging, especially in pseudonymous or cross-border transactions. UAE courts can award damages, but preventing harm before execution remains a challenge, Some have suggested building "kill switches" or pause functions into smart contracts to allow human intervention – indeed, the EU is moving in this direction for certain use cases *(Ledger Insights, 2023).*

c) Interpretation of Code

Judges must determine whether a smart contract's code aligns with contractual intent, yet legal proceedings in UAE are conducted in Arabic, not code. Courts may appoint IT experts to interpret the code, but the final ruling is made by judges with legal—not programming—expertise. This creates uncertainty in judicial approaches: some judges may strictly enforce the code, while others may consider external evidence of the parties' expectations. To mitigate risks, parties should provide natural-language agreements alongside coded terms to guide interpretation *(Muhami Legal, 2024).*

d) Dispute Resolution and Remedies

Disputes in smart contracts often arise due to their automated nature, reliance on external data sources (oracles), and the lack of human intervention in execution. This makes it difficult to determine who is responsible when errors, fraud, or system failures occur. In UAE, courts apply the to resolve such disputes, but enforcement is challenging, especially when transactions are executed on decentralized platforms. A common issue is manipulated oracles, which can trigger incorrect payments or contract terms. Additionally, it is unclear whether liability falls on developers, users, or platform operators. To address these challenges, on-chain arbitration mechanisms and Dubai's Smart Courts Initiative have introduced blockchain-based dispute resolution methods, offering faster and more transparent case handling. However, to ensure fair enforcement, clear regulations and standardized arbitration clauses must be established to define liability, dispute resolution processes, and legal remedies for affected parties.

In conclusion, while UAE law supports smart contracts, enforcement and dispute resolution remain untested in many respects. Courts must balance automation with contractual fairness, and procedural innovations—such as integrated arbitration clauses, fallback mechanisms, and insurance protections—can help mitigate risks. As case law develops, clearer judicial guidance will emerge, refining how smart contracts are handled in UAE legal forums.

e) Consumer Protection

Lack of Smart Contract-Specific Consumer Protections as any existing consumer laws do not explicitly cover smart contracts, leaving uncertainties about recourse for automated transactions gone wrong.

5. REGULATORY OVERSIGHT OF BLOCKCHAIN & VIRTUAL ASSETS

5.1 SCA

The UAE's primary federal regulator of financial markets, overseeing virtual asset trading, token issuance, and investor protection. The SCA duly mandates that crypto exchanges, custodians, and brokers obtain licenses, ensuring compliance with market integrity and anti-money laundering (AML) laws. The Cabinet Resolution No. (111) of 2022 further expanded its authority, requiring all virtual asset activities outside financial-free zones to be licensed by the SCA or a recognized local regulator. Since smart contracts are frequently used in crypto trading, tokenized securities, and decentralized finance (DeFi) protocols, they must comply with SCA regulations to ensure investor protection, financial transparency, and legal enforceability. The SCA further ensures that virtual asset service providers (VASPs) implement anti-fraud and transparency measures in line with financial market regulationsThe SCA's oversight ensures that self-executing smart contracts involved in financial transactions adhere to regulatory standards, preventing fraudulent or unlawful use (*SCA Decision No. 23,26/R.M of 2020*).

5.2 VARA

VARA was established under Dubai Law No. 4 of 2022 to oversee virtual asset transactions, exchanges, and blockchain-based financial services within Dubai (excluding DIFC). The Virtual Assets and Related Activities Regulations 2023 set out licensing and compliance requirements for crypto exchanges, token issuers, and DeFi platforms, ensuring that virtual asset transactions align with financial security, AML laws, and investor protections. Many smart contracts facilitate tokenized transactions, automated lending, and decentralized trading, and VARA ensures that such agreements are legally valid and secure. By regulating blockchain-based agreements, VARA plays a key role in preventing financial misconduct and ensuring the enforceability of smart contracts used in digital asset transactions *(VARA Virtual Assets and Related Activities Regulations 2023, Dubai Law No. 4 of 2022).*

5.3 CBUAE

CBUAE oversees banking institutions and financial services interacting with blockchain and virtual assets, particularly in AML compliance, stablecoin regulations, and blockchain-powered payment systems. In 2023, CBUAE issued guidelines for financial institutions integrating smart contract automation in banking services, ensuring compliance with financial security measures. Since smart contracts are widely used in banking for trade finance, remittance processing, and blockchain-based payment automation, CBUAE ensures that these transactions comply with financial security regulations and consumer protection laws. Any blockchain-based financial agreement executed via smart contracts—such as an automated remittance or self-executing loan contract—must align with CBUAE's regulations to ensure transparency, prevent financial crime, and protect users (*Federal Decree-Law No. 20 of 2018 on AM).*

5.4 Financial Free Zones

It is also worth mentioning that within UAE, the financial free zones have developed their own regulatory frameworks for crypto assets, which, while technically outside the federal civil law system, contribute to the country's overall legal landscape on blockchain. The Abu Dhabi Global Market (ADGM) through its Financial Services Regulatory Authority was a regional trailblazer, issuing comprehensive regulations for crypto asset exchanges and intermediaries as early as 2018.

Dubai International Financial Centre (DIFC) followed suit via the Dubai Financial Services Authority, which in 2021–2022 created rules for "Investment tokens" and later for broader crypto tokens. These regimes, largely aligning with international financial regulations, treat crypto assets within the existing categories of securities or commodities, adapting compliance rules to the digital context (e.g., requiring IT audits for DLT systems). While ADGM and DIFC laws apply only within those free zones, their presence underscores the UAE's multi-layered regulatory approach. Companies in those zones benefit from clear rules, and lessons from those jurisdictions often inform onshore policy development. For example, the SCA and VARA frameworks have drawn on terminology and standards that ADGM first introduced. There is ongoing cooperation to ensure consistency where possible, and the free zone experiments have positioned the UAE as having some of the most developed crypto laws globally *(Global Legal Post, 2024)*

In sum, the UAE's sector-specific regulations create a comprehensive mosaic: SCA and VARA license and supervise crypto asset activities; CBUAE oversees the intersection with the traditional monetary system; and the free zone regulators provide additional models for regulation. This mosaic is being continuously refined to reduce regulatory arbitrage and uncertainty. The result is that, unlike in some countries where crypto falls into a legal grey zone, in the UAE a business dealing with blockchain assets can identify a regulatory pathway and legal requirements. However, the division of oversight among multiple authorities also means participants must be mindful of overlapping rules and coordinate with the correct regulator(s) – a complexity that the UAE government is addressing through inter-agency cooperation. The effectiveness of this framework in practice, and any remaining ambiguities, are discussed in later sections focusing on challenges.

6. CURRENT LEGAL FRAMEWORK IN THE UAE

6.1 Federal Laws and Regulations Governing Digital Transactions and Blockchain Applications

The United Arab Emirates has taken significant legislative steps to regulate digital transactions, data protection, and financial integrity, thereby laying a foundational legal framework for blockchain technology and smart contracts. However, despite this progressive trajectory, existing federal legislation remains only partially adapted to the distinctive technical and legal characteristics of blockchain-based systems.

6.1.1 Federal Law No. (46) of 2021 on Electronic Commerce and Transactions

Federal Law No. (46) of 2021 on Electronic Commerce and Transactions represents a cornerstone of the UAE's digital legal infrastructure. The law provides formal recognition of electronic data, electronic records, and electronic signatures, thereby ensuring the legal validity and enforceability of digital contracts. By establishing functional equivalence between electronic and traditional paper-based transactions, the law facilitates the widespread adoption of digital contracting mechanisms across both public and private sectors.

From a smart contract's perspective, the law offers an essential legal basis by recognizing automated electronic transactions and affirming the admissibility of electronic evidence. This framework supports the enforceability of contracts concluded or executed through digital means, including those embedded within blockchain environments. Nevertheless, the law was primarily drafted with conventional electronic commerce in mind and does not explicitly address decentralized architectures, distributed ledger technologies, or self-executing contractual code.

Rapid technological developments—particularly in blockchain, edge computing, and fog computing—have exposed regulatory gaps within the law. Key challenges arise in relation to data governance, cybersecurity obligations, and liability allocation in decentralized systems. The law does not provide clear guidance on responsibility for data breaches, system failures, or erroneous automated execution in blockchain-based smart contracts. As a result, parties may face uncertainty when disputes arise from code-driven performance rather than human intervention.

6.1.2 Personal Data Protection Law No. (45) of 2021

The enactment of Federal Decree-Law No. (45) of 2021 on the Protection of Personal Data marked a significant milestone in aligning the UAE's data protection regime with international standards, particularly the European Union's General Data Protection Regulation (GDPR). The law incorporates core principles such as lawful processing, purpose limitation, data minimization, and the rights of data subjects, including the right to erasure (the "right to be forgotten"(Awad, A., Al-fil, N. Z., Dganni, K. M., Aldabousi, A. M., & Ahmad Obeidat, M. (2024).

However, the application of these principles to blockchain technology raises complex legal and technical tensions. Blockchain systems are inherently designed to ensure immutability, transparency, and permanence of records, characteristics that conflict directly with the right to erasure and data rectification. The law does not provide explicit mechanisms for reconciling these competing values, nor does it clarify whether techniques such as off-chain storage, encryption, or anonymization satisfy statutory erasure requirements.

This regulatory ambiguity creates compliance challenges for blockchain developers, platform operators, and users. Without explicit guidance, entities operating blockchain-based smart contracts may face legal risk when processing personal data, particularly in permissionless or cross-border blockchain networks. Consequently, while the Personal Data Protection Law establishes a robust normative framework, its effectiveness in the blockchain context remains constrained by the absence of technology-specific rules or interpretive guidance.

6.1.3 Anti-Money Laundering (AML) Regulations

The UAE has developed a comprehensive anti-money laundering and counter-terrorism financing framework, reflecting its commitment to international financial integrity and compliance with global standards. AML regulations impose stringent obligations on financial institutions and designated non-financial businesses, including customer due diligence, transaction monitoring, and reporting of suspicious activities.

In the context of blockchain and cryptocurrencies, these regulations play a critical role in mitigating risks associated with anonymity, illicit financial flows, and cross-border transactions. Nevertheless, the decentralized and borderless nature of blockchain-based finance presents ongoing regulatory challenges. Traditional AML mechanisms are often premised on centralized intermediaries, whereas decentralized finance (DeFi) platforms operate without identifiable controlling entities.

While the UAE has made substantial progress in aligning its AML regime with Financial Action Task Force (FATF) recommendations, further harmonization and adaptation are required to effectively address blockchain-specific risks. This includes clearer regulatory treatment of virtual asset service providers, enhanced international cooperation, and tailored compliance mechanisms capable of addressing decentralized transaction structures.

6.2 Synthesis of the Federal Legal Framework

Collectively, UAE federal laws provide a solid foundational framework for digital transactions, data protection, and financial compliance. However, they remain only partially responsive to the unique features of blockchain technology and smart contracts. Key areas requiring further legislative development include data protection in immutable systems, cross-border regulatory compliance, liability allocation in automated execution, and the legal characterization of emerging applications such as decentralized finance (DeFi) and non-fungible tokens (NFTs). Without targeted reforms or interpretive guidance, regulatory uncertainty may persist despite the overall robustness of the federal framework.

6.3 Dubai's Law No. (4) of 2022 on Digital Assets

6.3.1 Core Provisions and Regulatory Objectives

Dubai's Law No. (4) of 2022 on Digital Assets represents a landmark development in the regional regulation of blockchain-based finance. The law explicitly recognizes digital currencies and digital assets, thereby providing long-awaited legal clarity regarding their legitimacy and regulatory status. It establishes a structured regulatory environment for digital asset activities, including issuance, trading, and custody.

A notable feature of the law is its allocation of responsibilities to authorized companies, requiring them to implement risk management systems, cybersecurity measures, and mechanisms to prevent criminal activity. By imposing compliance obligations on regulated entities, the law seeks to balance innovation with financial stability and consumer protection. Furthermore, the law offers legislative guarantees that enhance market confidence and reduce legal uncertainty for investors and service providers.

6.3.2 Enforcement Mechanisms and Institutional Oversight

The law introduces clear enforcement mechanisms through regulatory oversight by Dubai's competent authorities. This centralized oversight model enhances supervisory effectiveness and facilitates consistent application of regulatory standards. Legislative clarity regarding risk allocation and compliance responsibilities further strengthens the enforceability of the regulatory regime.

Importantly, the law provides a transparent legal basis for regulatory intervention, enabling authorities to address misconduct, systemic risks, and market abuse in the digital asset sector. This proactive approach distinguishes Dubai from jurisdictions that rely primarily on ex post enforcement or judicial interpretation.

6.3.3 Regulatory Impact and Regional Significance

Dubai's digital asset law positions the Emirate as a regulatory pioneer in the Middle East and beyond. By offering legal certainty and a structured compliance framework, Dubai has enhanced its attractiveness as a global hub for blockchain innovation and digital finance. The law also serves as a potential model for other Emirates and Muslim-majority jurisdictions seeking to regulate digital assets in a manner consistent with both economic development and legal certainty.

6.4 Synthesis: The Need for National Harmonization

Despite its significance, Dubai's Law No. (4) of 2022 is limited by its emirate-specific scope. The coexistence of advanced local regulation alongside broader federal frameworks underscores the need for harmonized national legislation governing blockchain, smart contracts, and digital assets. Without such harmonization, regulatory fragmentation may emerge between Emirates, potentially undermining legal certainty and cross-jurisdictional coherence within the UAE.

In conclusion, while the UAE's current legal framework demonstrates substantial progress and regulatory ambition, further integration and adaptation are necessary to fully address the legal complexities of blockchain technology. A harmonized, technology-aware legislative approach would consolidate the UAE's position as a global leader in digital regulation and ensure sustainable legal certainty for emerging blockchain-based applications.

7. COMPARATIVE INTERNATIONAL INSIGHTS

7.1 International Regulatory Approaches to Blockchain and Smart Contracts

The regulation of blockchain technology and smart contracts has emerged as a critical legal challenge across jurisdictions, reflecting a broader tension between technological innovation and legal certainty. Comparative analysis reveals significant divergence in regulatory philosophies, institutional design, and legislative techniques, particularly when contrasting the European Union (EU), the United States (US), and selected specialized jurisdictions with the approach adopted by the United Arab Emirates (UAE).

7.1.1 The European Union and the United States: Fragmentation and Jurisdictional Complexity

Both the European Union and the United States face structurally similar challenges in regulating blockchain-based activities and smart contracts. In the EU, despite recent legislative efforts such as the Markets in Crypto-Assets Regulation (MiCA), regulatory competence remains fragmented across multiple legal instruments and institutional actors. Member States retain varying degrees of discretion in implementation, resulting in divergent national interpretations, inconsistent enforcement practices, and legal uncertainty for cross-border blockchain operations. Jurisdictional ambiguities are further exacerbated by the decentralized nature of blockchain technology, which often defies traditional territorial concepts underpinning EU private and public law.

Similarly, the United States exhibits a highly fragmented regulatory landscape, characterized by overlapping federal and state-level competencies. Agencies such as the Securities and Exchange Commission (SEC), the Commodity Futures Trading Commission (CFTC), and state financial regulators apply differing legal classifications to blockchain assets and smart contract-based transactions. This regulatory pluralism creates enforcement gaps and uncertainty, particularly regarding the legal status of smart contracts, the allocation of liability, and the applicability of existing contract doctrines. The absence of a unified federal framework specifically addressing smart contracts has resulted in reliance on judicial interpretation and administrative guidance, which often lags technological development.

In both jurisdictions, the regulatory response has largely been reactive rather than strategic, focusing on adapting existing legal concepts rather than developing comprehensive, technology-specific frameworks. This approach, while preserving legal continuity, risks inhibiting innovation and discouraging investment due to unpredictability and compliance complexity.

7.1.2 Specialized Jurisdictions: Innovation-Friendly but Limited Models

In contrast, certain jurisdictions such as Switzerland and Malta have adopted specialized regulatory frameworks designed to accommodate blockchain technology and smart contracts more directly. Switzerland's "Crypto Valley" ecosystem benefits from regulatory clarity, flexible legal interpretations, and proactive engagement by supervisory authorities. Similarly, Malta has positioned itself as a "blockchain island" through dedicated legislation addressing distributed ledger technology (DLT) and virtual financial assets.

These jurisdictions demonstrate that tailored regulatory frameworks can foster innovation, enhance legal certainty, and attract technology-driven investment. However, their models are not universally adopted and face inherent limitations. First, their relatively small market size and specific economic structures limit the scalability of their regulatory approaches. Second, the success of such models often depends on strong institutional capacity and regulatory expertise, which may not be easily replicated in larger or more complex legal systems. Consequently, while these jurisdictions offer valuable experimentation platforms, their approaches cannot be mechanically transplanted into broader regulatory contexts without structural adaptation.

7.2 The UAE's Proactive and Centralized Regulatory Approach

Against this comparative backdrop, the UAE presents a distinctive regulatory model characterized by proactivity, centralization, and strategic integration across sectors. Rather than reacting to technological developments, the UAE has pursued a government-led approach grounded in clear national strategies, such as the UAE Blockchain Strategy, which explicitly integrates blockchain applications into public administration, finance, logistics, and digital governance.

Unlike the fragmented models observed in the EU and the US, the UAE's regulatory architecture emphasizes coordination among federal and local authorities, sectoral regulators, and technological stakeholders. This centralized governance structure enables coherent policy formulation, reduces regulatory overlap, and enhances enforcement efficiency. Moreover, the UAE's approach reflects a functional understanding of smart contracts, recognizing their economic and legal significance beyond purely technical considerations.

Importantly, the UAE has demonstrated a willingness to adapt its legal framework to accommodate digital transformation, including the recognition of electronic records, digital signatures, and automated execution mechanisms. This adaptability enhances legal certainty and facilitates the enforceability of smart contracts within the existing contractual framework, while preserving fundamental principles such as consent, intention, and good faith.

7.3 Synthesis: Lessons from the UAE Model

The comparative analysis suggests that the UAE's model of government-led, sector-integrated blockchain regulation offers valuable lessons for jurisdictions struggling with regulatory fragmentation. By aligning national strategy with legislative reform and institutional coordination, the UAE mitigates the jurisdictional ambiguities and enforcement gaps that characterize more decentralized regulatory systems.

The UAE experience demonstrates that effective blockchain regulation does not require abandoning traditional legal principles but rather reinterpreting and operationalizing them within a technologically informed framework. This synthesis underscores the importance of strategic planning, regulatory coherence, and institutional capacity in addressing the legal challenges posed by smart contracts and blockchain technology.

7.4 Lessons from Saudi Arabia's Hybrid Regulatory Model

4.4.1 The Hybrid Legal Model

Saudi Arabia provides an additional comparative perspective through its hybrid regulatory model, which seeks to balance technological innovation with regulatory oversight. Rather than adopting fully autonomous smart contract regimes, Saudi Arabia emphasizes integration with existing legal and administrative systems, particularly in areas such as digital identity verification, authentication, and mutual consent mechanisms.

This model reflects a cautious yet pragmatic approach, ensuring that smart contracts operate within a legally recognizable environment. The incorporation of digital identity tools enhances trust, accountability, and traceability, addressing one of the core challenges associated with decentralized technologies. Moreover, the emphasis on mutual consent mechanisms reinforces traditional contractual doctrines, thereby facilitating judicial acceptance and enforceability.

7.4.2 Legal and Practical Challenges

Despite its strengths, the Saudi model faces notable challenges, particularly in aligning smart contract functionality with traditional legal doctrines such as offer and acceptance, capacity, and remedies for breach. The automated and self-executing nature of smart contracts raises complex questions regarding intention, mistake, and force majeure, which are not always easily reconciled with code-based execution.

Ensuring enforceability remains a central concern, as courts and enforcement authorities must interpret and assess technologically complex arrangements within conventional procedural frameworks. These challenges highlight the need for continuous legal adaptation and judicial capacity-building to support the effective integration of smart contracts.

7.4.3 Applicability to the UAE Context

For the UAE, the Saudi experience reinforces the importance of complementary legal infrastructure, particularly digital identity systems, electronic signatures, and clear statutory recognition of technologically mediated consent. While the UAE's regulatory approach is more centralized and strategic, incorporating elements of Saudi Arabia's hybrid model could further strengthen legal certainty and enhance cross-border interoperability.

In this respect, the comparative insight suggests that the optimal regulatory model lies not in purely autonomous smart contract regimes, nor in rigid adherence to traditional doctrines, but in a calibrated integration that preserves legal certainty while accommodating technological innovation.

CONCLUSION

UAE has a well-defined legal framework for blockchain and smart contracts through a combination of federal legislation and sector-specific regulations. ETTSL has provided a solid foundation for the legal recognition of digital contracts and automated transactions, ensuring their enforceability within the UAE's legal system. Regulatory bodies such as SCA and VARA have implemented licensing requirements and compliance guidelines, helping to regulate blockchain-related businesses. Additionally, UAE courts have demonstrated judicial recognition of digital transactions, as evidenced by a 2024 Dubai Court ruling that upheld cryptocurrency as a valid form of salary payment, reinforcing confidence in the legitimacy of blockchain-based contracts. These legal and regulatory advancements have positioned the UAE as a leader in blockchain adoption and innovation, making it an attractive destination for blockchain startups and investors.

However, despite these positive developments, several challenges remain in the practical application and enforcement of smart contracts. The interpretation of smart contracts under UAE law remains largely untested, raising questions about how courts will handle disputes arising from automated contract execution. Technical errors, contract ambiguity, and unintended consequences in self-executing agreements pose legal risks that require further judicial clarification. Additionally, jurisdictional complexities arise in cross-border blockchain transactions, as smart contracts often operate on decentralized networks without clear governing laws. Moreover, the lack of explicit legal provisions addressing error correction and dispute resolution in smart contracts leaves businesses and individuals uncertain about their legal remedies when an issue arises. Addressing these challenges will be crucial for ensuring the smooth integration of smart contracts into the UAE's legal and commercial landscape.

RECOMMENDATIONS

To enhance the legal certainty and enforceability of blockchain-based agreements, UAE should enact a unified "Virtual Assets and Blockchain Act" that consolidates existing regulations under SCA, VARA, and the Central Bank. This legislation should clearly define digital assets, smart contracts, and tokenized securities, ensuring that businesses and individuals can operate within a well-regulated legal environment. Furthermore, smart contracts should be explicitly recognized as legally binding, with provisions detailing their enforceability and the legal mechanisms available for addressing contract errors or disputes. This would provide greater clarity to businesses and investors while also minimizing the risks associated with automated contract execution. Additionally, the UAE should formally recognize crypto assets as a distinct class of property under civil law, ensuring that ownership rights and claims related to digital assets are legally protected.

Judicial and regulatory mechanisms should also be strengthened to facilitate the resolution of smart contract disputes. The UAE's courts should develop guidelines for interpreting smart contracts, ensuring that legal disputes involving blockchain-based agreements are resolved effectively. Furthermore, the creation of specialized arbitration or mediation centers for blockchain-related cases could provide a more efficient and technically informed approach to resolving disputes. Given the global nature of blockchain transactions, cross-border legal cooperation should be expanded, ensuring that smart contract disputes with international elements can be adjudicated fairly and efficiently. Finally, continuous legal reform and regulatory adaptation will be necessary to ensure that UAE remains at the forefront of blockchain innovation while maintaining legal certainty for businesses and individuals engaging in smart contract transactions.

REFERENCES

Al Barghuthi, N. B., Ncube, C., & Said, H. (2019). *State of art of the effectiveness in adopting blockchain technology: UAE survey study. In 2019 Information Technology Trends (ITT): Emerging Technologies Blockchain and IoT*. IEEE., DOI: 10.1109/ITT48889.2019.9075108

Al Tamimi & Company. (2021, October). Sign of the times: The UAE's new Federal Electronic Transactions Law and Trust Services. *Law Update*. https://www.tamimi.com/law-update-articles/sign-of-the-times-the-uaes-new-federal-electronic-transactions-law-and-trust-services/

Aldabousi, A. M. (2022). Legal problems of conclusion of intelligent software agent for smart commercial contracts in the era of blockchain: U.A.E as a model. *Universidad y Sociedad*, *14*(S3), 713–728. https://rus.ucf.edu.cu/index.php/rus/article/view/3005

Aldabousi, A. M. (2023). The legal problems facing the conclusion of cloud computing contracts. *Universidad y Sociedad*, *15*(3), 602–611. https://rus.ucf.edu.cu/index.php/rus/article/view/3815

Awad, A., Al-fil, N. Z., Dganni, K. M., Aldabousi, A. M., & Ahmad Obeidat, M. (2024). Optimizing dormant account management in UAE banking: Legal gaps and proposed reforms. *Banks and Bank Systems*, *19*(4), 10. Advance online publication. DOI: 10.21511/bbs.19(4).2024.10

Hussein, S., & Serria, E. (2024). *Understanding the crucial legal implications of edge and fog computing in data privacy and security laws in the UAE. In 2024 IEEE Future Networks World Forum (FNWF 2024)*. IEEE.

Law Library of Congress. (2025, January). Regulation of cryptocurrencies in the Gulf Cooperation Council countries (Part one). *In Custodia Legis*. https://blogs.loc.gov/law/2025/01/falqs-regulation-of-cryptocurrencies-in-the-gulf-cooperation-council-countries-part-one/

Muhami Legal. (2024). Blockchain & smart contracts in UAE real estate: Legal challenges & opportunities. https://muhami.ae/articles/blockchain-and-smart-contracts-revolutionising-rea/

News, D. L. (2024). Dubai court recognises crypto salaries in a precedent-setting decision. https://www.dlnews.com/articles/people-culture/dubai-court-recognises-crypto-salaries-in-landmark-decision/

United Arab Emirates. (2021). Federal Decree-Law No. (46) of 2021 on electronic transactions and trust services. https://tdra.gov.ae/-/media/About/Trust-Services/Laws-and-regulations/Federal-Decree-Law-No-46-OF-2021-On-Electronic-Transactions-and-Trust-Services-EN.ashx

United Arab Emirates. (2022). Cabinet Resolution No. (111) of 2022 concerning the regulation of virtual assets and their service providers. https://blogs.loc.gov/law/2025/01/falqs-regulation-of-cryptocurrencies-in-the-gulf-cooperation-council-countries-part-one/

United Arab Emirates Government Portal. (n.d.). Blockchain in the UAE government. https://u.ae/en/about-the-uae/digital-uae/digital-technology/blockchain-in-the-uae-government

ADDITIONAL READING

ADGM FSRA – Virtual Assets Regulatory Framework. (gateway). https://www.adgm.com/operating-in-adgm/financial-services/regulation/virtual-assets

Civil Transactions Law, U. A. E. (Federal Law No. 5 of 1985) – official portal. https://uaelegislation.gov.ae/en/legislations

DIFC DFSA – Crypto Token regime (gateway). https://www.dfsa.ae/

Dubai Law No. 4 of 2022 Regulating Virtual Assets (official). https://dlp.dubai.gov.ae/Legislation%20Reference/2022/Law%20No.%20%284%29%20of%202022%20Regulating%20Virtual%20Assets.html

OECD – Blockchain policy resources (gateway). https://www.oecd.org/digital/blockchain/

UAE ETTS Law. (Federal Decree-Law No. 46 of 2021) – official portal. https://uaelegislation.gov.ae/en/legislations

UNCITRAL Model Law on Electronic Commerce. (1996). https://uncitral.un.org/en/texts/ecommerce/modellaw/electronic_commerce

VARA Rulebooks – entry point. https://rulebooks.vara.ae/

KEY TERMS AND DEFINITIONS

Auditability: Ability to trace actions/transactions for compliance and evidentiary proof.

Automated Electronic System: A system that can form/perform contracts without direct human intervention under certain legal frameworks.

Blockchain: A distributed ledger technology that records transactions in tamper-resistant blocks validated by network consensus.

Dispute Resolution Clause: Contractual mechanism (courts/arbitration) defining forum and rules for smart-contract disputes.

Electronic Transactions and Trust Services: Framework recognising electronic records/signatures and trust services supporting authenticity and non-repudiation.

Liability Allocation: Rules assigning responsibility for code defects, security breaches, and failed performance.

Offer and Acceptance: Core contract formation elements; must be shown even when performance is automated.

Oracle: External data feed used by smart contracts; manipulation or error can create disputes.

Regulatory Fragmentation: Multiple regulators and regimes (federal vs emirate/free zones) creating compliance complexity.

SCA: Securities and Commodities Authority regulating certain securities/markets and related virtual asset activities federally.

Smart Contract: Self-executing code that performs contractual steps when conditions are met; enforceability depends on legal consent and legality.

VARA: Dubai's Virtual Assets Regulatory Authority regulating many virtual asset activities in Dubai (excluding DIFC).

Chapter 9
Criminal Jurisdiction and Modern Technology:
A Comparative Study

Abdulghani Al-Shuaibi
http://orcid.org/0000-0002-6679-0151
Umm Al Quwain University, UAE

Ahmed Aldabousi
Umm Al Quwain University, UAE

Abdalla Alhosani
http://orcid.org/0000-0002-9073-7254
Emirates National Oil Company, UAE

Fatma Lashkaran Alraees
Umm Al Quwain University, UAE

Ayman Fekry
Al Buraimi, BUC, Oman

ABSTRACT

This study explores criminal jurisdiction in the context of modern technological developments, focusing on the United Arab Emirates (UAE) legal framework and comparing it with other legal systems, particularly those of the United States and France. It highlights the legal challenges arising from transnational cybercrimes, which have complicated the application of traditional jurisdictional principles. The research analyses the UAE's legislative framework governing criminal jurisdiction, including Federal Law No. 39 of 2006 on international judicial cooperation in criminal matters, Federal Decree-Law No. 38 of 2022 enhancing the role of federal

DOI: 10.4018/979-8-3373-7961-6.ch009

courts in cross-border crime prosecution, and Federal Decree-Law No. 34 of 2021 on cybercrimes, which establishes a balance between international cooperation and national sovereignty.

1. INTRODUCTION

Jurisdiction is one of the most important aspects of any legal order. It proves the authority to enforce the law upon individuals and institutions within the jurisdiction of each state. The technological revolution has advanced the era in numerous ways and has appropriately created new challenges for the legislature. Now, with advanced modern technology, there have been advancements in e-commerce. Also, Cybercrimes can originate in one country and be completed in another country . (Awoyemi et al., 2021)

This study aims to explain what jurisdiction is and how effective it is in enforcing laws. The research focuses on the UAE's extraterritorial jurisdiction laws and compares them to similar laws in the United States and French, which have strong legal systems and large economies. It highlights the need for laws to address threats from computer crimes and suggests what qualifies courts to handle electronic world issues in today's cyber age.

2. OVERVIEW OF CRIMINAL JURISDICTION AND MODERN TECHNOLOGY

Criminal jurisdiction refers to the authority of a court to hear and adjudicate criminal cases. It determines which court has the legal power to prosecute and pass judgment on criminal offenses based on factors such as geographical location, the nature of the crime, and the defendant's nationality or status. Criminal jurisdiction can be territorial, meaning it is based on where the crime occurred, or it can be based on other factors like the nationality of the defendant or the victim, especially in international law contexts, Merriam-Webster(Ramadan et al., 2025).

Legal principals have adapted to address the risks of cross-border cybercrime, evolving alongside technology and changing legal systems. Jurisdiction rules have become more flexible, allowing states to protect their interests globally. While criminal jurisdiction aims to limit sovereign power, it must balance sovereignty with equality between states. Modern technology has greatly influenced how criminal laws are enforced, reshaping jurisdiction and regulation over time (Chimni, 2022; Ramirez et al., 2024; Yılmaz, 2024).

2.1 The Concept of Criminal Jurisdiction

Jurisdiction refers to the legal authority according to Article 78 of the UAE Constitution; justice is a fundamental right guaranteed to all UAE citizens. This principle is upheld through a legal framework that emphasizes justice, complies with international treaties, and assigns jurisdiction appropriately. Jurisdiction is closely tied to territorial boundaries, within which relevant authorities have the power to make decisions. In a broader sense, jurisdiction allows a legal system to prosecute individuals for crimes committed outside its physical territory. (Dutton, 2023)(Rabkin & Lerner, 2022)

2.2 The Impact of Modern Technology on Criminal Jurisdiction

Modern technology has altered traditional concepts of territorial jurisdiction, especially concerning the internet. The jurisdiction of cyberspace presents a significant challenge for law enforcement, as it is often difficult to apply existing domestic laws to online activities. This difficulty arises from new global communication technologies that allow information to move across and be accessed from jurisdictions. The growing ability to conduct global communication and online transactions introduces new challenges to the traditional enforcement of territorial jurisdiction (Aldabousi et al., 2025)

The internet, especially the World Wide Web, makes it easy to transfer data across borders. However, one challenge in managing online activities is the growing anonymity of users. In the past, it was easier to trace online activities because computers were often fixed in one location, like corporate offices, and users could be identified. Online transactions also went through servers in specific areas, making it easier to monitor user actions (Babikian, 2023; Rawat, 2021; Kong et al., 2022)

3. JURISDICTION UNDER UAE LEGISLATION AND COMPARATIVE PERSPECTIVES

The UAE legislator has enacted several laws that provide legal solutions to the issue of criminal court jurisdiction, which will be discussed below:

3.1 Jurisdiction Under the Repealed Federal Law No. 35 of 1992 and Modern Technology

Criminal jurisdiction in the United Arab Emirates is regulated by Federal Law No. 35 of 1992. Article 144 grants UAE authority's international jurisdiction, enabling them to investigate and prosecute individuals who commit crimes targeting the country's computer systems from outside its borders. This provision addresses criminal activities that continue to pose security risks and societal harm, complementing territorial jurisdiction by extending legal authority beyond the UAE's physical borders (Çolak & Yıkıcı, 2024)(Stanton, 2024)

3.2 Jurisdiction Under Federal Decree-Law No. 38 of 2022 (Criminal Procedure) and Technology

The UAE legislator has allocated the first chapter of the third book of the new Criminal Procedures Law to the rules of jurisdiction of criminal courts.

The UAE legislator regulated the rules of territorial jurisdiction of criminal courts in the previous Criminal Procedures Law under Articles 142 to 144, which adopted the principle of territoriality alongside complementary principles for addressing crimes committed outside the United Arab Emirates. This approach has been maintained in the new Criminal Procedures Law, specifically in Articles 143 to 145. Additionally, the new law explicitly grants jurisdiction over crimes committed abroad that harm the interests of the United Arab Emirates to the Union Courts located in the capital, thereby centralizing judicial authority for such cases to ensure consistency and effective enforcement.

By issuing the Criminal Procedures Law, Federal Decree-Law No. of 2022, the UAE legislator addressed the issue of the one-day court in Article 140/3, which includes: provision grants authority to the President of the Federal Judicial Council and the heads of local judicial authorities, depending on the circumstances and in accordance with the applicable laws, to establish special rules for the operation of "One-Day Courts" within misdemeanor courts. These rules are an exception to the general provisions of the law and include some procedures. This text highlights the legislature's intent to enhance judicial efficiency through specialized mechanisms, such as the "One-Day Court," while ensuring that these mechanisms operate within a regulated and lawful framework.

3.3 Jurisdiction Under Federal Decree-Law No. 34 of 2021 (Combating Rumors & Cybercrime)

Pursuant to the provisions of Article 69, the scope of the law is extended to encompass crimes committed beyond the territorial boundaries of the state, provided certain specific conditions are met. This ensures that the jurisdiction of the state covers acts that have substantial connections to or significant impacts on its sovereignty, security, or national interests. The article outlines four distinct circumstances under which the provisions of the law shall apply to such offenses (Aldabousi, 2025).

- Crimes Targeting Digital Systems: The law applies if crime involves an electronic information system, a network, a website, or any technological means directly associated with the state or one of its institutions.
- Preparation or Facilitation within the State: If the crime was prepared, planned, directed, supervised, or financed from within the UAE, the law applies to the offender.
- Impact on State Security or Interests: If crime threatens the internal or external security of the UAE, its interests, or causes harm to its citizens or residents, the provisions of the law are enforceable.
- Presence of the Offender in the State: The law applies if the perpetrator is found within the State after committing crimes abroad and has not been extradited.
- Legal effects for applying this text:
- Jurisdiction Beyond Borders: The provision establishes the extraterritorial jurisdiction of UAE law, ensuring accountability for crimes that affect the state's security, interests, or systems, regardless of where they occur.
- Protection of National Interests: By addressing crimes that harm national security, the law safeguards the state's sovereignty and its citizens' well-being.
- Obligation to Prosecute: The presence of the offender within the UAE creates a duty for the state to prosecute if extradition does not occur, reinforcing the principle of no impunity(Aldabousi, 2024).

This text reflects the UAE's commitment to combat transnational crimes that have a nexus to its territory, security, or interests. It underscores the state's proactive stance in addressing threats originating from outside its borders, ensuring both accountability and protection of its sovereignty in a technologically interconnected world.

3.4 Jurisdiction and International Judicial Cooperation (Federal Law No. 39 of 2006) in the Digital Era

According to this law by with Article from it which determined of Conditions for Extradition of individuals. The requirements emphasize the dual criminality principle, the severity of the offense, and the remaining penalty duration. The conditions are as follows:

1.The crime for which extradition is sought must be punishable under the laws of the requesting state by a custodial sentence of at least one year or a more severe penalty.
2.The act must also constitute a punishable crime in the state receiving the extradition request, with sentence of at least one year .

If the extradition request is for the execution of a custodial sentence, the remaining period of the sentence must not be less than six months.

Differences in the designation, description, or legal elements of the crime between the two states do not affect the determination of whether the act constitutes a punishable offense under both legal systems.

This article reflects several key principles in international law:

Dual Criminality Principle: The requirement for the act to be punishable in both the requesting and requested states ensures mutual respect for the legal systems of both jurisdictions.

Severity Threshold: By setting a minimum threshold for punishment (one year for offense or six months for the remaining sentence), the law ensures that extradition is reserved for serious crimes, preventing misuse for minor offenses.

Flexibility in Legal Definitions: The provision allowing differences in naming or defining crimes acknowledges the diversity of legal systems while maintaining the focus on substantive justice.

The condition requiring a minimum remaining sentence ensures that extradition requests are practical .

This article underscores the UAE's commitment to international judicial cooperation while safeguarding procedural fairness and respecting the principles of dual criminality and proportionality. By balancing these considerations, the provision facilitates effective extradition processes while upholding the rule of law and international obligations. Also law includes some cases not allowing extradition in the Article:

If the individual whose extradition is requested holds the nationality of the state.

If the law of the state grants jurisdiction to its judicial authorities over the crime for which extradition is requested.

If the crime subject to the extradition request is a political crime or is connected to a political crime. However, crimes such as terrorism, war crimes, genocide, crimes against the head of state or their representative, a member of their family, the vice president, a member of the Supreme Council, the prime minister, or a family member of any of these individuals, as well as crimes against state facilities and its essential interests, shall not be considered political crimes.

If the crime for which extradition is requested relates solely to the violation of military duties.

If there are serious reasons to believe that the request for extradition is made with the intent to prosecute or punish the person for reasons related to their race, religion, nationality, political opinions, or that extradition may harm the person's status due to any of these reasons.

If the individual whose extradition is requested has already been subject to investigation or trial in the state for the same crime.

If the person has been previously tried for the crime subject to the extradition request and was either acquitted or convicted, and the sentence has been fully served.

If a final judgment has already been issued by the courts of the state for the crime subject to the extradition request.

If the criminal case has been dismissed or the penalty has been extinguished due to the expiration of the statutory limitation period at the time of the extradition request.

If the individual is at risk of being subjected to torture, inhumane or degrading treatment, or punishment in the requesting state that is disproportionate to the crime. Additionally, extradition shall not be permitted if the person will not be guaranteed the minimum standards of procedural safeguards provided under the Criminal Procedures Law.

This article demonstrates a robust framework for protecting fundamental human rights and ensuring procedural fairness in extradition matters. It strikes a balance between international judicial cooperation and safeguarding the sovereignty of the state and the rights of individuals. By enumerating clear conditions for refusal, the article minimizes the risk of misuse or politically motivated extradition requests, while reinforcing the commitment to human dignity and justice.

3.5 Other Jurisdictions for Comparisons

This section offers an overview of how some jurisdictions stat address the challenges of criminal jurisdiction arising from advancements in technology. While this is not an exhaustive analysis of all countries, it highlights key examples that may complement the UAE's approach. A comprehensive and accurate comparative study would require further research; however, the selected jurisdictions provide valuable insights. The study includes an examination of laws and practices from several countries, such as United States of USA, French . These examples showcase diverse strategies for dealing jurisdictional in the digital age (Uzougbo et al., 2024)

3.6 Judicial Jurisdiction in United States Law and Modern Technology

From this we can reach to that The United States and France have adapted their judicial jurisdiction to address modern technological challenges, particularly in combating cybercrimes:

1. United States:
   - o Uses the "effects doctrine" to assert jurisdiction over crimes committed abroad if they significantly impact U.S. territory or citizens.

- o Relies on cases like United States v. Al Kassar and statutes such as 18 U.S.C. § 2332b to prosecute threats to national security and domestic harm from foreign actions.

2. France:
   - o Enacted the Loi pour une République numérique in 2016 to enhance jurisdiction over digital crimes.
   - o Applies territorialité augmentée to claim jurisdiction over online crimes with effects in France.
   - o Collaborates internationally through the Budapest Convention on Cybercrime.

Both nations aim to balance national sovereignty with global cooperation to address the complexities of cybercrime.

4. PROBLEMS OF APPLYING TRADITIONAL PRINCIPLES OF JURISDICTION AND MODERN TECHNOLOGY

4.1 Legal Challenges in Applying Jurisdiction to Cybercrimes

Enforcing jurisdiction in cyberspace presents significant legal challenges. One major issue is applying criminal laws to cybercrimes, especially when defining terms like the "location" or "place" of the crime or its effects. Unlike traditional crimes, cybercrimes involve digital data, making it hard to pinpoint the offender's location or identity. Criminals often use anonymizing tools to conceal their actions, further complicating enforcement, revealing the challenges of identifying and prosecuting cybercriminals (Atrey, 2023).

The challenges in investigating and prosecuting cybercrimes due to technical and legal issues. These include a lack of concrete evidence, unknown server locations, and offenders who know how to hide their whereabouts. Investigations often focus on the user's side rather than the sender's. Similar issues arise in prosecuting cyber-criminals, such as differing national laws and international legal challenges. Even with adequate text laws, technical barriers make it difficult to catch suspects. These problems show that judicial systems are struggling to keep up with advancements in cybercrime (Atrey, 2023; Arnell & Faturoti, 2023; Sarkar & Shukla, 2023)

4.2 Opportunities for Enhancing Jurisdiction through Technological Innovations

Technological innovations offer significant opportunities to improve criminal jurisdiction, particularly through advancements in digital forensics. Digital tools have transformed criminal investigations by enabling new methods for data collection and processing. Unlike traditional hard copy evidence, which required physical transportation to labs for examination, electronic evidence can now be transmitted instantly between law enforcement and Relevant institutions . This facilitates real-time collaboration among international teams of investigators (Khashashneh et al., 2023)(Yadav et al., 2023)

The Budapest Convention on Cybercrime (Convention 185) aims to standardize practices related to jurisdiction in cybercrime cases. It promotes international cooperation through technology-driven and operational initiatives, facilitating coordinated responses to cyber incidents. These efforts have already begun yielding results, fostering collaboration across different regions of the world (Iu & Wong, 2024)

5. JUDICIAL JURISDICTION AND ITS APPLICATIONS IN THE ERA OF MODERN TECHNOLOGY

These cases highlight the jurisdictional challenges that arise in dealing with cybercrimes. They aim to help policymakers understand the need to update laws to address these threats effectively. By analyzing international cases, we identify similarities and differences in how such crimes are handled. Our goal is to learn lessons from these examples to improve future practices (Richet, 2022; Sarkar & Shukla, 2023)

6. HIGH-PROFILE CASES IN UAE INVOLVING MODERN TECHNOLOGY

Case 1: The "TK-1" Case

Criminal Acts:

In January 2010, the defendant Hamza Chammam, also known as "TK-1," utilized the business center at the Shangri-La Hotel in Abu Dhabi to send suspicious emails. These activities raised suspicions among hotel staff, who promptly reported the matter to the police.

Legal Issues:

- The authorities were unable to trace the defendant using internet usage records in the area.
- The lack of an arrest warrant was attributed to the requirement of direct presidential authorization, coupled with concerns that the defendant might flee to Afghanistan.
- This situation highlights the challenges associated with monitoring online activities and enforcing laws against transnational cybercrimes.

Case 2: The Mohammed Saeed Investment Dispute
Criminal Acts:

- Emirati investor Mohammed Saeed sought an injunction to halt the publication of tweets from the account "Smart Growth Limited," alleging that these tweets harmed his business interests.

Legal Issues:

- The case raises concerns about the impact of social media content on commercial activities and the need for legal frameworks to address defamatory or harmful online posts.

Case 3: Breach of the Ruling Family's Data
Criminal Acts:

- A group was involved in hacking into the computer system of a member of the ruling family, leading to the leak of confidential information related to family investments.
- The family was subjected to extortion and threats, including harm to their members and assets.

Legal Issues:

- Safeguarding the confidentiality of sensitive personal and institutional data.
- Combating cyber extortion and personal threats.
- Developing cybercrime laws to address non-material threats and crimes with far-reaching implications (Aldabousi & Ali, 2025)

These cases illustrate the legal challenges arising from modern technology, including cross-border crimes, internet misuse, and cyber extortion. They also underscore the urgent need for advanced legal frameworks that account for technological developments to ensure justice and protect individuals and institutions effectively.

6.1 Comparative Analysis of International Cases

A comparative study of international cases highlights how jurisdictions address techno-crimes and how their methods influence their jurisdictional authority. Examining case outcomes based on jurisdictional principles is essential to evaluate the effectiveness and success of modern national legal systems in handling similar cases resolved in other jurisdictions. Additionally, this study proposes the foundational principles that should guide jurisdiction and the rationale for adopting these standards. The goal is to identify potential gaps in a country's domestic legal framework and suggest improvements (Davis & Arrigo)

While taking any comparative law, it shall be noted in the conclusion that we are not suggesting any national procedural law or substantive law but merely proposing a framework. The framework constructed shall further illustrate the basic requirements that must be satisfied to establish jurisdiction and what the consequences of the accused's act will be. The consequences must directly or indirectly affect the other state (Hebous et al., 2024)

6.2 The Most Prominent Case Highlighting Jurisdictional Issues in Cybercrimes

Case: "Microsoft v. United States"

Facts:

This case revolved around the U.S. government's request to access data stored on Microsoft's servers located outside the United States. The matter began when the U.S. Department of Justice issued a warrant compelling Microsoft to provide emails belonging to a suspect in a criminal investigation. The data in question was stored in the company's data center in Ireland. Microsoft refused to comply, arguing that U.S. law does not extend to data stored outside its borders.

Legal Issues:

1. Cross-Border Jurisdiction:
    - o Can U.S. courts issue warrants for data stored in foreign jurisdictions?
    - o How should national laws apply to digital information in a global context?
2. National Sovereignty:
    - o The case raised concerns about Ireland's sovereignty, as the U.S. warrant appeared to overstep territorial boundaries.

3. Privacy Protection:
   - o The case questioned the implications of cross-border warrants on user privacy, particularly when data is protected under local privacy laws.
4. Defining “Location” in the Digital World:
   - o It highlighted the difficulty of defining the physical location of data in a cloud-based technological environment.

The U.S. Supreme Court declared the case moot after Congress passed the CLOUD Act (Clarifying Lawful Overseas Use of Data Act). This law permits U.S. authorities to request data stored abroad while respecting local laws through international cooperation agreements. This case exemplifies the challenges legal systems face with cross-border data and cybercrimes. It underscores the importance of international treaties to address jurisdictional disputes and ensure that cybercrime laws are applied equitably and effectively Microsoft Corp. v. United States, 584 U.S. ___

7. THE FUTURE OF JUDICIAL COMPETENCE AND MODERN TECHNOLOGY

7.1 The Importance of International Cooperation

In addressing the complexities of court jurisdiction under international agreements, it is imperative to anticipate future challenges and implement appropriate legal reforms. This research aims to provide lawmakers and decision-makers with insights into effective regulatory frameworks and guiding principles.

First, fostering advanced research and robust international dialogue is essential to harmonize jurisdictional standards and practices. Second, jurisdictions must prioritize the attainment of justice, ensuring that offenders are held accountable without overextending the scope of their laws beyond established norms of international law and misuse of jurisdictional principles to unduly expand authority must be avoided.

Third, Where specific practices contravene international standards or norms, legal systems must undergo rigorous reform and refinement through collaborative international consultation. It is the substantive application and practical implementation of legal principles, rather than the formal text of international agreements, that defines the normative framework of criminal jurisdiction. Such an approach ensures that legal systems remain aligned with global standards while effectively addressing transnational crimes. (Mensah et al., 2023)(Mahdavich, 2023)

The study, recognition, and prediction of appropriate legal solutions, along with the assessment of their effectiveness, are fundamentally influenced by modernity, technological advancements, and the digital revolution.

The conventional legal and political frameworks established by state and international authorities have struggled to keep pace with the rapid evolution of technology. These advancements demand the creation of new legal instruments that align with technological realities, ensuring a fair balance between legal, criminal, and socio-international dimensions. (Abulibdeh et al., 2024).

The use of modern technology in international crimes remains one of the greatest challenges to the rules of jurisdiction. The modern criminal rules of jurisdiction should adapt to the technology that we use today, and the big challenge is how to make it practical between the different states. Therefore, in practical terms, jurisdictional rules shall seek to facilitate the application of justice.

8. SOLUTIONS FOR APPLYING CRIMINAL JURISDICTION TO MODERN TECHNOLOGICAL CRIMES

The researcher suggests that this issue can be addressed through the following measures:

Adopting International Conventions: Encourage states to ratify conventions such as the Budapest Convention on Cybercrime to promote a unified approach to investigating and prosecuting cybercrimes.

Enhance and streamline MLAT procedures to facilitate real-time evidence sharing and cross-border investigations.

Addressing Legal Gaps and Jurisdictional Overlaps by implementing a one-day court system through digital courts, as seen in the United Arab Emirates and other advanced legal systems. This system can resolve jurisdictional conflicts by allowing the state affected by the crime to initiate criminal proceedings in the courts of the state where the offender is present. When extradition is not possible due to conflicting legal rules or conditions, this approach ensures that trial procedures take place effectively in the offender's country of residence, promoting justice and addressing the complexities of transnational crimes."

Encourage further research on "Criminal Jurisdiction and Modern Technology" to evaluate the influence of technology not only on international jurisdiction but also on domestic jurisdictional rules.

9. DIGITAL EVIDENCE AND PROCEDURAL SAFEGUARDS IN THE UAE

Overall, the UAE's modern legislative architecture provides a strong foundation for addressing transnational cybercrime. The next step is consistent implementation through clear procedures, skilled institutions, and fast, lawful cooperation that preserves evidence and protects rights. With these elements in place, jurisdiction in the digital era can remain both effective and legitimate.

9.1 One-Day Courts And Accelerated Procedures: Relevance To Cyber-Enabled Misdemeanors

One emerging procedural theme in several jurisdictions is the use of accelerated or specialized court sessions for high-volume, lower-severity offenses. The UAE Criminal Procedures Law includes a mechanism allowing competent judicial authorities to set special operational rules for "One-Day Courts" within misdemeanor courts, as an exception to general procedures, with the aim of improving efficiency while maintaining legality (Federal Decree-Law No. 38 of 2022). In cyber-enabled contexts, accelerated procedures can be relevant for certain categories of offenses where the evidentiary record is relatively standardized (for example, clear platform logs, authenticated screenshots with supporting metadata, or straightforward unlawful access attempts).

However, cyber-enabled misdemeanors can still raise technical disputes—such as attribution, integrity, or authenticity—that require careful handling. An efficiency-oriented court model should therefore be paired with safeguards: (1) minimum evidentiary standards for digital exhibits; (2) access to qualified forensic expertise; (3) procedures for the defense to challenge extraction methods and request verification; and (4) clear disclosure rules to prevent "trial by screenshot" without underlying data. If these safeguards are implemented, accelerated procedures can reduce backlog and improve timely justice while preserving fair trial rights.

From a jurisdictional perspective, faster procedures also reduce the risk of losing volatile evidence. Delay is an evidentiary problem in cybercrime: platform logs may be retained only for limited periods; cloud artifacts may be overwritten; and devices may be reset or destroyed. Streamlined workflows—starting from prompt preservation requests and ending with efficient adjudication—therefore strengthen the practical enforceability of jurisdictional claims.

Finally, the UAE's experience with modernization can be linked to the broader international discussion about digital courts and electronic litigation. Proposals for "transnational cybercrime courts" or enhanced cross-border mechanisms emphasize that timeliness and procedural clarity are essential in cyber investigations (Iu & Wong, 2024). While such proposals raise complex sovereignty questions, domestic reforms that improve speed and reliability can achieve many practical goals without requiring new supranational institutions.

International cooperation is not optional in transnational cybercrime: it is the mechanism that converts a jurisdictional claim into an enforceable case. The UAE's international judicial cooperation law sets out channels for requests, conditions for extradition, and grounds for refusal, including protections related to double criminality, political offenses, ne bis in idem, and human rights safeguards (Federal Law No. 39 of 2006). At the multilateral level, the Budapest Convention (ETS No. 185) provides widely referenced standards for cybercrime cooperation, including jurisdictional provisions and procedural powers designed to facilitate timely preservation and sharing of data (Council of Europe, 2001). Even when a state is not a party to a given convention, these instruments can function as persuasive models for drafting domestic procedures and bilateral cooperation arrangements.

Comparative analysis is valuable in this area because multiple legal systems face the same structural problem: cyber offenses often produce effects in many jurisdictions simultaneously, and evidence is frequently held by foreign intermediaries. The United States has relied on effects-based reasoning and statutory grants for extraterritorial reach in national security and cyber contexts, while also evolving mechanisms to obtain electronic evidence held abroad (United States v. Al Kassar, 2011; U.S. Congress, 2018). France has combined domestic digital regulation with international cooperation commitments, including alignment with cybercrime cooperation standards and a willingness to assert jurisdiction when conduct produces effects within French territory (Cassim, 2019). For the UAE, the central strategic question is not whether jurisdiction can be asserted—UAE law already provides a basis in key scenarios—but whether procedures will consistently secure reliable evidence, protect rights, and withstand challenges to admissibility and fairness.

Building on the foregoing, several pragmatic reform directions can strengthen UAE practice without compromising sovereignty or due process. First, specialized digital evidence protocols should be standardized across investigative bodies, including minimum documentation, hashing requirements, secure storage standards, and expert reporting templates, to reduce variability and enhance judicial confidence. Second, specialized judicial training and designated cyber benches can improve consistency in handling complex technical disputes. Third, cooperation timelines can be improved through pre-agreed points of contact, streamlined request templates, and enhanced digital channels for urgent preservation requests, consistent with international best practices (Federal Law No. 39 of 2006; Council of Europe, 2001). Fourth, to address jurisdictional conflicts where extradition is not feasible, structured options such as remote testimony, secure electronic litigation tools, and coordinated prosecution strategies can reduce impunity while avoiding unilateral overreach.

Limitations include the rapid evolution of cross-border investigative technologies and the uneven availability of attribution evidence. Future research should evaluate how UAE courts operationalize digital integrity tests, including hash verification, metadata validation, and expert testimony standards, and should assess whether regional cooperation mechanisms improve timeliness of mutual legal assistance in cyber-enabled cases.

This article also draws on additional comparative and doctrinal sources that inform the discussion of cybercrime jurisdiction, digital evidence, and transnational enforcement (Alkhseilat et al., 2024; Arnell & Faturoti, 2023; Awad et al., 2024; Babikian, 2023; Davis & Arrigo, n.d.; Gawer, 2022; Glasze et al., 2023; Hatam, 2024; Hessick & Hessick, 2021; Hussein & Mohammed, 2024; Kagita et al., 2022; Kaplan et al., 2021; McDonald & Swaak-Goldman, 2023; Rawat, 2021; Richet, 2022; Sarkar & Shukla, 2023; Scher-Zagier, 2024; Sharma, 2024; Sviatun et al., 2021; U.S. Code, 2023).

REFERENCES

Aldabousi, A. M. (2024). The joint responsibility of the air carrier established in accordance with international conventions on the status of air terrorism. *Pakistan Journal of Criminology*, *16*(2), 133–144. DOI: 10.62271/pjc.16.2.133.144

Aldabousi, A. M. (2025). Managing commercial space activities: Legal and regulatory challenges in UAE's space sector. *Problems and Perspectives in Management*, *23*(2), 423–432. Advance online publication. DOI: 10.21511/ppm.23(2).2025.30

Aldabousi, A. M., Awad, A., Hassan, H. E. M., Abdullah, S. S., & Ghonim, A. (2025). Arbitration in Islamic banking: Exploring legal and practical implications for dispute resolution. *Banks and Bank Systems*, *20*(2), 15–26. DOI: 10.21511/bbs.20(2).2025.02

Alkhseilat, A., Al-Billeh, T., Albazi, M., & Ali, N. A. (2024). The authenticity of digital evidence in criminal courts: A comparative study. *International Journal of Electronic Security and Digital Forensics*, *16*(6), 720–738. DOI: 10.1504/IJESDF.2024.142010

Arnell, P., & Faturoti, B. (2023). The prosecution of cybercrime—Why transnational and extraterritorial jurisdiction should be resisted. *International Review of Law Computers & Technology*, *37*(1), 29–51. DOI: 10.1080/13600869.2022.2061888

Atrey, I. (2023). Cybercrime and its legal implications: Analysing the challenges and legal frameworks surrounding cybercrime, including issues related to jurisdiction, privacy, and digital evidence. *International Journal of Research and Analytical Reviews*. https://ssrn.com/abstract=4542139

Awad, A., Al-Fil, N. Z., Dganni, K. M., Aldabousi, A. M., & Obeidat, M. A. (2024). Optimizing dormant account management in UAE banking: Legal gaps and proposed reforms. *Banks and Bank Systems*, *19*(4), 124–135. DOI: 10.21511/bbs.19(4).2024.10

Awoyemi, B. O., Omotayo, O. A., & Mpapalika, J. J. (2021). Globalization and cybercrimes: A review of forms and effects of cybercrime in Nigeria. *Internal Journal of Interdisciplinary Research and Modern Education, 7*(1), 18–25. https://www.researchgate.net/publication/353706017

Babikian, J. (2023). Navigating legal frontiers: Exploring emerging issues in cyber law. *Revista Española de Documentación Científica*. https://www.researchgate.net/publication/371914009

Cassim, F. (2019). *Cybercrime and international law: A comparative approach.* Cambridge University Press., https://www.cambridge.org/core/books/cybercrime-and-international-law

Chimni, B. S. (2022). The international law of jurisdiction: A TWAIL perspective. *Leiden Journal of International Law*. https://archive.org/details/internationallawofjurisdiction

Code, U. S. (2023). *Title 18—Crimes and criminal procedure*. https://uscode.house.gov/view.xhtml?path=/prelim@title18

Davis, S., & Arrigo, B. (n.d.). The dark web and anonymizing technologies: Legal pitfalls, ethical prospects, and policy directions from radical criminology. *Crime*. https://link.springer.com/article/10.1007/s10611-021-09972-z

Dutton, Y. M. (2023). Prosecuting atrocities committed in Ukraine: A new era for universal jurisdiction? *Case Western Reserve Journal of International Law*. https://ssrn.com/abstract=4513158

Gawer, A. (2022). Digital platforms and ecosystems: Remarks on the dominant organizational forms of the digital age. *Innovation (North Sydney, N.S.W.)*, *24*(1), 110–124. Advance online publication. DOI: 10.1080/14479338.2021.1965888

Glasze, G., Cattaruzza, A., Douzet, F., Dammann, F., Bertran, M. G., Bômont, C., & Zanin, C. (2023). Contested spatialities of digital sovereignty. *Geopolitics*, *28*(2), 919–958. DOI: 10.1080/14650045.2022.2050070

Hatam, M. A. (2024). *Crime rate analysis and e-crime prevention in Dubai using machine learning* [Master's thesis]. https://repository.rit.edu/theses/11798/

Hessick, F. A., & Hessick, C. B. (2021). Nondelegation and criminal law. *Virginia Law Review*. https://ssrn.com/abstract=3828486

Hussein, S., & Mohammed, S. (2024, February). Analyzing the legal framework and implications of Federal Decree-Law No. 34/2021 in combatting cyber blackmail in the UAE. In *2024 2nd International Conference on Cyber Resilience (ICCR)* (pp. 1–6). IEEE. https://doi.org/DOI: 10.1109/ICCR61006.2024.10533025

Iu, K. Y., & Wong, V. M. Y. (2024). The trans-national cybercrime court: Towards a new harmonisation of cyber law regime in ASEAN. *International Cybersecurity Law Review*. https://link.springer.com/article/10.1365/s43439-023-00105-x

Kagita, M. K., Thilakarathne, N., Gadekallu, T. R., Maddikunta, P. K. R., & Singh, S. (2022). A review on cybercrimes on the internet of things. In *Deep learning for security and privacy preservation in IoT* (pp. 83–98). Springer., DOI: 10.1007/978-3-031-05390-0_5

Kaplan, J., Weisberg, R., & Binder, G. (2021). *Criminal law: Cases and materials*. https://www.buffalo.edu/classics/documents/criminal-law.html

Khashashneh, T., Al-Billeh, T., Al-Hammouri, A., & Belghit, R. (2023). The importance of digital technology in extracting electronic evidence: How can digital technology be used at crime scenes? *Pakistan Journal of Criminology*, *15*(4). https://www.pjcriminology.com/wp-content/uploads/2023/11/5.-The-Importance-of-Digital-Technology.pdf

Kong, X., Wu, Y., Wang, H., & Xia, F. (2022). Edge computing for internet of everything: A survey. *IEEE Internet of Things Journal*. https://ieeexplore.ieee.org/document/9734901

Mahdavich, R. (2023). Beyond the borders: The rise of judicial corruption and universal jurisdiction. *University of Miami Race & Social Justice Law Review, 14*(2). https://repository.law.miami.edu/umrsjlr/vol14/iss2/6/

McDonald, G. K., & Swaak-Goldman, O. (2023). *Substantive and procedural aspects of international criminal law: The experience of international and national courts* (Vol. 1). Cambridge University Press., https://www.cambridge.org/core/books/substantive-and-procedural-aspects-of-international-criminal-law

Mensah, G. B., Addy, A., & Frimpong, P. O. (2023). Comparative legal analysis of the medical negligence landscape: The Ghanaian and Commonwealth criminal jurisprudence. *JL Pol'y & Globalization*. https://iiste.org/Journals/index.php/JLPG/article/view/61538

Rabkin, J. A., & Lerner, C. S. (2022). Criminal justice is local: Why states disregard universal jurisdiction for human rights abuses. *Vanderbilt Journal of Transnational Law*. https://scholarship.law.vanderbilt.edu/vjtl/vol55/iss4/2/

Ramadan, S. A., Qasim, A., & Raslan, L. (2025). The impact of scientific and technological advancements on judicial evidence methods: An applied study on UAE law. In *IoT and digital transformation: Innovating business models for the connected world* (pp. 187–197). Springer., DOI: 10.1007/978-3-032-00450-5_20

Ramirez, M., Boni, A., Wade, I., & Byrne, R. (2024). How does transformative innovation policy travel across physical and cognitive spaces? Exploring the role of mutable fluid space in experimental policy engagements. *Environmental Innovation and Societal Transitions, 52*, 100881. https://www.sciencedirect.com/science/article/pii/S2210422423000660. DOI: 10.1016/j.eist.2024.100881

Rawat, M. (2021). Transnational cybercrime: Issue of jurisdiction. *International Journal of Law Management & Humanities*. https://www.ijlmh.com/paper/transnational-cybercrime-issue-of-jurisdiction/

Richet, J. L. (2022). How cybercriminal communities grow and change: An investigation of ad-fraud communities. *Technological Forecasting and Social Change*. https://www.sciencedirect.com/science/article/pii/S0040162521007162

Sarkar, G., & Shukla, S. K. (2023). Behavioral analysis of cybercrime: Paving the way for effective policing strategies. *Journal of Economic Criminology*. https://www.sciencedirect.com/science/article/pii/S2949791423000340

Scher-Zagier, E. (2024). Jurisdictional creep: The UN cybercrime convention and the expansion of passive personality jurisdiction. *Yale Journal of Law & Technology*. https://ssrn.com/abstract=4759987

Sharma, S. P. (2024, February 10). Territorial acquisition, disputes and international law. *E-International Relations*. https://www.e-ir.info/2024/02/10/territorial-acquisition-disputes-and-international-law/

Stanton, J. (2024). In search of constitutional supremacy in Malta. *European Public Law*. https://openaccess.city.ac.uk/32972/

Sviatun, O. V., Goncharuk, O. V., Roman, C., Kuzmenko, O., & Kozych, I. V. (2021). Combating cybercrime: Economic and legal aspects. *WSEAS Transactions on Business and Economics, 18*, 751–762. https://www.academia.edu/53767740

Uzougbo, N. S., Ikegwu, C. G., & Adewusi, A. O. (2024). International enforcement of cryptocurrency laws: Jurisdictional challenges and collaborative solutions. *Magna Scientia Advanced Research and Reviews, 11*(1), 68–83. https://magnascientiapub.com/journals/index.php/MSARR/article/view/2147

Yadav, S., Yadav, S., Verma, P., Ojha, S., & Mishra, S. (2023). Artificial intelligence: An advanced evolution in forensic and criminal investigation. *Current Forensic Science, 1*(1), e190822207706. https://www.benthamscience.com/article/125626

Yılmaz, H. K. E. (2024). Legal issues of the metaverse: Public international law perspective. *Law & Justice Review*. https://dergipark.org.tr/en/pub/lawandjusticereview/issue/85441

ADDITIONAL READING

3. Council of Europe – Budapest Convention on Cybercrime. https://www.coe.int/en/web/cybercrime/the-budapest-convention

2. Criminal Procedure Law, U. A. E. (Federal Decree-Law No. 38 of 2022) – official portal. https://uaelegislation.gov.ae/en/legislations

1. Cybercrimes Law, U. A. E. (Federal Decree-Law No. 34 of 2021) – official portal. https://uaelegislation.gov.ae/en/legislations

6. INTERPOL – Cybercrime cooperation resources. https://www.interpol.int/en/Crimes/Cybercrime

7. OECD – Cross-border data and governance resources (gateway). https://www.oecd.org/digital/

5. UNODC – Mutual legal assistance tools (gateway). https://www.unodc.org/unodc/en/legal-tools/index.html

4. U.S. CLOUD Act (overview) – U.S. DOJ. https://www.justice.gov/dag/cloudact

KEY TERMS AND DEFINITIONS

Cloud Evidence: Evidence stored on distributed infrastructures, raising sovereignty and access issues.

Criminal Jurisdiction: A state's authority to investigate, try, and punish criminal conduct within legally defined boundaries.

Cross-Border Data Access: Legal mechanisms for obtaining data held abroad (MLA, agreements, provider disclosures).

Digital Evidence: Electronic records critical for cyber-enabled offences; often stored cross-border in cloud platforms.

Due Process: Procedural safeguards ensuring lawful collection, disclosure, and fair trial rights.

Effects Doctrine: Approach asserting jurisdiction where harmful effects occur within the forum state.

Extradition: Surrender of a suspect/convicted person under treaty/statute subject to safeguards (dual criminality, thresholds).

Extraterritorial Jurisdiction: Jurisdiction over conduct occurring abroad when sufficient legal nexus exists (nationality, protective, effects).

Forum Selection: Decision on the most appropriate jurisdiction based on nexus, evidence access, fairness, and practicality.

Mutual Legal Assistance (MLA): Formal inter-state cooperation for evidence collection, service, and investigative assistance.

Preservation Request: Rapid request to preserve data before deletion while legal processes proceed.

Territoriality: Jurisdiction based on where conduct or result occurs within the state's territory.

Chapter 10
Digital Evidence and Procedural Enforcement of Noise Pollution in the UAE

Emad Ibrahim
http://orcid.org/0009-0009-8571-315X
Umm Al Quwain University, UAE

Ehab Alrousan
Umm Al Quwain University, UAE

Amira Badr
http://orcid.org/0009-0005-6245-5806
Umm Al Quwain University, UAE

Muhammad Ibrahim Sarhan
Umm Al Quwain University, UAE

ABSTRACT

Noise pollution is a serious threat to human life and a significant source of concern. While noise has always been a part of human existence, it has now become a crime and a clear violation of one's quality of life. This is especially true in modern times, where advancements in civilization and industrial development, such as airplanes, trains, cars, and factories of all types and sizes, have greatly intensified noise levels. This contradicts the natural disposition of a healthy individual, law.

DOI: 10.4018/979-8-3373-7961-6.ch010

1. INTRODUCTION AND CHAPTER SCOPE

Urbanization, round-the-clock commercial activity, and intensified mobility have made environmental noise one of the most visible quality-of-life issues in contemporary cities. The legal question is no longer whether noise harms individuals and communities, but how the state should classify and respond to that harm. In many jurisdictions, noise is addressed through a layered model: (a) environmental regulation setting measurable exposure limits; (b) administrative enforcement and municipal fines for nuisance and public-serenity disturbance; and (c) criminal law in aggravated cases where harm is severe, repeated, or associated with other offences. In the United Arab Emirates (UAE), the regulatory foundation for noise control is embedded in the national environmental framework. Federal Law No. 24 of 1999 on the Protection and Development of the Environment explicitly requires that persons and entities undertaking activities - particularly those involving machines, equipment, warning devices, and loudspeakers - must not exceed permissible noise limits (Article 54) (United Arab Emirates, 1999). This federal baseline is operationalized through implementing rules, sector-specific guidance, and emirate-level public-serenity regimes. Abu Dhabi, for instance, has developed a comprehensive enforcement approach under its public-serenity framework, supported by schedules of violations and fines. (Abu Dhabi Department of Municipalities and Transport, 2024). This chapter fits the book's theme - Digital Evidence and Procedural Law in the UAE - by analyzing how noise disputes increasingly rely on digital traces: calibrated sound-level meters, event logs, CCTV systems with audio capture, mobile-phone recordings, and smart-city sensors. Digitalization creates a paradox: it can make enforcement more accurate and transparent, but it also raises procedural questions about authenticity, calibration, chain of custody, privacy, and the probative value of electronic records. The UAE legal system has responded through a modern evidence framework recognizing electronic evidence in civil and commercial proceedings, including rules on verification and judicial assessment of probative value (United Arab Emirates, 2022a). In addition, the federal law on electronic transactions and trust services confirms that electronic documents and signatures are not inadmissible merely because they are electronic, while setting conditions for authenticity (United Arab Emirates, 2021a). Accordingly, the chapter's main objective is to provide a structured, practice-oriented synthesis of noise pollution as an actionable offence in the UAE, with a focus on the procedural pathway from complaint to decision and on the evidentiary requirements for modern, digitally mediated proof. The discussion is designed for legal scholars, practitioners, municipal enforcement bodies, and policy makers concerned with fair and effective enforcement. Three contributions are emphasized. First, the chapter translates a 'quality-of-life' problem into a legally operational framework by distinguishing substantive routes (environmental, nuisance, administrative) and linking each route to concrete evidentiary requirements. Second, it connects measurement technology to procedural safeguards, showing how authenticity and chain-of-custody questions are now central in disputes. Third, it proposes an implementation roadmap that can be adopted by municipalities and regulators to standardize practice without waiting for major legislative reform.

2. CONCEPTUAL AND PUBLIC-HEALTH FOUNDATIONS OF NOISE REGULATION

Noise is commonly defined as unwanted or harmful sound. Legally, the term is often operationalized through measurable indicators rather than purely subjective perceptions. Modern governance typically relies on a combination of: (a) sound pressure level measures (e.g., A-weighted decibels, dB(A)); (b) exposure time; and (c) context (residential, mixed-use, industrial, sensitive receptors such as hospitals and schools). International standards such as ISO 1996-1 provide widely used quantities and assessment procedures for community noise description and evaluation (International Organization for Standardization, 2016). Sound-level meters used for regulatory measurements are also commonly specified against standards like IEC 61672-1, which differentiates performance classes and technical requirements (International Electrotechnical Commission, 2013). The rationale for treating noise as a legal wrong is strengthened by public-health evidence. Large-scale reviews and guideline processes identify links between environmental noise exposure and annoyance, sleep disturbance, cardiovascular outcomes, and cognitive impacts (Basner et al., 2014; Stansfeld & Matheson, 2003). The World Health Organization's Environmental Noise Guidelines for the European Region (2018) provide evidence-based recommendations for major noise sources and emphasize the burden of disease attributable to environmental noise exposure (World Health Organization Regional Office for Europe, 2018). Earlier WHO work on night noise similarly highlights the importance of protecting sleep through lower nighttime exposure (World Health Organization Regional Office for Europe, 2009). From a legal-theoretical perspective, noise cases illustrate the tension between individual freedom (e.g., business activity, celebration, mobility) and the collective right to tranquility and health. This is why many legal systems treat noise through a graduated enforcement ladder, where the same conduct may be an administrative violation at one stage (fine/closure order) and a criminal offence at another (repeated non-compliance, intentional disturbance, or harm). In the UAE context, the layering is particularly visible because federal environmental law sets a general obligation, while emirate-level regimes operationalize 'public serenity' as an enforceable public interest. Empirical literature focusing specifically on the Arab region remains comparatively fragmented, even though the

UAE is frequently included in regional datasets. A recent scientometric analysis of noise pollution studies across 22 Arab countries highlights the uneven distribution of research outputs and emphasizes the need for policy-relevant research agendas and standardized methodologies, which is consistent with the chapter's argument on measurement and evidentiary standardization (Bouzir et al., 2024). Classic syntheses in public-health literature have long argued that the evidence for non-auditory effects of environmental noise is strongest for annoyance, sleep disturbance, and cognitive outcomes, with additional associations to hypertension and cardiovascular disease (Stansfeld & Matheson, 2003). Systematic reviews commissioned for the WHO guideline process also document effects on cognition and wellbeing, supporting a preventive approach where vulnerable groups and nighttime exposure receive special protection (Clark & Paunovic, 2018). At the policy level, international instruments such as the OECD Recommendation on Strengthening Noise Abatement Policies emphasize integrated planning, emission standards, and coordinated enforcement, reinforcing the idea that sanctioning should be embedded in a broader abatement program (Organisation for Economic Co-operation and Development, 2024).

3. LEGAL FRAMEWORK IN THE UAE

3.1 Federal Baseline: Environmental Protection and Permissible Noise Limits

UAE Federal Law No. 24 of 1999 establishes a general legal duty not to exceed permissible noise limits when undertaking activities, especially those involving machines, equipment, warning devices, and loudspeakers (Article 54) (United Arab Emirates, 1999). The law's approach is important for two reasons. First, it frames noise as an environmental pollutant, placing it within a broader regulatory architecture that includes monitoring, inspection, and administrative measures. Second, the explicit reference to “permissible limits” implies that enforcement should be anchored in quantification rather than pure subjectivity, which is directly relevant to the use of digital and instrument-based evidence.

3.2 Emirate-Level Enforcement: Public Serenity and Municipal Governance (Abu Dhabi as Example)

At the emirate level, public-serenity and municipal frameworks provide operational tools: licensing conditions, inspection powers, violation schedules, and fines. Abu Dhabi's enforcement architecture illustrates how noise is conceptualized as a disturbance of ‘public serenity' - i.e., a state of tranquility and quietness in roads, public places, and residential areas, ensuring comfort against actions causing disturbance or noise in any form. Such definitions matter because they connect noise regulation to public-order rationales (annoyance, panic, provocation) rather than only environmental exposure. (Abu Dhabi Department of Municipalities and Transport, 2024). These regimes often distinguish between: (a) situational noise events (e.g., loudspeakers, late-night parties, construction outside permitted hours); (b) chronic exposure (e.g., repeated venue non-compliance); and (c) traffic-related noise. In practice, the enforcement toolkit includes inspections, warnings, administrative penalties, and (where relevant) referral to police or prosecution when conduct escalates beyond administrative non-compliance. Public-facing guidance may also facilitate complaint channels. Media guidance directed to residents frequently connects complaints to the federal environmental duty not to exceed permissible noise limits.

3.3 Sector-Specific Rules and Technical Guidance (Dubai Example)

Beyond general legal duties, emirates and municipalities may issue technical guidance that translates legal standards into operational rules. Dubai Municipality, for instance, has issued technical guidelines for controlling noise at entertainment areas, referencing local orders and specifying measurement and compliance expectations (e.g., boundary measurements, monitoring, and mitigation). Such documents are highly relevant in litigation because they are often used to determine whether the "permissible limit" was exceeded, how measurements should be taken, and whether documentation meets the evidentiary threshold. (Dubai Municipality, 2021).

3.4 Emerging Enforcement Technologies

Recent initiatives in the UAE also illustrate how technology is integrated into enforcement. For example, Dubai has deployed and expanded traffic 'noise radar' capabilities to detect excessively loud vehicles and deter nuisance behavior through fines and administrative measures. Although media reports are not primary legal sources, they show that public authorities increasingly rely on sensor-based detection and automated logging, which inevitably raises procedural and evidentiary questions about device certification, error rates, and due process. (Gulf News, 2025).

3.5 Where 'Procedural Law' Enters the Noise Framework

The book's emphasis on procedural law is especially relevant because noise regulation is not merely about substantive prohibitions; it is also about who measures, how records are created, and how those records are evaluated. Two procedural layers matter.

First, administrative procedure governs municipal inspections, issuance of violation notices, and the internal review of sanctions. Emirate-level schedules of violations and fines operationalize this layer by defining standardized violation descriptions and associated penalties. Even when the legal basis is administrative, the quality of procedure determines the legitimacy of sanctions.

Second, judicial procedure becomes relevant when disputes escalate to courts, either through challenges to administrative sanctions, civil claims (e.g., tenancy and neighborhood disputes), or criminal referrals. In criminal contexts, the UAE's Criminal Procedures Law provides the overarching procedural framework for investigation, evidence gathering, and expert involvement (United Arab Emirates, 2022b). Although this chapter is not a commentary on criminal procedure, recognizing the procedural context helps authors and reviewers evaluate whether an evidentiary claim is institutionally realistic and legally sustainable.

At the system level, this procedural perspective supports a key proposition: noise enforcement succeeds when measurement technology is integrated with legally robust procedures for documentation, notification, challenge, and review.

4. DOCTRINAL ROUTES FOR LIABILITY: ENVIRONMENTAL OFFENCE, NUISANCE, AND ADMINISTRATIVE SANCTIONS

In doctrinal terms, 'noise pollution as a crime' in the UAE is best conceptualized through three legal routes, each with distinct elements and procedural implications.

First, noise may be treated as an environmental offence grounded in federal environmental law and its implementing standards. Here, the wrong is exceeding permissible limits and thereby harming environmental quality and public health. The evidence focus is on measurement (intensity and exposure time), compliance with implementing regulations, and documentation by authorized inspectors. (United Arab Emirates, 1999).

Second, noise may be treated as a public-order or nuisance offence under emirate-level public-serenity frameworks. The wrong is the disturbance of tranquility in public or residential spaces. Because 'disturbance' has subjective components, these cases often combine objective evidence (measurements, recordings) with contextual factors (time of day, location, repetition, warnings).

Third, noise may be addressed as an administrative violation through municipal regulations (e.g., licensing conditions, construction hours, entertainment permits). In practice, this route often handles the majority of complaints because it is faster and more flexible than criminal prosecution. However, administrative cases still benefit from procedural rigor, especially when sanctions are high or include closure orders.

Across all routes, escalation criteria are central. Repeated violations after warnings, deliberate disregard of orders, or demonstrable harm can justify moving from a purely administrative response to a more coercive enforcement model. In aggravated circumstances - for example, where conduct is intentional, persistent, or linked to broader public-order harms - general offences and sanctions under the federal Crimes and Penalties framework may become relevant, subject to the specific facts and the applicable procedural safeguards (United Arab Emirates, 2021c). A fair system should therefore specify escalation triggers and preserve proportionality.

4.1 Sanction Calibration and Proportionality

Sanction design in noise governance must satisfy two objectives that can pull in opposite directions: deterrence and social acceptability. Overly mild sanctions risk normalizing late-night disturbance and shifting costs to residents (sleep disruption, reduced wellbeing). Overly harsh sanctions may be perceived as arbitrary, especially where measurement uncertainty exists or where a venue has made reasonable mitigation efforts.

A proportional approach typically considers: (a) time sensitivity (nighttime disturbance is treated more seriously); (b) recurrence (repeat violations after notice justify escalation); (c) affected receptor (hospitals, schools, and residential buildings); (d) degree of exceedance above the permitted level; and (e) mitigation behavior (whether the operator cooperates, installs barriers, adjusts operations).

Procedurally, proportionality also requires that enforcement bodies document the reasoning for escalation. For example, if a closure order is imposed, the file should show prior warnings, measured exceedances, and the failure of mitigation. This reduces contestability and signals that enforcement is rule-based rather than discretionary.

Finally, proportionality should be linked to prevention. In mixed-use urban development, a purely punitive approach is often less effective than combining sanctions with licensing conditions, acoustic design requirements, and communication with affected communities. This integrated logic reinforces the chapter's core argument: the legal treatment of noise is inseparable from the evidentiary and procedural system that produces enforceable, reviewable decisions.

5. CONSTITUENT ELEMENTS OF NOISE-RELATED OFFENCES

To promote legal certainty, enforcement bodies and courts should articulate noise offences through identifiable elements, even when the legal basis is framed broadly.

(a) Conduct (actus reus): a measurable emission or an audible disturbance attributable to a person or entity (e.g., operating loudspeakers, machinery, construction, entertainment activities, or vehicle behavior).
(b) Unlawfulness: exceeding permissible limits (quantitative) and/or violating applicable time/place restrictions, licensing conditions, or public-serenity rules. Federal environmental law emphasizes the former (permissible limits), while emirate regimes often emphasize the latter (disturbance in residential/public areas).
(c) Attribution and causation: linking the noise event to the responsible operator or individual. This is particularly relevant in urban settings with multiple noise sources (traffic + construction + venues). Instrument placement, time synchronization, and geo-location documentation are therefore critical.
(d) Mental element (mens rea) or negligence (where relevant): In many systems, minor noise violations are strict or quasi-strict (liability triggered by exceedance), while aggravated cases require intent or knowing disregard. Even in an administrative context, intentionality affects sanction calibration and escalation.
(e) Harm or risk: While some violations are established by exceedance alone, others depend on demonstrated nuisance, disturbance, or risk to health. Public health evidence strengthens the legitimacy of preventive enforcement because it shows harm can occur even without immediate, visible injury (Basner et al., 2014; World Health Organization Regional Office for Europe, 2018).

These elements guide evidence collection: if liability depends on exceedance, the measurement method becomes decisive; if it depends on disturbance, contextual and corroborative evidence becomes more important.

6. DIGITAL EVIDENCE IN NOISE CASES

Noise events are ephemeral. They occur in time, often fluctuate, and may not leave physical traces. This makes evidentiary design central to enforcement.

6.1 Categories of Digital Evidence in Noise Cases

Noise cases may involve several categories of electronic evidence, and the evidentiary weight of each category depends on how it was generated and preserved.

In practice, enforcement files commonly draw on instrument-based readings and logs from calibrated sound-level meters or fixed sensors; inspection reports and photographs that contextualize the alleged source (equipment, venue, construction site, or vehicle); audio/video recordings from CCTV systems or mobile devices; and administrative-system records such as complaint tickets, GPS coordinates, and time stamps. Where official measurements are relied upon, standardized concepts and device performance requirements should be aligned with widely used technical standards and measurement procedures, including ISO 1996-1 and IEC 61672-1, while empirical reviews emphasize that deviations from protocol can materially affect exposure estimates and legal conclusions (Barrigón Morillas et al., 2016; International Electrotechnical Commission, 2013; International Organization for Standardization, 2016).

6.2 Authenticity, Reliability, and Chain of Custody

The probative value of digital evidence turns on authenticity, integrity, and reliability. UAE law provides a basis for admitting and evaluating electronic materials: the federal framework on electronic transactions and trust services prevents exclusion solely because a record is electronic and sets authenticity conditions (United Arab Emirates, 2021a). In criminal matters involving electronic systems, the cybercrimes decree-law recognizes the evidential value of digital traces extracted from devices, subject to procedural legality and forensic safeguards (United Arab Emirates, 2021b).

In civil and commercial disputes, the UAE evidence law similarly recognizes electronic evidence and addresses verification challenges. Where verification is not possible for reasons not attributable to the parties, the court may still assess probative value based on the circumstances (United Arab Emirates, 2022a). This principle is significant for noise cases because recordings may be imperfect yet still probative when corroborated by other evidence (for example, official measurements, multiple independent recordings, witness statements, or inspection reports).

6.3 Practical Protocol for Noise Measurements and Electronic Proof

To reduce litigation risk and strengthen due process, enforcement bodies should adopt a structured documentation protocol covering the full measurement and data-handling lifecycle.

The protocol should record device identification (model, class, serial number), calibration certificates, and compliance class; measurement conditions (location coordinates, height, distance from source, weather and background noise considerations where relevant); time synchronization (use of a reliable time source and consistent timestamps across devices); data integrity measures (secure storage, controlled export, access logs, and, where feasible, hash verification); and linkage between the measurement record and the alleged source through scene photographs, setup documentation, and contemporaneous notes (International Organization for Standardization, 2016; International Organization for Standardization & International Electrotechnical Commission, 2012).

Where a case relies primarily on a resident's smartphone recording, best practice is to treat it as corroborative evidence and to obtain official measurements where feasible. Smartphone microphones are not designed for regulatory-grade measurement; however, recordings can capture qualitative severity (e.g., nighttime disturbance) and support a decision to inspect.

6.4 Privacy and Proportionality

Audio capture, especially in residential settings, can implicate privacy. A proportionate approach is needed: collect the minimum necessary data to prove exceedance/disturbance, avoid capturing unrelated private conversations, and ensure that any monitoring is grounded in a clear legal basis and procedural authorization. A well-designed evidentiary protocol protects both public interests (quiet, health) and individual rights.

6.5 Audio Authenticity, Editing Risks, and the Need for Forensic Protocols

Digital recordings are persuasive because they appear 'direct'. Yet modern editing software makes it easy to cut, splice, filter, or re-encode audio in ways that are not obvious to non-experts. In contested cases, parties may argue that an audio file was modified, that the recording device distorted the sound, or that the captured sound originated from a different source. Accordingly, the evidentiary task shifts from merely producing a recording to demonstrating its authenticity and contextual integrity.

International forensic practice has developed structured approaches to these challenges. The Scientific Working Group on Digital Evidence (SWGDE) provides best-practice guidance for handling forensic audio, emphasizing documentation of the recording's provenance, preservation of original files, careful management of copies, and transparent reporting of analytical steps (SWGDE, 2022). Complementary guidance exists for audio authentication examinations, including evaluation of waveform continuity, spectrogram consistency, compression artifacts, metadata, and indicators of pause/restart events (SWGDE, 2018). In Europe, the European Network of Forensic Science Institutes (ENFSI) has published a Best Practice Manual for Digital Audio Authenticity Analysis that outlines quality assurance expectations, handling requirements, and interpretive cautions for authenticity claims (ENFSI, 2022).

In the UAE context, these forensic standards are not automatically binding. However, they serve as persuasive benchmarks for what constitutes 'reasonable' professional practice when authenticity is disputed. Where courts appoint experts or rely on municipal laboratory assessments, referencing established best-practice manuals can improve methodological transparency and reduce the risk of over-claiming.

6.6 ISO/IEC Digital Evidence Handling Principles

Beyond audio-specific guidance, digital evidence handling should follow general principles aimed at preserving integrity. ISO/IEC 27037 provides guidelines for identification, collection, acquisition, and preservation of potential digital evidence (International Organization for Standardization & International Electrotechnical Commission, 2012). Applying these principles to noise cases implies: (a) capturing data in a manner that minimizes alteration (e.g., exporting logs directly from devices); (b) preserving originals; (c) documenting every transfer and access; and (d) maintaining auditability.

6.7 From 'Decibels' to 'Proof': Structuring Evidentiary Inference

Courts and administrative decision makers rarely decide cases on raw decibel values alone. They must infer unlawfulness from a combination of facts. A structured inferential approach can be summarized as follows:

(1) Was the measurement valid? The device class, calibration status, and measurement protocol determine whether the reported value is trustworthy. (2) Was the exceedance attributable? Location, time synchronization, and source identification must link the exceedance to the defendant. (3) Was the limit applicable? The legal

threshold depends on context (land use, time period, permit conditions). (4) Was the response proportionate? Administrative penalties should be justified by severity and repetition; criminal escalation should be reserved for aggravated patterns.

Presenting evidence in this sequence improves due process because it clarifies what must be challenged and where uncertainty lies.

6.8 Trust Services, Electronic Signatures, and Time-Stamping

One practical way to strengthen the evidentiary weight of noise measurement records is to integrate trust services and secure time-stamping. When sensor data are exported as signed reports, or when inspection records are digitally signed by authorized officers, the record becomes easier to authenticate and harder to repudiate. The UAE's electronic transactions and trust services framework provides the conceptual and legal foundation for this approach by recognizing electronic signatures and trust services as tools for establishing authenticity and integrity. (United Arab Emirates, 2021a).

In operational terms, municipalities and enforcement bodies can implement systems where: (a) sensor datasets are automatically time-stamped by a secure service; (b) inspection reports are generated from tamper-evident templates; and (c) each issuance of a violation notice produces a verifiable audit trail. Such measures reduce disputes about ‘when' the event occurred, whether the record was altered, and whether the reported exceedance is connected to the defendant.

6.9 Handling Resident-Supplied Digital Materials

Resident recordings and neighborhood WhatsApp messages are increasingly common in noise disputes. These materials raise three recurring issues.

First, the authenticity issue: a file may be edited, re-encoded, or forwarded with stripped metadata. ENFSI and SWGDE guidance recommends preserving original files where possible, documenting the acquisition process, and recording the device and application used for capture.

Second, the relevance issue: a loud event may be intermittent, and short clips may misrepresent the overall exposure. Authorities should treat resident material as a trigger for inspection rather than as a substitute for official measurement.

Third, the privacy issue: recordings may inadvertently capture private conversations or identifiable individuals. Collection and retention should therefore be proportionate, and disclosure should be limited to what is necessary for adjudication.

6.10 Digital Forensics Governance and Incident-Response Logic

Many principles used in digital forensics and incident response translate well to noise enforcement because both rely on preserving volatile data and maintaining integrity. Guidance such as NIST's incident-response forensics publications emphasizes disciplined collection, documentation, and preservation to prevent contamination and to support later review. Similarly, NIST guidance on mobile device forensics highlights the need for consistent procedures when evidence resides on personal devices. While these materials are primarily developed for cybersecurity investigations, the underlying integrity principles are directly applicable to digitally mediated nuisance enforcement. (Kent et al., 2006; Ayers et al., 2014).

International organizations also link these ideas to cross-jurisdictional cooperation. For example, UNODC educational guidance references ISO/IEC 27037 as a foundational standard for identification, collection, acquisition, and preservation of digital evidence, supporting harmonized expectations where evidence might be exchanged between agencies or used in proceedings with different procedural cultures. (United Nations Office on Drugs and Crime, n.d.).

7. PROCEDURAL PATHWAYS AND SAFEGUARDS

Because noise cases frequently begin as community complaints, procedural pathways should be clear and predictable.

7.1 Complaint Intake and Initial Assessment

Authorities should record the complaint with essential metadata: time, location, alleged source, and nature of disturbance. When possible, the system should support attaching digital materials (photos, short recordings) as preliminary indicators. Public guidance in the UAE often directs residents to municipal channels and emphasizes that excessive noise should not exceed permissible limits. (Khaleej Times, 2025; United Arab Emirates, 1999).

7.2 Inspection, Sampling Strategy, and Risk-Based Prioritization

Inspection resources are limited. A risk-based approach - prioritizing repeated complaints, sensitive locations (hospitals, schools), and nighttime disturbances - can improve outcomes. The EU Environmental Noise Directive illustrates how strategic mapping and action planning can support risk-based governance of environmental noise exposures. While the EU model is not directly transplanted, it offers useful institutional design lessons: data aggregation, transparency, and targeted intervention. (European Parliament and Council, 2002).

7.3 Administrative Decision-Making and Judicial Review

When an administrative fine or closure order is imposed, a written reasoning and an evidence packet should accompany the decision: measurements, calibration evidence, photographs, notices, and prior warnings. This increases fairness and reduces the likelihood of successful challenges.

7.4 Civil Litigation and Tenancy Disputes

Noise also appears in civil contexts such as tenancy and neighborhood disputes. In such settings, the legal acceptance of electronic evidence (messages, notices, time-stamped logs) becomes especially relevant. Professional analyses of UAE litigation trends emphasize that federal evidence rules have reinforced recognition of digital materials, provided authenticity requirements are satisfied (Taylor Wessing, 2022; BSA Ahmad Bin Hezeem & Associates LLP, 2025).

7.5 Expert Evidence and Judicial Evaluation of Technical Proof

Noise litigation often turns on expert assessment: whether measurements were properly taken, whether the device was appropriately calibrated, and whether recordings show indications of tampering. An expert may also be needed to distinguish between multiple sources (e.g., traffic vs. venue music), to interpret impulsive noise events, or to explain psychoacoustic factors affecting perception.

Best practice in forensic reporting emphasizes that experts should separate observations from interpretation, disclose limitations, and avoid categorical conclusions that exceed the data. In authenticity assessments, for instance, a careful examiner will articulate what the analysis can and cannot establish, rather than declaring absolute authenticity in the absence of a clear testable claim.

7.6 Procedural Fairness: Access to Evidence and the Right to Challenge

Because digital evidence can be complex, fairness requires disclosure and a meaningful opportunity to challenge the evidence. Practically, this means providing the full measurement report (device details, calibration, setup), preserving and disclosing relevant metadata and logs, and supplying recordings in original formats where feasible. When authenticity or methodology is contested, counter-expertise and transparent reporting of limitations help protect procedural rights (European Network of Forensic Science Institutes, 2022; Scientific Working Group on Digital Evidence, 2022).

These safeguards align with broader procedural principles: decisions should be based on reliable evidence, and parties should be able to test reliability. (European Network of Forensic Science Institutes, 2022).

7.7 Administrative Enforcement as 'Procedural Law in Practice'

Although the book's focus is often on courtroom procedure, the practical reality is that most noise cases are resolved administratively. Administrative enforcement therefore functions as a form of procedural law-in-action: it determines what counts as evidence, how it is recorded, and how sanctions are imposed. A rigorous administrative process reduces the burden on courts and can prevent escalation.

In the UAE, the combination of (a) the federal environmental baseline, (b) emirate-level violation schedules, and (c) recognition of electronic records provides a strong platform for this approach. (Abu Dhabi Department of Municipalities and Transport, 2024; United Arab Emirates, 1999; United Arab Emirates, 2022a).

7.8 A Worked Procedural Scenario (Illustrative)

Consider a scenario: residents in a mixed-use neighborhood report repeated late-night music from an entertainment venue. The complaint includes a short smartphone recording captured at 1:30 a.m. The venue holds a valid license but is alleged to exceed permitted noise levels.

Step 1: Complaint record and triage. The authority registers the complaint, logs the time and location, and stores the resident file as a preliminary indicator.

Step 2: Inspection and measurement. Inspectors attend during the relevant time window. They document device details and calibration certificates, record location coordinates, and measure both background noise and venue-related noise using a defensible protocol. Readings are logged electronically and exported with a secure audit trail.

Step 3: Attribution. Inspectors document the venue's operations at the time of measurement (music system active, doors open) and capture contextual photographs. If multiple sources exist, they take comparative measurements at different positions.

Step 4: Notice and mitigation opportunity. The venue receives an electronic notice summarizing the exceedance and mitigation expectations. Follow-up inspections are scheduled.

Step 5: Escalation. If the venue repeatedly violates limits after warnings, sanctions escalate. Administrative penalties may include higher fines and temporary closure. In aggravated cases, the file may be referred to police/prosecution depending on the applicable legal route.

Step 6: Challenge and review. If the venue challenges the sanction, the authority provides the full evidence packet, including raw logs, calibration documentation, and any recordings relied upon. The venue may submit counter-expertise.

This scenario illustrates how digital evidence, if properly handled, improves both enforcement efficiency and procedural fairness. It also shows how escalation should be evidence-driven, with transparency at each stage.

7.9 Minimizing Disputes Through Standard Forms

One low-cost reform is the use of standardized evidence forms and templates. For instance, a 'Noise Measurement Record' can include mandatory fields for calibration, environmental conditions, device placement, and time synchronization. A 'Digital Evidence Chain-of-Custody' form can record each transfer, export, and access. These practices align with ISO/IEC digital evidence handling principles (International Organization for Standardization & International Electrotechnical Commission, 2012) and reduce vulnerability to procedural challenges.

7.10 Escalation Into Criminal Procedure: When, Why, and How

Most noise matters are resolved administratively; however, escalation into criminal procedure may occur in aggravated situations, such as repeated defiance of closure orders, intentional disturbance linked to other offences, or cases where conduct contributes to a broader public-order incident. In such situations, procedural questions become more formal: who is authorized to seize devices, how recordings are collected, and how expert examinations are requested.

The UAE's Criminal Procedures Law (Federal Decree-Law No. 38 of 2022) (United Arab Emirates, 2022b) modernizes criminal procedure and provides the backbone for investigation and evidence handling in criminal matters. For a noise-related file, the practical implications include: (a) clearer documentation standards for investigative actions; (b) structured opportunities for expert involvement; and (c) the need to ensure that digital records presented to prosecution are traceable to lawful collection steps.

Importantly, the existence of a modern criminal procedure framework does not mean that every nuisance becomes a crime. Rather, it provides a legally coherent escalation path that can be activated in exceptional cases. The chapter's policy recommendation is therefore not 'criminalize everything', but 'ensure that escalation, when it occurs, is procedurally defensible and evidence-based'.

7.11 Standards of Proof and Decision Thresholds

Decision thresholds differ across forums:

Standards of proof and evaluation differ across pathways. In administrative enforcement, decision-makers typically rely on reasonable satisfaction based on official inspection records and measurements. In civil disputes, courts balance the totality of evidence while assigning probative value to electronic materials under the evidence framework (United Arab Emirates, 2022a). In criminal contexts, the standard is higher, and disputes about measurement integrity, authenticity, and procedural legality can be decisive (United Arab Emirates, 2022b).

Recognizing these differences helps authors draft chapters that remain internally consistent: a measurement approach that is acceptable for an administrative fine may require additional expert validation if it is used to support criminal liability.

7.12 Linking Evidence Law Concepts to Noise Cases

UAE Evidence Law provisions on formal and informal electronic evidence are especially instructive for how digital records should be generated. For example, the legislation notes that formal electronic evidence may have the same probative value as formal instruments if statutory conditions are met, including documents automatically generated by electronic systems of public entities or entities entrusted with a public service. This encourages public entities to design systems that generate tamper-evident, automatically logged records for inspections and measurements. In noise enforcement, this can include automated sensor logs and digitally signed inspection reports. (United Arab Emirates, 2022a).

At the same time, unofficial electronic evidence (e.g., resident recordings) can be valuable, but courts will weigh its probative value in light of authenticity challenges and corroboration.

8. COMPARATIVE PERSPECTIVE AND POLICY LESSONS

A brief comparative lens helps situate the UAE approach.

8.1 European Union

The EU Environmental Noise Directive (2002/49/EC) focuses on assessment and management of environmental noise exposure and requires strategic noise mapping and action plans for major sources. The directive illustrates a policy architecture where measurement, mapping, and public information are central. Its emphasis is not criminalization per se, but prevention, transparency, and health protection. (European Parliament and Council, 2002).

8.2 Implications for the UAE

The UAE's legal architecture already contains the essential building blocks for an evidence-based noise governance model: a federal duty anchored in permissible limits (Federal Law No. 24/1999), emirate-level public-serenity enforcement, and a modern evidence regime recognizing electronic records. The comparative lesson is that robust governance depends on standardized measurement practices and data-driven prioritization, not only on sanctions. (Abu Dhabi Department of Municipalities and Transport, 2024; United Arab Emirates, 1999; United Arab Emirates, 2022a).

8.3 Comparative Criminalization Considerations

Criminal law is typically reserved for serious or repeated conduct. If the UAE chooses to strengthen criminal pathways, legal certainty requires clear thresholds (e.g., repeated exceedance, intentional disturbance, harm), while procedural law must ensure defendants can challenge device accuracy and measurement methodology. The core comparative insight is that when enforcement becomes technologically sophisticated, procedural protections must advance in parallel.

European policy discussions are also informed by periodic assessments of exposure and health impacts, such as the European Environment Agency's reports on environmental noise in Europe, which consolidate exposure estimates and highlight policy gaps. (European Environment Agency, 2020).

9. CONCLUSIONS AND RECOMMENDATIONS

Based on the analysis, several recommendations can improve compliance, fairness, and evidentiary robustness. They are consistent with the general international trend toward strengthening noise abatement policies through standardized measurement, transparent governance, and targeted interventions (Organisation for Economic Cooperation and Development, 2024; World Health Organization Regional Office for Europe, 2018).

Practical reforms can be implemented without major legislative change. Enforcement bodies should codify measurement and documentation standards that reference applicable local guidance and recognized ISO/IEC specifications to reduce methodological disputes (Dubai Municipality, 2021; International Electrotechnical Commission, 2013; International Organization for Standardization, 2016). Calibration governance should be strengthened through periodic device testing and clear documentation of uncertainty margins. Finally, agencies should standardize digital chain-of-custody practices - secure storage, controlled export, and audit logs - consistent with digital evidence handling principles (International Organization for Standardization & International Electrotechnical Commission, 2012).

Noise pollution will remain a central governance issue in rapidly developing cities. The UAE's legal framework is already positioned to handle the challenge, but the legitimacy and effectiveness of enforcement increasingly depend on how digital evidence is collected, authenticated, and assessed. Aligning enforcement technology with procedural safeguards is therefore essential to the book's broader theme of digital evidence and procedural law.

Implementation Roadmap (Practical Steps)

Institutions can adopt a staged roadmap: start with standardized templates for complaints, inspections, and measurement records; move to digital case files with time-stamping and audit trails; build training and limited forensic capacity for contested cases; and use aggregated data for prevention and planning (European Parliament and Council, 2002).

DECLARATION

Declaration of AI-Assisted Language Editing

The authors confirm that AI-assisted tools were used solely for language editing purposes (improving clarity, grammar, and academic style) and not for generating original legal analysis, research data, or substantive conclusions. Specifically, QuillBot and Grammarly were used to refine English language expression, correct grammatical errors, and enhance readability. The authors reviewed, verified, and take full responsibility for the final content.

REFERENCES

Abu Dhabi Department of Municipalities and Transport. (2024). *Administrative Decision No. (220) of 2024 on the schedule of violations, fines and administrative penalties related to Law No. (2) of 2012 regarding the public serenity and the appearance of the city (Abu Dhabi).* https://pages.dmt.gov.ae/-/media/592AA5F85BA9410D82F3FEDAB95C1AD1.ashx

Ahmad Bin Hezeem, B. S. A., & Associates. LLP. (2025). *UAE evidence law: Admissibility of electronic evidence in legal disputes.* https://bsaah.com/uae-evidence-law/

Ayers, R., Brothers, S., & Jansen, W. (2014). *Guidelines on mobile device forensics* (NIST Special Publication 800-101 Rev. 1). National Institute of Standards and Technology. https://nvlpubs.nist.gov/nistpubs/SpecialPublications/NIST.SP.800-101r1.pdf

Barrigón Morillas, J. M., Rey-Gozalo, G., & Montes González, D. (2016). A review of the measurement procedure of the ISO 1996 standard. In Licitra, A. (Ed.), *Noise mapping in the EU: Models and procedures* (pp. 67–85). CRC Press., DOI: 10.1201/b19188-4

Basner, M., Babisch, W., Davis, A., Brink, M., Clark, C., Janssen, S., & Stansfeld, S. (2014). Auditory and non-auditory effects of noise on health. *Lancet*, *383*(9925), 1325–1332. DOI: 10.1016/S0140-6736(13)61613-X PMID: 24183105

Bouzir, L., Tabbakh, T., & Aydin, A. (2024). Noise pollution impacts on physical and mental well-being: A cross-sectional study. *BMC Public Health*, *24*, 970. DOI: 10.1186/s12889-024-18300-8

Clark, C., & Paunovic, K. (2018). WHO environmental noise guidelines for the European region: A systematic review on environmental noise and cognition. *International Journal of Environmental Research and Public Health*, *15*(2), 285. DOI: 10.3390/ijerph15020285 PMID: 29414890

Dubai Municipality. (2021). *Technical guidelines for monitoring and controlling noise at entertainment areas in Dubai* (Technical Guideline No. 9). https://www.dubaiehs.gov.ae/docs/default-source/technical-guidelines/noise-at-entertainment-areas.pdf

European Environment Agency. (2020). *Environmental noise in Europe—2020.* https://www.eea.europa.eu/en/analysis/publications/environmental-noise-in-europe

European Network of Forensic Science Institutes. (2022). *Best practice manual for the forensic examination of digital technology* (Version 1). https://enfsi.eu/wp-content/uploads/2022/07/ENFSI-BPM-Digital-Forensics.pdf

European Parliament and Council. (2002). *Directive 2002/49/EC of the European Parliament and of the Council of 25 June 2002 relating to the assessment and management of environmental noise.* https://eur-lex.europa.eu/eli/dir/2002/49/oj

Gulf News. (2025, November 19). Explained: How Dubai's new radars will curb noise pollution on the roads. https://gulfnews.com/uae/explained-how-dubais-new-radars-will-curb-noise-pollution-on-the-roads-1.500351645

International Electrotechnical Commission. (2013). *IEC 61672-1:2013: Electroacoustics—Sound level meters—Part 1: Specifications.* https://webstore.iec.ch/en/publication/5708

International Organization for Standardization. (2016). *ISO 1996-1:2016: Acoustics—Description, measurement and assessment of environmental noise—Part 1: Basic quantities and assessment procedures.* https://www.iso.org/standard/59766.html

International Organization for Standardization, & International Electrotechnical Commission. (2012). *ISO/IEC 27037:2012: Guidelines for identification, collection, acquisition and preservation of digital evidence.* https://www.iso.org/standard/44381.html

Kent, K., Chevalier, S., Grance, T., & Dang, H. (2006). *Guide to integrating forensic techniques into incident response* (NIST Special Publication 800-86). National Institute of Standards and Technology. https://nvlpubs.nist.gov/nistpubs/Legacy/SP/nistspecialpublication800-86.pdf

Khaleej Times. (2025, January 18). Abu Dhabi introduces new fines for noise pollution in public areas. https://www.khaleejtimes.com/uae/abu-dhabi-introduces-new-fines-for-noise-pollution-in-public-areas

Organisation for Economic Co-operation and Development. (2024). *Recommendation of the Council on integrated policies to reduce noise pollution.* https://legalinstruments.oecd.org/en/instruments/OECD-LEGAL-0507

Scientific Working Group on Digital Evidence. (2018). *SWGDE best practices for forensic audio authentication* (Version 2.0). https://www.swgde.org/documents/published

Scientific Working Group on Digital Evidence. (2022). *SWGDE best practices for forensic audio* (Version 1.0). https://www.swgde.org/documents/published

Stansfeld, S. A., & Matheson, M. P. (2003). Noise pollution: Non-auditory effects on health. *British Medical Bulletin, 68*(1), 243–257. DOI: 10.1093/bmb/ldg033 PMID: 14757721

Taylor Wessing. (2022, August 23). *UAE—Evidence and electronic evidence.* https://www.taylorwessing.com/en/insights-and-events/insights/2022/08/uae---evidence-and-electronic-evidence

United Arab Emirates. (1999). *Federal Law No. 24 of 1999 on the protection and development of the environment.* https://uaelegislation.gov.ae/en/legislations/411/download

United Arab Emirates. (2021a). *Federal Decree-Law No. 46 of 2021 on electronic transactions and trust services.* https://assets.u.ae/download/205f84f0-33d1-4241-af37-e8e79ed6b816/Federal-Decree-Law-No-46-of-2021.pdf

United Arab Emirates. (2021b). *Federal Decree-Law No. 34 of 2021 on combatting rumours and cybercrimes.* https://uaelegislation.gov.ae/en/legislations/1526/download

United Arab Emirates. (2021c). *Federal Decree-Law No. 31 of 2021 promulgating the crimes and penalties law.* https://uaelegislation.gov.ae/en/legislations/1547/download

United Arab Emirates. (2022a). *Federal Decree-Law No. 35 of 2022 on evidence in civil and commercial transactions.* https://uaelegislation.gov.ae/en/legislations/1919/download

United Arab Emirates. (2022b). *Federal Decree-Law No. 38 of 2022 promulgating the criminal procedures law.* https://uaelegislation.gov.ae/en/legislations/2197/download

United Nations Office on Drugs and Crime. (n.d.). *Handling digital evidence.* https://www.unodc.org/e4j/en/cybercrime/module-10/key-issues/handling-digital-evidence.html

World Health Organization Regional Office for Europe. (2009). *Night noise guidelines for Europe.* https://iris.who.int/items/272ff6f8-24ea-409e-b772-06b34210fb1c

World Health Organization Regional Office for Europe. (2018). *Environmental noise guidelines for the European region.* https://iris.who.int/bitstream/handle/10665/279952/9789289053563-eng.pdf?sequence=1

ADDITIONAL READING

Evidence Law, U. A. E. (Federal Decree-Law No. 35 of 2022) – official portal. https://uaelegislation.gov.ae/en/legislations

IEC 61672-1: Electroacoustics — Sound level meters (catalog). https://webstore.iec.ch/publication/5708

ISO 1996-1: Acoustics — Description, measurement and assessment of environmental noise (catalog). https://www.iso.org/standard/59766.html

OECD Recommendation on Strengthening Noise Abatement Policies. (2024). https://legalinstruments.oecd.org/en/instruments/OECD-LEGAL-0567

UAE Federal Law No. 24 of 1999 on Protection and Development of the Environment – official portal. https://uaelegislation.gov.ae/en/legislations

UAE Government Portal – Virtual litigation (procedural context). https://u.ae/en/information-and-services/justice-safety-and-the-law/litigation-procedures/virtual-litigation

WHO Environmental Noise Guidelines for the European Region. (2018). https://www.who.int/europe/publications/i/item/9789289053563

KEY TERMS AND DEFINITIONS

Administrative Sanction: Municipal/environmental penalty (fine, closure) imposed through administrative procedures.

Calibration Certificate: Documentation proving an instrument was calibrated to standards, supporting reliability of measurements.

CCTV/Audio Recording: Digital recording used as corroboration; requires integrity, legality, and privacy controls.

Chain of Custody: Documentation of collection/export/storage of measurement data and recordings.

Complaint Ticket: Digitally recorded complaint initiating inspection/enforcement workflow.

Measurement Protocol: Standardised method for where/how measurements are taken (distance, height, time period, background noise).

Metadata and Timestamps: Technical attributes supporting event sequencing and authenticity of recordings/logs.

Noise Pollution: Unwanted or harmful sound regulated via environmental/public-order rules and enforced through measurable thresholds.

Proportionality: Balancing enforcement severity with evidence strength and privacy considerations.

Public Serenity: Regulatory concept linking noise control to public order and community tranquility.

Sensor-Based Enforcement: Use of fixed sensors/noise radars generating logs used for enforcement and later review.

Sound Level Meter (SLM): Instrument measuring sound pressure levels (dB(A)); evidentiary value depends on calibration and protocol.

Compilation of References

Abdullah, F. M. (2020). *Civil liability for damages resulting from the use of artificial intelligence in the medical profession* [Thesis]. United Arab Emirates University. https://scholarworks.uaeu.ac.ae/all_theses/1016

Aboelazm, K. S. (2025). A new era of public procurement: Critical issues of procuring artificial intelligence systems to produce public services. *International Journal of Law and Management.* https://doi.org/DOI: 10.1108/IJLMA-06-2024-0208

Aboelazm, K. (2025). The effects of Supreme Constitutional Court decision of unconstitutionality legislative omission: A comparative study. *Lex Scientia Law Review*, *9*(2), 1446–1483. Advance online publication. DOI: 10.15294/lslr.v9i2.8801

Abu Dhabi Department of Municipalities and Transport. (2024). *Administrative Decision No. (220) of 2024 on the schedule of violations, fines and administrative penalties related to Law No. (2) of 2012 regarding the public serenity and the appearance of the city (Abu Dhabi).* https://pages.dmt.gov.ae/-/media/592AA5F85BA9410D82F3FEDAB95C1AD1.ashx

Abu Dhabi Judicial Department. (n.d.). Auctions. Retrieved February 20, 2026, from https://www.adjd.gov.ae/ar/pages/auctions.aspx

Abu Dhabi Judicial Department. (n.d.). Remote Court Hearings. Retrieved February 22, 2026, from https://www.adjd.gov.ae/en/Pages/RemoteCourtHearings.aspx

Ahmad Bin Hezeem, B. S. A., & Associates. LLP. (2025). *UAE evidence law: Admissibility of electronic evidence in legal disputes.* https://bsaah.com/uae-evidence-law/

Ahmed Abd El-Zaher. (2020). The road to artificial intelligence in the legal profession. *Egyptian Bar Association.* https://egyls.com/%D8%A7%D9%84%D8%B7%D8%B1%D9%8A%D9%82-%D8%A5%D9%84%D9%89-%D8%A7%D9%84%D8%B0%D9%83%D8%A7%D8%A1

Ahmed Qasim Farah. (2019). Virtual currencies in the United Arab Emirates: The need for a legal framework to address their risks—A comparative study. *University of Sharjah Journal of Legal Sciences, 16*(2). https://old.sharjah.ac.ae/ar/Research/spu/Journallaw/Pages/V16.aspx

Al Barghuthi, N. B., Ncube, C., & Said, H. (2019). *State of art of the effectiveness in adopting blockchain technology: UAE survey study. In 2019 Information Technology Trends (ITT): Emerging Technologies Blockchain and IoT*. IEEE., DOI: 10.1109/ITT48889.2019.9075108

Al Tamimi & Company. (2021, October). Sign of the times: The UAE's new Federal Electronic Transactions Law and Trust Services. *Law Update*. https://www.tamimi.com/law-update-articles/sign-of-the-times-the-uaes-new-federal-electronic-transactions-law-and-trust-services/

Al-Aboudi, A. R. (2020). *E-litigation and its impact on judicial procedures*. Dar Al Nahda Al Arabiya.

Al-Adba, N. M. M. A. (2025). AI and the future of decision-making in international arbitration: Redefining the boundaries of human judgment. *International Arbitration Law Review, 28*(3), 172–192.

Albatal, S., Awad, A., & Aldabousi, A. M. (2025). The influence of social media marketing on customer knowledge management: The role of confidentiality in UAE public banks. *Banks and Bank Systems, 20*(1), 1–10. DOI: 10.21511/bbs.20(1).2025.01

Aldabousi, A. M. (2025). Governance as a means to protect family businesses from collapse according to the laws of the United Arab Emirates. In *Advances in Science, Technology and Innovation* (pp. 123–138). Springer. DOI: 10.1007/978-3-031-92135-3_13

Aldabousi, A. M. (2022). Legal problems of conclusion of intelligent software agent for smart commercial contracts in the era of blockchain: U.A.E as a model. *Universidad y Sociedad, 14*(S3), 713–728. https://rus.ucf.edu.cu/index.php/rus/article/view/3005

Aldabousi, A. M. (2022). Legal problems of conclusion of intelligent software agent for smart commercial contracts in the era of blockchain: UAE as a model. *Universidad y Sociedad, 14*, 713–728.

Aldabousi, A. M. (2022). Legal problems of electronic pollution according to UAE and Egyptian law. *Arab World Geographer, 25*(2–3), 154–168. DOI: 10.64903/1480-6800-25.2.154

Aldabousi, A. M. (2023). The legal problems facing the conclusion of cloud computing contracts. *Universidad y Sociedad, 15*(3), 602–611. https://rus.ucf.edu.cu/index.php/rus/article/view/3815

Aldabousi, A. M. (2024). The joint responsibility of the air carrier established in accordance with international conventions on the status of air terrorism. *Pakistan Journal of Criminology*, *16*(2), 133–144. DOI: 10.62271/pjc.16.2.133.144

Aldabousi, A. M. (2025). Managing commercial space activities: Legal and regulatory challenges in UAE's space sector. *Problems and Perspectives in Management, 23*(2), 423–432. Advance online publication. DOI: 10.21511/ppm.23(2).2025.30

Aldabousi, A. M., & Ali, I. M. S. (2025). Legal safeguards against market rumors in UAE securities: A comparative commercial law study. *Investment Management and Financial Innovations*, *22*(4), 227–236. DOI: 10.21511/imfi.22(4).2025.18

Aldabousi, A. M., Awad, A., Hassan, H. E. M., Abdullah, S. S., & Ghonim, A. (2025). Arbitration in Islamic banking: Exploring legal and practical implications for dispute resolution. *Banks and Bank Systems*, *20*(2), 15–28. DOI: 10.21511/bbs.20(2).2025.02

Alenezi, A. M. (2023). Digital and cloud forensic challenges. arXiv. https://arxiv.org/abs/2305.03059

Al-Falasi, A. A. M. (2019). Criminal liability resulting from artificial intelligence errors. *Legal Journal*. https://jlaw.journals.ekb.eg/article_190836_001cd12821ed784ae2d063d3a6832284.pdf

Alhiniti, Y., & Zaid, M. Y. A. (2026). Future prospects of electronic commercial arbitration in light of modern technologies and artificial intelligence. In *Studies in Systems, Decision and Control*. https://www.scopus.com/pages/publications/105027061756

Al-Kattan, M. S. (2024). Bounced cheque as an enforceable instrument: A comparative study between the United Arab Emirates (UAE) & French legislations, (SSRN Scholarly Paper No. 5159907). Social Science Research Network. DOI: 10.24857/rgsa.v18n1-198

Al-Kattan, M. S. (2024). *Digital justice "model of the United Arab Emirates", 6-9 (SSRN Scholarly Paper No. 5159911)*. Social Science Research Network., DOI: 10.2139/ssrn.5159911

Al-Khateeb, H. M., Epiphaniou, G., & Daly, H. (2019). Blockchain for modern digital forensics: The chain-of-custody as a distributed ledger. In Jahankhani, H., Kendzierskyj, S., Jamal, A., Epiphaniou, G., & Al-Khateeb, H. (Eds.), *Blockchain and clinical trial: Securing patient data* (pp. 149–168). Springer., DOI: 10.1007/978-3-030-11289-9_7

Alkhseilat, A., Al-Billeh, T., Albazi, M., & Ali, N. A. (2024). The authenticity of digital evidence in criminal courts: A comparative study. *International Journal of Electronic Security and Digital Forensics, 16*(6), 720–738. DOI: 10.1504/IJESDF.2024.142010

Allah Rakha, N. (2023). Ensuring cyber-security in remote workforce: Legal implications and best international practices. *International Journal of Law and Policy, 1*(3). Advance online publication. https://irshadjournals.com/index.php/ijlp/article/view/43. DOI: 10.59022/ijlp.43

Al-Motawalli Qandil, M. (2024). *A concise treatise on forced enforcement in accordance with the UAE Civil Procedure Law* (7th ed.). Al-Afaq Publishing.

Al-Sherman, N., & Aldabousi, A. M. (2024). The complementary penalties enforced to combat corporate crimes in UAE law. *Pakistan Journal of Criminology, 16*(3), 635–648. DOI: 10.62271/pjc.16.3.635.648

Al-Tawil, T. N. (2023). Anti-money laundering regulation of cryptocurrency: UAE and global approaches. *Journal of Money Laundering Control*. https://www.scopus.com/pages/publications/85137537374

Angerschmid, A., Zhou, J., Theuermann, K., Chen, F., & Holzinger, A. (2022). Fairness and explanation in AI-informed decision making. *Machine Learning and Knowledge Extraction, 4*(2), 556–579. DOI: 10.3390/make4020026

Antwi-Boasiako, A., & Venter, H. (2017). A model for digital evidence admissibility assessment. In Peterson, G., & Shenoi, S. (Eds.), *Advances in digital forensics XIII* (pp. 23–38). Springer., DOI: 10.1007/978-3-319-67208-3_2

Antwi-Boasiako, A., & Venter, H. S. (2017). A model for digital forensic readiness for cloud computing environments. *Journal of Forensic Sciences, 62*(6), 1534–1544. DOI: 10.1111/1556-4029.13434 PMID: 28230894

Arjmand, S., & Kondori, N. F. (2025). Identifying functions and benefits of artificial intelligence in judgement using the metasynthesis method. Iranian Journal of Information Processing and Management. https://jipm.irandoc.ac.ir/article_728675_en.html

Arnell, P., & Faturoti, B. (2023). The prosecution of cybercrime—Why transnational and extraterritorial jurisdiction should be resisted. *International Review of Law Computers & Technology, 37*(1), 29–51. DOI: 10.1080/13600869.2022.2061888

Arthur, W. B. (2009). *The nature of technology: What it is and how it evolves.* Free Press.

Atrey, I. (2023). Cybercrime and its legal implications: Analysing the challenges and legal frameworks surrounding cybercrime, including issues related to jurisdiction, privacy, and digital evidence. *International Journal of Research and Analytical Reviews.* https://ssrn.com/abstract=4542139

Awad, A., & Aldabousi, A. M. (2024). Analyzing thc impact of viral markcting on brand equity dimensions in Egypt's home appliances sector: A customer and legal perspective. *Innovative Marketing, 20*(4), 100–111. https://www.businessperspectives.org/images/pdf/applications/publishing/templates/article/assets/21026/IM_2024_04_Awad.pdf

Awad, A., & Aldabousi, A. M. (2024). Analyzing the impact of viral marketing on brand equity dimensions in Egypt's home appliances sector: A customer and legal perspective. *Innovative Marketing, 20*(4), 100–111. DOI: 10.21511/im.20(4).2024.09

Awad, A., Al-fil, N. Z., Dganni, K. M., Aldabousi, A. M., & Obeidat, M. A. (2024). Optimizing dormant account management in UAE banking: Legal gaps and proposed reforms. *Banks and Bank Systems, 19*(4), 124–135. DOI: 10.21511/bbs.19(4).2024.10

Awoyemi, B. O., Omotayo, O. A., & Mpapalika, J. J. (2021). Globalization and cybercrimes: A review of forms and effects of cybercrime in Nigeria. *Internal Journal of Interdisciplinary Research and Modern Education, 7*(1), 18–25. https://www.researchgate.net/publication/353706017

Ayers, R., Brothers, S., & Jansen, W. (2014). *Guidelines on mobile device forensics* (NIST Special Publication 800-101 Rev. 1). National Institute of Standards and Technology. https://nvlpubs.nist.gov/nistpubs/SpecialPublications/NIST.SP.800-101r1.pdf

Aykul, A., & Uddin, A. H. M. E. (2025). Evaluating the influence of doubt (shubhah) in the implementation of hudud penalties. Ahkam. *Jurnal Ilmu Syariah, 25*(1), 87–104. DOI: 10.15408/ajis.v25i1.37953

Azab, R. S., & Ismail, H. H. (2024). AI as a tool to enhance digital arbitration effectiveness: Analytical study under Silicon Valley Arbitration Center guidelines. *Edelweiss Applied Science and Technology, 8*(6), 1723–1734. DOI: 10.55214/25768484.v8i6.2333

Babikian, J. (2023). Navigating legal frontiers: Exploring emerging issues in cyber law. *Revista Española de Documentación Científica*. https://www.researchgate.net/publication/371914009

Badawi, A., & Al-Haija, Q. A. (2021). Detection of money laundering in Bitcoin transactions. *IET Conference Proceedings*. https://www.scopus.com/pages/publications/85139870704

Baker McKenzie. (2020, March 30). COVID-19 in the UAE: Overview and FAQs (client alert). https://www.bakermckenzie.com/-/media/files/insight/publications/2020/03/bmham-client-alert--covid19-in-the-uae--overview-and-faqs--30-mar-2020_final_v3.pdf

Barrigón Morillas, J. M., Rey-Gozalo, G., & Montes González, D. (2016). A review of the measurement procedure of the ISO 1996 standard. In Licitra, A. (Ed.), *Noise mapping in the EU: Models and procedures* (pp. 67–85). CRC Press., DOI: 10.1201/b19188-4

Basner, M., Babisch, W., Davis, A., Brink, M., Clark, C., Janssen, S., & Stansfeld, S. (2014). Auditory and non-auditory effects of noise on health. *Lancet*, *383*(9925), 1325–1332. DOI: 10.1016/S0140-6736(13)61613-X PMID: 24183105

Bielova, M., & Byelov, D. (2023). Challenges and threats of personal data protection in working with artificial intelligence. *Uzhhorod National University Herald. Series: Law*. DOI: 10.24144/2307-3322.2023.79.2.2

Bouzir, L., Tabbakh, T., & Aydin, A. (2024). Noise pollution impacts on physical and mental well-being: A cross-sectional study. *BMC Public Health*, *24*, 970. DOI: 10.1186/s12889-024-18300-8

Cadiet, L. (2020). *Le procès civil à l'ère numérique*. LGDJ.

Cassim, F. (2019). *Cybercrime and international law: A comparative approach*. Cambridge University Press., https://www.cambridge.org/core/books/cybercrime-and-international-law

Chambre nationale des commissaires de justice. (n.d.). Outils numériques professionnels. https://commissaire-justice.fr

Charles Russell Speechlys. (2026, January 27). An overview of electronic signatures in the UAE. https://www.charlesrussellspeechlys.com/en/insights/expert-insights/corporate/2026/an-overview-of-electronic-signatures-in-the-uae/

Chimni, B. S. (2022). The international law of jurisdiction: A TWAIL perspective. *Leiden Journal of International Law*. https://archive.org/details/internationallawofjurisdiction

Chopade, M., Khan, S., Shaikh, U., & Pawar, R. (2019). Digital forensics: Maintaining chain of custody using blockchain. In 2019 Third International Conference on I-SMAC (IoT in Social, Mobile, Analytics and Cloud) (pp. 744-747). IEEE. https://doi.org/DOI: 10.1109/I-SMAC47947.2019.9032693

Clark, C., & Paunovic, K. (2018). WHO environmental noise guidelines for the European region: A systematic review on environmental noise and cognition. *International Journal of Environmental Research and Public Health, 15*(2), 285. DOI: 10.3390/ijerph15020285 PMID: 29414890

Code, U. S. (2023). *Title 18—Crimes and criminal procedure*. https://uscode.house.gov/view.xhtml?path=/prelim@title18

Commissaires de justice. (n.d.). Gestion numérique des dossiers d'exécution. https://commissaire-justice.fr

Commissaires de justice. (n.d.). Signification électronique des actes. https://commissaire-justice.fr

Conseil national des barreaux. (n.d.). e-Barreau. https://www.cnb.avocat.fr/fr/webinaire-e-barreau

Davis, S., & Arrigo, B. (n.d.). The dark web and anonymizing technologies: Legal pitfalls, ethical prospects, and policy directions from radical criminology. *Crime*. https://link.springer.com/article/10.1007/s10611-021-09972-z

Direction générale des Finances publiques. (n.d.). Échanges numériques avec les commissaires de justice. https://www.impots.gouv.fr

Dubai Court of Cassation. (2011, September 18). Rights guaranteed by the Dubai Court of Cassation ruling in Case No. 2011/119 (Real Estate Appeal) [Legal rule]. Retrieved March 10, 2020, from https://www.dc.gov.ae/SubscribedServices/LegalRule

Dubai Court of Cassation. (2016, November 27). Rule derived from judgment in Appeal No. 2016/453 (Commercial Appeal) [Legal rule]. Retrieved March 25, 2020, from https://www.dc.gov.ae/SubscribedServices/LegalRule

Dubai Court of Cassation. (2017, May 10). Rights guaranteed by the Dubai Court of Cassation ruling in Case No. 2016/496 (Real Estate Appeal) [Legal rule]. Retrieved March 20, 2020, from https://www.dc.gov.ae/SubscribedServices/LegalRule

Dubai Courts. (n.d.). Official website of Dubai Courts. Retrieved February 20, 2026, from https://www.dc.gov.ae

Dubai Municipality. (2021). *Technical guidelines for monitoring and controlling noise at entertainment areas in Dubai* (Technical Guideline No. 9). https://www.dubaiehs.gov.ae/docs/default-source/technical-guidelines/noise-at-entertainment-areas.pdf

Dutton, Y. M. (2023). Prosecuting atrocities committed in Ukraine: A new era for universal jurisdiction? *Case Western Reserve Journal of International Law*. https://ssrn.com/abstract=4513158

Emarat Al Youm. (2024). https://www.emaratalyoum.com/local-section/other/2024-10-18-1.1890425

Emirates Auction. (n.d.). Emirates Auction. Retrieved February 20, 2026, from https://www.emiratesauction.com/ar

European Commission for the Efficiency of Justice. (2016). Guidelines on how to drive change towards cyberjustice. Council of Europe. https://rm.coe.int/16807482de

European Commission for the Efficiency of Justice. (2018). European ethical charter on the use of artificial intelligence in judicial systems and their environment, 59 Council of Europe.

European Commission. (2016). Online platforms and the digital single market: Opportunities and challenges for Europe. Publications Office of the European Union. https://eur-lex.europa.eu/legal-content/EN/TXT/?uri=celex:52016DC0288

European Environment Agency. (2020). *Environmental noise in Europe—2020.* https://www.eea.europa.eu/en/analysis/publications/environmental-noise-in-europe

European Network of Forensic Science Institutes. (2022). *Best practice manual for the forensic examination of digital technology* (Version 1). https://enfsi.eu/wp-content/uploads/2022/07/ENFSI-BPM-Digital-Forensics.pdf

European Parliament and Council. (2002). *Directive 2002/49/EC of the European Parliament and of the Council of 25 June 2002 relating to the assessment and management of environmental noise.* https://eur-lex.europa.eu/eli/dir/2002/49/oj

European Parliament. (2018, July). *Cryptocurrencies and blockchain: Legal context and implications for financial crime, money laundering, and tax evasion.* https://www.europarl.europa.eu/cmsdata/150761/TAX3%20Study%20on%20cryptocurrencies%20and%20blockchain

European Union Agency for Fundamental Rights. (2023). *Digitalising justice: A fundamental rights-based approach.* Publications Office of the European Union.

European Union. (2014). Regulation (EU) No 910/2014 of the European Parliament and of the Council of 23 July 2014 on electronic identification and trust services for electronic transactions in the internal market (eIDAS). Official Journal of the European Union, L 257, 73-114.

European Union. (2016). Regulation (EU) 2016/679 of the European Parliament and of the Council of 27 April 2016 (General Data Protection Regulation – GDPR). Official Journal of the European Union, L 119, 1-88.

Extance, A. (2018). How AI technology can tame the scientific literature. *Nature*, *561*(7722), 273–274. DOI: 10.1038/d41586-018-06617-5 PMID: 30202054

Feng, S., & Shen, W. (2025). Selecting arbitrators by AI: Theoretical analysis and institutional responses. *International Journal of Legal Discourse*, *10*(2), 333–360. DOI: 10.1515/ijld-2025-2018

Financial Action Task Force (FATF). (2020). *Mutual evaluation report.*

France. Code civil [Civil Code], arts. 1366-1367. France. Code de procédure civile [Code of Civil Procedure], art. 662-1; arts. 748-1–748-9.

Garrie, D. B., & Morrissy, J. D. (2014). Digital forensic evidence in the courtroom: Understanding content and quality. *Northwestern Journal of Technology and Intellectual Property*, *12*(2), 121–128. https://scholarlycommons.law.northwestern.edu/njtip/vol12/iss2/1/

Gawer, A. (2022). Digital platforms and ecosystems: Remarks on the dominant organizational forms of the digital age. *Innovation (North Sydney, N.S.W.)*, *24*(1), 110–124. Advance online publication. DOI: 10.1080/14479338.2021.1965888

Ghonim, A., & Awad, A. (2024). Leveraging e-marketing for enhancing customer knowledge management: A systematic review of tourism strategies in the Saudi Arabian context. *Journal of Ecohumanism*, *3*(8), 2729–2745. DOI: 10.2478/jeh-2024-0056

Glasze, G., Cattaruzza, A., Douzet, F., Dammann, F., Bertran, M. G., Bômont, C., & Zanin, C. (2023). Contested spatialities of digital sovereignty. *Geopolitics*, *28*(2), 919–958. DOI: 10.1080/14650045.2022.2050070

Goltz, N., & Dondoli, G. (2019). A note on science, legal research and artificial intelligence. *Information & Communications Technology Law*, *28*(3), 239–251. DOI: 10.1080/13600834.2019.1644065

Government, U. A. E. (2025, November 19). Virtual litigation. The Official Portal of the UAE Government. https://u.ae/en/information-and-services/justice-safety-and-the-law/litigation-procedures/virtual-litigation

Granja, F. M., & Rafael, G. D. R. (2017). The preservation of digital evidence and its admissibility in the court. *International Journal of Electronic Security and Digital Forensics*, *9*(1), 1–19. DOI: 10.1504/IJESDF.2017.081749

Gulf News. (2025, November 19). Explained: How Dubai's new radars will curb noise pollution on the roads. https://gulfnews.com/uae/explained-how-dubais-new-radars-will-curb-noise-pollution-on-the-roads-1.500351645

Hatam, M. A. (2024). *Crime rate analysis and e-crime prevention in Dubai using machine learning* [Master's thesis]. https://repository.rit.edu/theses/11798/

Hessick, F. A., & Hessick, C. B. (2021). Nondelegation and criminal law. *Virginia Law Review*. https://ssrn.com/abstract=3828486

Hosseini, M., Resnik, D., & Holmes, K. (2023). The ethics of disclosing the use of artificial intelligence tools in writing scholarly manuscripts. *Research Ethics*, *19*(4), 449–465. DOI: 10.1177/17470161231180449 PMID: 39749232

Hussein, S., & Mohammed, S. (2024, February). Analyzing the legal framework and implications of Federal Decree-Law No. 34/2021 in combatting cyber blackmail in the UAE. In *2024 2nd International Conference on Cyber Resilience (ICCR)* (pp. 1–6). IEEE. https://doi.org/DOI: 10.1109/ICCR61006.2024.10533025

Hussein, S., & Serria, E. (2024). *Understanding the crucial legal implications of edge and fog computing in data privacy and security laws in the UAE. In 2024 IEEE Future Networks World Forum (FNWF 2024)*. IEEE.

Hussin, N., & Majdah, M. (2013). The application of the rule of "avoiding hudud due to shubhah" in Islamic criminal law. In Proceedings of the Islamic Law and Contemporary Issues Conference (ISLAC 2013). https://irep.iium.edu.my/34400/1/ISLAC_2013_final_papcr-_Dr.Nasimah_%26_Dr.Majdah_%28UIAM%29.pdf

Igonor, O. S., Amin, M. B., & Garg, S. (2025). The application of blockchain technology in the field of digital forensics: A literature review. *Blockchains*, *3*(1), 5. DOI: 10.3390/blockchains3010005

International Chamber of Commerce. (2020). ICC Force Majeure and Hardship Clauses (PDF). https://iccwbo.org/wp-content/uploads/sites/3/2020/03/icc-forcemajeure-hardship-clauses-march2020.pdf

International Chamber of Commerce. (2020, March 24). ICC Force Majeure and Hardship Clauses. https://iccwbo.org/news-publications/icc-rules-guidelines/icc-force-majeure-and-hardship-clauses/

International Electrotechnical Commission. (2013). *IEC 61672-1:2013: Electroacoustics—Sound level meters—Part 1: Specifications.* https://webstore.iec.ch/en/publication/5708

International Organization for Standardization, & International Electrotechnical Commission. (2012). *ISO/IEC 27037:2012: Guidelines for identification, collection, acquisition and preservation of digital evidence.* https://www.iso.org/standard/44381.html

International Organization for Standardization. (2016). *ISO 1996-1:2016: Acoustics—Description, measurement and assessment of environmental noise—Part 1: Basic quantities and assessment procedures.* https://www.iso.org/standard/59766.html

ISO/IEC. (2012). ISO/IEC 27037:2012—Information technology—Security techniques—Guidelines for identification, collection, acquisition and preservation of digital evidence. International Organization for Standardization. https://www.iso.org/standard/44381.html

Iu, K. Y., & Wong, V. M. Y. (2024). The trans-national cybercrime court: Towards a new harmonisation of cyber law regime in ASEAN. *International Cybersecurity Law Review*. https://link.springer.com/article/10.1365/s43439-023-00105-x

K&L Gates. (2020, March 11). COVID-19: Force majeure in the United Arab Emirates. https://www.klgates.com/COVID-19-Force-Majeure-in-the-United-Arab-Emirates-03-11-2020

Kagita, M. K., Thilakarathne, N., Gadekallu, T. R., Maddikunta, P. K. R., & Singh, S. (2022). A review on cybercrimes on the internet of things. In *Deep learning for security and privacy preservation in IoT* (pp. 83–98). Springer., DOI: 10.1007/978-3-031-05390-0_5

Kaplan, J., Weisberg, R., & Binder, G. (2021). *Criminal law: Cases and materials*. https://www.buffalo.edu/classics/documents/criminal-law.html

Kent, K., Chevalier, S., Grance, T., & Dang, H. (2006). *Guide to integrating forensic techniques into incident response* (NIST Special Publication 800-86). National Institute of Standards and Technology. https://nvlpubs.nist.gov/nistpubs/Legacy/SP/nistspecialpublication800-86.pdf

Khaleej Times. (2025, January 18). Abu Dhabi introduces new fines for noise pollution in public areas. https://www.khaleejtimes.com/uae/abu-dhabi-introduces-new-fines-for-noise-pollution-in-public-areas

Khashashneh, T., Al-Billeh, T., Al-Hammouri, A., & Belghit, R. (2023). The importance of digital technology in extracting electronic evidence: How can digital technology be used at crime scenes? *Pakistan Journal of Criminology*, *15*(4). https://www.pjcriminology.com/wp-content/uploads/2023/11/5.-The-Importance-of-Digital-Technology.pdf

Kong, X., Wu, Y., Wang, H., & Xia, F. (2022). Edge computing for internet of everything: A survey. *IEEE Internet of Things Journal*. https://ieeexplore.ieee.org/document/9734901

Korbatieh, S. (2018). The law of evidence in the Islamic criminal justice system: A critical appraisal in the light of modern technology (Doctoral thesis, Macquarie University). *Figshare*. https://figshare.mq.edu.au/articles/thesis/The_law_of_evidence_in_the_Islamic_criminal_justice_system_a_critical_appraisal_in_the_light_of_modern_technology/19440422

Korbatieh, S. (2020). Evidence rules in sharia and the impact of modern technology and DNA testing. *Australian Journal of Islamic Studies*, *5*(3), 4–29. https://ajis.com.au/index.php/ajis/article/view/303. DOI: 10.55831/ajis.v5i3.303

Koul, P. (2023). Disclosing use of artificial intelligence: Promoting transparency in publishing. *Lung India : Official Organ of Indian Chest Society*, *40*(5), 401–403. DOI: 10.4103/lungindia.lungindia_370_23 PMID: 37787350

Kumar, S. G. K., Shreenidhi, P. L., Rahman, S. Z., & Munagalachetty, C. (2025). Secure AI frameworks for detecting cross-border tax fraud. *Industry Applications*. https://www.scopus.com/pages/publications/105021944630

Labanieh, M. F., Alshamsi, A. A. S. S., Ayub, Z. A., & Wahab, H. A. (2025). The potential benefits of establishing an AI-arbitration legal framework in Malaysia. Multidisciplinary Science Journal. https://malque.pub/ojs/index.php/msj/article/view/10180

Laudon, K. C., & Laudon, J. P. (2020). *Management information systems: Managing the digital firm* (16th ed.). Pearson.

Law Library of Congress. (2025, January). Regulation of cryptocurrencies in the Gulf Cooperation Council countries (Part one). *In Custodia Legis*. https://blogs.loc.gov/law/2025/01/falqs-regulation-of-cryptocurrencies-in-the-gulf-cooperation-council-countries-part-one/

Lucien, L. R. (2024). Challenges of trustworthy of digital evidence and its chain of custody on cloud computing environment: A systematic review. In Proceedings of the 26th International Conference on Enterprise Information Systems (ICEIS 2024) (Vol. 2, pp. 240-246). SCITEPRESS. https://doi.org/DOI: 10.5220/0012702800003690

Mahdavich, R. (2023). Beyond the borders: The rise of judicial corruption and universal jurisdiction. *University of Miami Race & Social Justice Law Review, 14*(2). https://repository.law.miami.edu/umrsjlr/vol14/iss2/6/

Matis, J. (2025). Digital evidence and its use for criminal proceedings. *Analytical and Comparative Jurisprudence*, *5*(3), 121–126. DOI: 10.24144/2788-6018.2025.03.3.19

McDonald, G. K., & Swaak-Goldman, O. (2023). *Substantive and procedural aspects of international criminal law: The experience of international and national courts* (Vol. 1). Cambridge University Press., https://www.cambridge.org/core/books/substantive-and-procedural-aspects-of-international-criminal-law

Mensah, G. B., Addy, A., & Frimpong, P. O. (2023). Comparative legal analysis of the medical negligence landscape: The Ghanaian and Commonwealth criminal jurisprudence. *JL Pol'y & Globalization*. https://iiste.org/Journals/index.php/JLPG/article/view/61538

Miller, A., & Singh, A. (2024). Chain of custody and evidence integrity verification using blockchain technology. In Proceedings of the International Conference on Cyber Warfare and Security (Vol. 19, Issue 1, pp. 168-176). Academic Conferences International. https://doi.org/DOI: 10.34190/iccws.19.1.2025

Ministère de la Justice (France). (n.d.). Portail du justiciable https://www.justice.fr/donnees-personnelles/portalis

Ministère de la Justice. (n.d.). Dématérialisation des actes judiciaires. https://www.justice.gouv.fr

Ministère de la Justice. (n.d.). Exécution des décisions de justice. https://www.justice.gouv.fr

Ministère de la Justice. (n.d.). La transformation numérique de la justice. https://www.justice.gouv.fr

Ministère de la Justice. (n.d.). Services numériques judiciaires. https://www.justice.gouv.fr

Ministry of Justice (UAE). (n.d.). The guideline for using remote trials (English). Retrieved February 22, 2026, from https://www.moj.gov.ae/assets/remote-trial-advisory-guide-in-english-638793604613261872

Ministry of Justice, United Arab Emirates. (n.d.). Digital and smart judicial services. Retrieved February 20, 2026, from https://www.moj.gov.ae

Motulsky, H. (1973). *Droit judiciaire privé* (2nd ed.). Dalloz.

Moussa, A. F. (2021). Electronic evidence and its authenticity in forensic evidence. *Egyptian Journal of Forensic Sciences*, *11*(1), 34. DOI: 10.1186/s41935-021-00234-6

Muhami Legal. (2024). Blockchain & smart contracts in UAE real estate: Legal challenges & opportunities. https://muhami.ae/articles/blockchain-and-smart-contracts-revolutionising-rea/

Narasimhan, P., & Kala, N. (2024). Ensuring the integrity of digital evidence: The role of the chain of custody in digital forensics. International Journal of Scientific Research in Computer Science. *Engineering and Information Technology*, *10*(6), 2438–2450. DOI: 10.32628/CSEIT2410612443

Nasreldin, M. M., El-Hennawy, M., Aslan, H. K., & El-Hennawy, A. E. (2015). Digital forensics evidence acquisition and chain of custody in cloud computing. *International Journal of Computer Science Issues*, *12*(1), 153–160. https://www.ijcsi.org/papers/IJCSI-12-1-1-153-160.pdf

National Institute of Standards and Technology. (2006). Guide to integrating forensic techniques into incident response (NIST Special Publication 800-86). https://csrc.nist.gov/pubs/sp/800/86/final

Nekit, K. (2023). Legal nature and types of digital assets in the activities of technology-oriented startups. *Juridical Tribune*. https://www.scopus.com/pages/publications/85167466698

News, D. L. (2024). Dubai court recognises crypto salaries in a precedent-setting decision. https://www.dlnews.com/articles/people-culture/dubai-court-recognises-crypto-salaries-in-landmark-decision/

Obeidat, M. A., Alfil, N. Z., Aldabousi, A. M., & Dganni, K. M. (2024). Criminal protection for the merchants from the crimes of electronic publishing about invasion of privacy in UAE legislation. *Pakistan Journal of Criminology*, *16*(3), 779–792. DOI: 10.62271/pjc.16.3.779.792

Organisation for Economic Co-operation and Development. (2020). *Digital government policy framework: Six dimensions of a digital government*. OECD Publishing., DOI: 10.1787/f64fed2a-

Organisation for Economic Co-operation and Development. (2020). *Regulatory approaches to the digital economy*. OECD Publishing., DOI: 10.1787/bb167041-

Organisation for Economic Co-operation and Development. (2024). *Recommendation of the Council on integrated policies to reduce noise pollution.* https://legalinstruments.oecd.org/en/instruments/OECD-LEGAL-0507

Othman, A. M., & ElDosh, E. M. E. (2024). Regulating digital currencies in the Emirate of Dubai: A comparative legislative review. *International Journal of Public Law and Policy*. https://www.scopus.com/pages/publications/85190089767

Parker, G. G., Van Alstyne, M. W., & Choudary, S. P. (2016). *Platform revolution: How networked markets are transforming the economy and how to make them work for you*. W. W. Norton & Company.

Penal Reform International. (2015). Sharia law and the death penalty: Would abolition of the death penalty be unfaithful to the message of Islam? https://cdn.penalreform.org/wp-content/uploads/2015/07/Sharia-law-and-the-death-penalty.pdf

Perera, D., & Tan, A. (2025). AI guidelines in international arbitration: Revolutionary or cautionary? A comparative analysis. *Journal of International Arbitration*. https://www.scopus.com/pages/publications/105018928452

Peters, R. (2006). *Crime and punishment in Islamic law: Theory and practice from the sixteenth to the twenty-first century*. Cambridge University Press., https://www.cambridge.org/core/books/crime-and-punishment-in-islamic-law/75C4EBE9B545F4F0FD7F41B62C4B3883 DOI: 10.1017/CBO9780511610677

Rabkin, J. A., & Lerner, C. S. (2022). Criminal justice is local: Why states disregard universal jurisdiction for human rights abuses. *Vanderbilt Journal of Transnational Law*. https://scholarship.law.vanderbilt.edu/vjtl/vol55/iss4/2/

Ramadan, S. A., Abdelsalam, T., Qasim, A., & Aldabousi, A. M. (2025). The role and impact of legal legislation in achieving sustainable development goals: An applied study on UAE legislation. In *Studies in Systems, Decision and Control*. Springer., DOI: 10.1007/978-3-031-96641-5_4

Ramadan, S. A., Qasim, A., & Raslan, L. (2025). The impact of scientific and technological advancements on judicial evidence methods: An applied study on UAE law. In *IoT and digital transformation: Innovating business models for the connected world* (pp. 187–197). Springer., DOI: 10.1007/978-3-032-00450-5_20

Ramadan, S. A., Qasim, A., & Raslan, L. (2025). The impact of scientific and technological advancements on judicial evidence methods: An applied study on UAE law. In *Lecture Notes in Networks and Systems* (Vol. 1575, pp. 187–197). Springer., https://www.springerprofessional.de/en/the-impact-of-scientific-and-technological-advancements-on-judic/51291204

Ramey, K. (2013, December 12). What is technology – Meaning of technology and its use. Use of Technology. https://www.useoftechnology.com/what-is-technology/

Ramirez, M., Boni, A., Wade, I., & Byrne, R. (2024). How does transformative innovation policy travel across physical and cognitive spaces? Exploring the role of mutable fluid space in experimental policy engagements. *Environmental Innovation and Societal Transitions*, *52*, 100881. https://www.sciencedirect.com/science/article/pii/S2210422423000660. DOI: 10.1016/j.eist.2024.100881

Rawat, M. (2021). Transnational cybercrime: Issue of jurisdiction. *International Journal of Law Management & Humanities*. https://www.ijlmh.com/paper/transnational-cybercrime-issue-of-jurisdiction/

Richet, J. L. (2022). How cybercriminal communities grow and change: An investigation of ad-fraud communities. *Technological Forecasting and Social Change*. https://www.sciencedirect.com/science/article/pii/S0040162521007162

Şahin, Ş., & Erkmen, B. (2023). Navigating the impact of artificial intelligence on scholarly authorship: Transparency and responsibility in the technological era. *European Journal of Therapeutics*, *29*(4), 994–995. Advance online publication. DOI: 10.58600/eurjther1811

Sarkar, G., & Shukla, S. K. (2023). Behavioral analysis of cybercrime: Paving the way for effective policing strategies. *Journal of Economic Criminology*. https://www.sciencedirect.com/science/article/pii/S2949791423000340

Sayedahmed, N. Y., & Anwar, S. (2025). AI adoption in tax fraud detection in Palestine: Insights from Arab countries on public policy and sustainable governance. *Engineering, and Sustainable Business*. https://www.scopus.com/pages/publications/105013207035

Schatzberg, E. (2018). *Technology: A critical history of a concept*. University of Chicago Press. DOI: 10.7208/chicago/9780226584027.001.0001

Scher-Zagier, E. (2024). Jurisdictional creep: The UN cybercrime convention and the expansion of passive personality jurisdiction. *Yale Journal of Law & Technology*. https://ssrn.com/abstract=4759987

Scientific Working Group on Digital Evidence. (2018). *SWGDE best practices for forensic audio authentication* (Version 2.0). https://www.swgde.org/documents/published

Scientific Working Group on Digital Evidence. (2022). *SWGDE best practices for forensic audio* (Version 1.0). https://www.swgde.org/documents/published

Scientific Working Group on Digital Evidence. (2025). SWGDE best practices for cloud service providers (Version 1.1). https://www.swgde.org/documents/published/2025-01-15%20SWGDE%20Best%20Practices%20for%20Cloud%20Service%20Providers%20Version%201.1.pdf

Securact. (n.d.). SECURACT – Signification électronique des actes. https://www.securact-huissier.fr

Sharma, S. P. (2024, February 10). Territorial acquisition, disputes and international law. *E-International Relations*. https://www.e-ir.info/2024/02/10/territorial-acquisition-disputes-and-international-law/

Soltan, K. R. (2025). Digital evidence as a means of proof in criminal proceedings in the UAE. Al Dhakheerah (UAE) repository. https://aldhakheerah.ae/handle/123456789/105076

Stansfeld, S. A., & Matheson, M. P. (2003). Noise pollution: Non-auditory effects on health. *British Medical Bulletin*, *68*(1), 243–257. DOI: 10.1093/bmb/ldg033 PMID: 14757721

Stanton, J. (2024). In search of constitutional supremacy in Malta. *European Public Law*. https://openaccess.city.ac.uk/32972/

Stoykova, R. (2023). The right to a fair trial as a conceptual framework for digital evidence rules in criminal investigations. *Computer Law & Security Review*, *49*, 105801. DOI: 10.1016/j.clsr.2023.105801

Surana, S., Dembla, S., & Bihani, P. (2022). Identifying contradictions in the legal proceedings using natural language models. *SN Computer Science*, *3*(3), 187. DOI: 10.1007/s42979-022-01075-3

Sviatun, O. V., Goncharuk, O. V., Roman, C., Kuzmenko, O., & Kozych, I. V. (2021). Combating cybercrime: Economic and legal aspects. *WSEAS Transactions on Business and Economics, 18*, 751–762. https://www.academia.edu/53767740

Taylor Wessing. (2022, August 23). *UAE—Evidence and electronic evidence*. https://www.taylorwessing.com/en/insights-and-events/insights/2022/08/uae---evidence-and-electronic-evidence

Tiwana, A. (2014). *Platform ecosystems: Aligning architecture, governance, and strategy*. Morgan Kaufmann. DOI: 10.1016/B978-0-12-408066-9.00001-1

Tripathi, K., & Mubarak, U. (2020). Protecting privacy in the era of artificial intelligence.

Tsuda, K., Ichino, J., & Shimizu, K. (2023). Gender effects on physical contact in social VR. In *Lecture Notes in Computer Science (including subseries Lecture Notes in Artificial Intelligence and Lecture Notes in Bioinformatics).* https://www.scopus.com/pages/publications/85171473708

UAE Ministry of Health and Prevention. (2020). *COVID-19 information center.* Retrieved April 24, 2020, from https://www.mohap.gov.ae/ar/AwarenessCenter/Pages/COVID19-Information-Center.aspx

UNCITRAL. (1980). United Nations Convention on Contracts for the International Sale of Goods (CISG). https://uncitral.un.org/en/texts/salegoods/conventions/sale_of_goods/cisg

UNIDROIT. (2016). UNIDROIT Principles of International Commercial Contracts 2016. https://www.unidroit.org/english/principles/contracts/principles2016/principles2016-e.pdf

United Arab Emirates Government Portal. (n.d.). Blockchain in the UAE government. https://u.ae/en/about-the-uae/digital-uae/digital-technology/blockchain-in-the-uae-government

United Arab Emirates Ministry of Justice. (n.d.). *Federal Civil Transactions Law (Federal Law No. 5 of 1985): Article 273* [Webpage]. Retrieved from https://elaws.moj.gov.ae/UAE-MOJ_LC-En/00_CIVIL%20TRANSACTIONS%20AND%20PROCEDURES/UAE-LC-En_1985-12-15_00005_Kait.html

United Arab Emirates. (1985). Federal Law No. (5) of 1985 concerning the issuance of the Civil Transactions Law of the United Arab Emirates. https://uaelegislation.gov.ae/en/legislations/1025/download

United Arab Emirates. (1985). *Federal Law No. 5 of 1985 (Civil Transactions Law). Official Gazette, 15*(158), December 29, 1985. (Amended by Federal Law No. 1 of 1987, *Official Gazette*, Issue 173; effective March 29, 1987).

United Arab Emirates. (1999). *Federal Law No. 24 of 1999 on the protection and development of the environment.* https://uaelegislation.gov.ae/en/legislations/411/download

United Arab Emirates. (2021). Electronic Transactions and Trust Services law (Federal Decree-Law No. 46 of 2021) (webpage and PDF). The Official Portal of the UAE Government. https://u.ae/en/about-the-uae/digital-uae/regulatory-framework/electronic-transactions-and-trust-services-law

United Arab Emirates. (2021). Federal Decree-Law No. (34) of 2021 on countering rumors and cybercrimes. UAE Legislation. https://uaelegislation.gov.ae/en/legislations/1526/download

United Arab Emirates. (2021). Federal Decree-Law No. (45) of 2021 on the protection of personal data. UAE Legislation. https://uaelegislation.gov.ae/en/legislations/1972/download

United Arab Emirates. (2021). Federal Decree-Law No. (46) of 2021 on electronic transactions and trust services. https://tdra.gov.ae/-/media/About/Trust-Services/Laws-and-regulations/Federal-Decree-Law-No-46-OF-2021-On-Electronic-Transactions-and-Trust-Services-EN.ashx

United Arab Emirates. (2021). Federal Decree-Law No. (46) of 2021 on electronic transactions and trust services. Telecommunications and Digital Government Regulatory Authority. https://tdra.gov.ae/-/media/About/Trust-Services/Laws-and-regulations/Federal-Decree-Law-No-46-OF-2021-On-Electronic-Transactions-and-Trust-Services-EN.ashx

United Arab Emirates. (2021). Federal Decree-Law No. 45 of 2021 concerning the protection of personal data.

United Arab Emirates. (2021a). Federal Decree-Law No. (31) of 2021 promulgating the crimes and penalties law. UAE Legislation. https://uaelegislation.gov.ae/en/legislations/1529

United Arab Emirates. (2021a). *Federal Decree-Law No. 46 of 2021 on electronic transactions and trust services.* https://assets.u.ae/download/205f84f0-33d1-4241-af37-e8e79ed6b816/Federal-Decree-Law-No-46-of-2021.pdf

United Arab Emirates. (2021b). Federal Decree-Law No. (34) of 2021 on combatting rumors and cybercrimes. UAE Legislation. https://uaelegislation.gov.ae/en/legislations/1418

United Arab Emirates. (2021b). *Federal Decree-Law No. 34 of 2021 on combatting rumours and cybercrimes.* https://uaelegislation.gov.ae/en/legislations/1526/download

United Arab Emirates. (2021c). *Federal Decree-Law No. 31 of 2021 promulgating the crimes and penalties law.* https://uaelegislation.gov.ae/en/legislations/1547/download

United Arab Emirates. (2022). Cabinet Resolution No. (111) of 2022 concerning the regulation of virtual assets and their service providers. https://blogs.loc.gov/law/2025/01/falqs-regulation-of-cryptocurrencies-in-the-gulf-cooperation-council-countries-part-one/

United Arab Emirates. (2022). Federal Decree-Law No. (35) of 2022 promulgating the law of evidence in civil and commercial transactions. UAE Legislation. https://uaelegislation.gov.ae/en/legislations/1612/download

United Arab Emirates. (2022). Federal Decree-Law No. (38) of 2022 promulgating the criminal procedures law. UAE Legislation. https://uaelegislation.gov.ae/en/legislations/1609/download

United Arab Emirates. (2022). Federal Decree-Law No. (42) of 2022 promulgating the civil procedure code. UAE Legislation. https://uaelegislation.gov.ae/en/legislations/1602/download

United Arab Emirates. (2022a). Federal Decree-Law No. (38) of 2022 on criminal procedures. UAE Legislation. https://uaelegislation.gov.ae/en/legislations/1609

United Arab Emirates. (2022a). *Federal Decree-Law No. 35 of 2022 on evidence in civil and commercial transactions.* https://uaelegislation.gov.ae/en/legislations/1919/download

United Arab Emirates. (2022b). *Federal Decree-Law No. 38 of 2022 promulgating the criminal procedures law.* https://uaelegislation.gov.ae/en/legislations/2197/download

United Arab Emirates. (2022b). Federal Law by Decree No. (35) of 2022 issuing the law of evidence in civil and commercial transactions. UAE Legislation. https://uaelegislation.gov.ae/en/legislations/1719

United Arab Emirates. (2023). Cabinet Resolution No. (28) of 2023 on the executive regulations of Federal Decree-Law on Electronic Transactions and Trust Services (English). https://uaelegislation.gov.ae/en/legislations/2199/download

United Nations Commission on International Trade Law. (1996). UNCITRAL Model Law on Electronic Commerce.

United Nations Office on Drugs and Crime. (n.d.). Cybercrime module 6: Handling of digital evidence. https://www.unodc.org/e4j/en/cybercrime/module-6/key-issues/handling-digital-evidence.html

United Nations Office on Drugs and Crime. (n.d.). *Handling digital evidence.* https://www.unodc.org/e4j/en/cybercrime/module-10/key-issues/handling-digital-evidence.html

Uzougbo, N. S., Ikegwu, C. G., & Adewusi, A. O. (2024). International enforcement of cryptocurrency laws: Jurisdictional challenges and collaborative solutions. *Magna Scientia Advanced Research and Reviews, 11*(1), 68–83. https://magnascientiapub.com/journals/index.php/MSARR/article/view/2147

Vincent, J., & Prévault, J. (1999). Voies d'exécution et procédures de distribution (19e éd.). Dalloz.

Wan Ismail, W. A. F., Baharuddin, A. S., Mutalib, L. A., & Alias, M. A. A. (2021). An appraisal of digital documents as evidence in Islamic law. *Academic Journal of Interdisciplinary Studies, 10*(3), 198–206. DOI: 10.36941/ajis-2021-0076

Weerasinghe, M., Macdonald, S., Fiani, C., et al., & Khamis, M. (2025). Beyond mute and block: Adoption and effectiveness of safety tools in social VR, from ubiquitous harassment to social sculpting. *IEEE Transactions on Visualization and Computer Graphics.* https://www.scopus.com/pages/publications/105004050119

World Health Organization Regional Office for Europe. (2009). *Night noise guidelines for Europe.* https://iris.who.int/items/272ff6f8-24ea-409e-b772-06b34210fb1c

World Health Organization Regional Office for Europe. (2018). *Environmental noise guidelines for the European region.* https://iris.who.int/bitstream/handle/10665/279952/9789289053563-eng.pdf?sequence=1

World Health Organization. (2020, March 11). WHO Director-General's opening remarks at the media briefing on COVID-19 – 11 March 2020. https://www.who.int/news-room/speeches/item/who-director-general-s-opening-remarks-at-the-media-briefing-on-covid-19---11-march-2020

Wu, Y. (2025). Arbitrators in the virtual world: The evolution of independence and impartiality and the safeguarding of procedural justice in metaverse dispute resolution. Arbitration: The International Journal of Arbitration. *Mediation and Dispute Management, 91*(4), 360–386. DOI: 10.54648/AMDM2025027

Yadav, S., Yadav, S., Verma, P., Ojha, S., & Mishra, S. (2023). Artificial intelligence: An advanced evolution in forensic and criminal investigation. *Current Forensic Science, 1*(1), e190822207706. https://www.benthamscience.com/article/125626

Yılmaz, H. K. E. (2024). Legal issues of the metaverse: Public international law perspective. *Law & Justice Review.* https://dergipark.org.tr/en/pub/lawandjusticereview/issue/85441

Zahid, A., Shariff, A. A. M., & Zulkifli, A. N. (2015). The use of qarinah in proving hudud and qisas crimes: An analysis of the debate between Islamic schools and the Malaysian syariah courts. *Mediterranean Journal of Social Sciences, 6*(2), 141–147.

About the Contributors

Hany Ganah is an Associate Professor of Biotechnology and the Vice Chancellor at Umm Al Quwain University (UAQU). Prior to joining UAQU, he served as Director of Quality Assurance and Institutional Effectiveness, Program Coordinator, and Dean of the College of Biotechnology. Dr. Hany has extensive experience in quality assurance and institutional effectiveness, particularly in university licensure, re-licensure, initial program accreditation, program re-accreditation, and international accreditation processes. He has also delivered numerous academic workshops focused on professional development for faculty members. As a Program Coordinator and Dean of the College of Biotechnology, Dr. Hany has been actively involved in both administrative and academic leadership. His responsibilities have included curriculum development, preparing and authoring self-study reports for new academic programs and specializations. His postdoctoral research focuses on biotechnology, and he has published multiple papers in areas such as: Follicular dynamics in dairy animals and its relationship to superovulation response and embryo quality; Factors affecting embryo production and transfer; In-vitro maturation and fertilization of rabbit oocytes, as well as semen processing. Additionally, Dr. Hany has contributed to research in: Studies on cytochrome allelic variants and clopidogrel metabolism in cardiovascular disease therapy; The role of FABP2 and PPAR-γ genes as risk factors for dyslipidemia in Type 2 Diabetes Mellitus in residents of the United Arab Emirates; Associations between PPAR and FABP2 gene polymorphisms with Type 2 Diabetes Mellitus (T2DM) and insulin resistance across different populations. Dr. Hany is an experienced educator, teaching both undergraduate and postgraduate courses in biotechnology. His teaching portfolio includes subjects such as Cell Biology and Physiology, Introductory Genetics, Molecular Biology, Immunology, and Biosafety. He employs modern and innovative teaching methods to enhance student engagement and learning outcomes. Furthermore, he has conducted various hands-on training sessions that promote critical thinking and experiential learning through experiments in biotechnology courses.

Ahmed Moustafa Aldabousi is an Associate Professor of Commercial and Maritime Law at the College of Law, Umm Al Quwain University, UAE, and a practicing arbitrator and legal consultant. He holds a PhD in Commercial Law and Arbitration from Mansoura University, Egypt, awarded with highest distinction ("Very Good with Honours"), and officially recognized in the UAE and the USA. He has over eleven years of academic experience in teaching and research across private law disciplines, including commercial law, arbitration, corporate law, maritime and aviation law, in addition to delivering specialized legal training programs. He also brings more than seventeen years of professional legal practice, serving as a legal advisor in Egypt and the UAE, particularly in construction, maritime, and real estate sectors.

Amer Fakhoury is Professor of Law at AUE (Dubai). His teaching and research intersect commercial/comparative law, dispute resolution, and the legal implications of emerging technologies; he contributes to practice-oriented curricula and professional development across the UAE.

Abdulghani Al-Shuaibi holds a Bachelor of Laws degree obtained in 1992 with a very good general grade with honors from the Faculty of Law at the University of Aden. Additionally, he earned a Diploma in General Law Studies from the Dubai Police Academy in 2003. He also obtained a Master's degree in Public Law in 2007 with a very good grade from the Dubai Police Academy. Furthermore, he earned a Doctorate in Public Law, specializing in Criminal Law, in March 2017 with a very good grade from the Dubai Police Academy. He holds a certificate of excellence in academic achievement awarded by the Yemeni Presidential Office in 1992. He has held various administrative positions, with the most recent being the Dean of the College of Law at Umm Al Quwain University from January 2020 until the present. Additionally, he is a member of several academic and scientific committees at Umm Al Quwain University. He is a member of several academic and scientific committees at Umm Al Quwain University. Additionally, he has participated in numerous local and international workshops, seminars, and conferences. He has also served on committees for the evaluation and judgment of master's theses in criminal sciences. He has authored numerous legal research papers and publications. Additionally, he serves as a member of the Board of Trustees of Um Al-Qura Private School in Umm Al Quwain and acts as the legal advisor to the school. He is also a member of the Yemeni Lawyers Union.

Abdelrehim Nader Awad is an Associate Professor of Business Administration at the University of Bisha, Saudi Arabia. His academic and research profile spans marketing, management, innovation, and digital business, with a growing focus on artificial intelligence, digital transformation, technological adaptation, and data-driven organizational development. He has published extensively in Scopus- and Web of Science-indexed journals and has edited and contributed to several scholarly books and chapters in areas related to AI, sustainability, branding, supply chains, and knowledge management. His current interests on the application of artificial intelligence and digital technologies to business strategy, marketing, governance, innovation ecosystems, and organizational performance. Alongside his research, he has substantial experience in teaching, supervision, academic leadership, innovation and entrepreneurship initiatives, and quality and accreditation activities in higher education.

***

Tarek Mahmoud Abdel Salam Mohamed is a Professor of Public Law at the Faculty of Law, Helwan University, and Dean of the College of Law at the American University in the Emirates (2014–2026), currently serving as Professor at Umm Al Quwain University. He specializes in Public Finance and Tax Legislation, holds a PhD with distinction and honors, and is an attorney before the Court of Cassation and the Supreme Constitutional Court with 27 years of expertise in tax evasion litigation. He has held leadership positions, including Director of the Institute of Financial and Tax Sciences, and has made significant academic and professional contributions in VAT regulation, tax policy, virtual asset taxation, environmental taxation, and UAE financial legislation.

Mhd Samer Al Kattan Professional Biography Dr. Mhd Samer Al Kattan is an Associate Professor of Law at Umm Al Quwain University in the United Arab Emirates, where he has served since 2018. With a career spanning over three decades in legal academia and practice, Dr. Al Kattan brings deep expertise in civil procedure, arbitration, enforcement law. Dr. Al Kattan earned his PhD in Criminal Sciences and Private Law from the University of Paris X (Nanterre) in 2004, with a thesis "Comparing arbitration enforcement in Syrian, Lebanese, and French law". He holds two Postgraduate diplomas which are together equivalent to a Master's Degree and both are from Damascus university, The first is in Private Law, 1989 (Thesis" Termination of Indivision of Agricultural Land"), the second in Criminal Sciences, 1990 (Thesis" Justification of criminal Judgments") He holds a Bachelor's Degree in Law from Damascus University, 1984. In addition to his academic credentials, he has been a licensed legal practitioner with the Syrian Bar Association since 1987-1994 and 2005-2010 and practiced law before various court levels, including the Court of Cassation. A prolific legal scholar, Dr. Al Kattan has authored several peer-reviewed studies and legal research, most notably his Book on UAE Civil Procedure Law. His research's issues such as digital justice "The UAE model", Bounced cheques as an enforceable instrument, One-session trial circuits, and The role of technology in remote litigation. His articles appear in reputable and indexed journals. Beyond publishing, Dr. Al Kattan has actively participated in academic conferences, legal workshops, and training seminars. He has organized and managed numerous legal seminars and mock trials and continues to mentor students through practical legal clinics and educational trips. He has also contributed to national legislative development, notably by advising on the UAE Federal Arbitration Law through consultations with the Federal National Council's legislative committee. Dr. Al Kattan is a Syrian national.

Naser Al-Sherman is an Associate Professor of Private Law and Commercial Law at the American University in the Emirates. His research interests focus on private law, commercial law, intellectual property law, environmental law, and sustainable development. He has published several peer-reviewed articles in international journals.

Ahmed Hassan, Associate Professor of Public Law, Faculty of Law, Abu Dhabi University. He received his PhD in 2014 from Mansoura University, Egypt. He also received his Master of Laws (LLM) in Public Law in 2002 from Mansoura University, Egypt, and his Bachelor of Laws (LLB) from Mansoura University, Egypt in 1996.

George Nabil Micheal is an Associate Professor of Commercial Law, Legal Expert at the Law Center of the Institute of Public Administration in Riyadh, legal consultant, and arbitrator specializing in commercial arbitration. Have over 23 years of legal and academic experience across Egypt, Saudi Arabia, and the United Arab Emirates, Fellow of the Chartered Institute of Arbitrators (FCIArb).

Mohamed Nagib Saleh holds a Bachelor of Law (LL.B) from the Faculty of Law, Menofia University (1999) and a Master's degree in International Commerce (2017). He obtained an International Diploma in Arbitration from the International Academy of Legal Sciences, Canada (2013) and was awarded an Honorary Doctorate in Commercial and Investment Laws (2017). He lectures in International Commercial Arbitration and has authored several legal publications, including the Comprehensive UAE Civil Encyclopedia.

Israa Taha Khudair Shujairi holds a Ph.D. in Public Law from the Faculty of Law, Mansoura University, and works at the College of Political Science, University of Baghdad. Her academic work focuses on Constitutional Law, Administrative Law, and Public Governance. She has contributed to a number of research studies in the field of Public Law and actively participates in scholarly discussions related to legal and political developments.

Index

A

B

C

D

E

I

L

M

O

P

R

S

U

V

W